W9-AVB-178

Catholic Identity
School Edition

Sadlier

WE•BELIEVE™

We Meet Jesus in the Sacraments

WITH PROJECT DISCIPLE

Pray
Learn
Celebrate
Share
Choose
Live

Grade Five

S® Sadlier

This advanced publication copy has been printed prior to final publication and pending ecclesiastical approval.

Acknowledgments

Excerpts from the English translation of *The Roman Missal*, © 2010, International Committee on English in the Liturgy, Inc. All rights reserved.

Excerpts from the English translation of the *Catechism of the Catholic Church* for the United States of America, copyright © 1994, United States Catholic Conference, Inc.—Libreria Editrice Vaticana. English translation of the *Catechism of the Catholic Church: Modifications from the Editio Typica* copyright © 1997, United States Catholic Conference, Inc.—Libreria Editrice Vaticana. Used with permission.

Scripture excerpts are taken from the *New American Bible with Revised New Testament and Psalms* Copyright © 1991, 1986, 1970, Confraternity of Christian Doctrine, Inc., Washington, D.C. Used with permission. All rights reserved. No part of the *New American Bible* may be reproduced by any means without permission in writing from the copyright owner.

Excerpts from the English translation of *Rite of Marriage* © 1969, International Committee on English in the Liturgy, Inc. (ICEL); excerpts from the English translation of *Rite of Baptism for Children* © 1969, ICEL; excerpts from the English translation of *Lectionary for Mass* © 1969, 1981, ICEL; excerpts from the English translation of *The Liturgy of the Hours* © 1974, ICEL; excerpts from the English translation of *Holy Communion and Worship of the Eucharist outside Mass* © 1974, ICEL; excerpts from the English translation of *Rite of Penance* © 1974, ICEL; excerpts from the English translation of *Rite of Confirmation* (2nd Edition) © 1975, ICEL; excerpts from the English translation of *Pastoral Care of the Sick* © 1982, ICEL; excerpts from the English translation of *A Book of Prayers* © 1982, ICEL; excerpts from the English translation of *Order of Christian Funerals* © 1985, ICEL; excerpts from the English translation of *Book of Blessings* © 1988, ICEL; excerpt from the English translation of the *Presidential Prayers for Experimental Use at Mass* © 1983, ICEL. All rights reserved.

Excerpts from *Catholic Household Blessings and Prayers (Revised Edition)* copyright © 2007, 1988 United States Conference of Catholic Bishops, Inc. (USCCB), Washington, D.C. Used with permission. All rights reserved.

English translation of the Glory Be to the Father, Apostles' Creed, Nicene Creed, Lord's Prayer and *Gloria in Excelsis* by the International Consultation on English Texts. (ICET)

Excerpt from Anima Christi from the Web site of the United States Catholic Conference Inc. Washington, D.C., http://www.usccb.org/prayer-and-worship/prayers-and-devotions/prayers/anima-christi.cfm

The seven themes of Catholic Social Teaching are taken from *Sharing Catholic Social Teaching, Challenges and Directions: Reflections of the U.S. Catholic Bishops*, USCCB, Washington, D.C. © 1998.

Excerpts from the Angelus message of Pope Francis on the Solemnity of the Most Holy Trinity, May 26, 2013, and on the Feast of the Holy Family of Nazareth on December 29, 2013.

Excerpt from *Lumen Gentium, Dogmatic Constitution on the Church*, Pope Paul VI, November 21, 1964.

Excerpt from Irenaeus, *Against Heresies*, Book III, Chapter 3, Verse 1, from The Church Fathers, http://www.churchfathers.org/.

His Holiness Pope Francis, Twitter posts, February 13, 2013, 2:13 a.m., February 14, 2013, 3:14 a.m., and August 9, 2013, 2:00 a.m. http://twitter.com/Pontifex

Quotation from Saint Pio of Pietrelcina from the Capuchin Franciscan Friars, Union City, NJ.

"Prayer for Discernment: Walking One Day at a Time," copyright © Salesian Sisters of St. John Bosco, Daughters of Mary Help of Christians, Western Province, USA. http://www.salesiansisterswest.org/pages.asp?pageid=104814 "We Believe, We Believe in God," © 1979, North American Liturgy Resources (NALR), 5536 NE Hassalo, Portland, OR 97213. All rights reserved. Used with permission. "Jesus Is with Us," © 1990, OCP Publications, 5536 NE Hassalo, Portland, OR 97213. All rights reserved. Used with permission. "Bring Forth the Kingdom," Marty Haugen. © 1986, G.I.A. Publications, Inc. All rights reserved. Used with permission. "We Are the Body of Christ (Somos el Cuerpo de Cristo)," © 1994, Jaime Cortez. Published by OCP Publications, 5536 NE Hassalo, Portland, OR 97213. All rights reserved. Used with permission. "We Belong to God's Family," © 1992, OCP Publications, 5536 NE Hassalo, Portland, OR 97213. All rights reserved. Used with permission. "Saints of God," (Enter the Journey Collection). © 2000, Mark Friedman and Janet Vogt. Published by OCP Publications, 5536 NE Hassalo, Portland, OR 97213. All rights reserved. Used with permission. "Envía Tu Espíritu," © 1988, Bob Hurd. Published by OCP Publications, 5536 NE Hassalo, Portland, OR 97213. All rights reserved. Used with permission. "I Am the Bread of Life," Suzanne Toolan, RSM, © 1970, G.I.A. Publications, Inc. All rights reserved. Used with permission. "Calling the Children," © 1991, Christopher Walker and Matthew Wooten. Published by OCP Publications, 5536 NE Hassalo, Portland, OR 97213. All rights reserved. Used with permission. "With Open Hands," © 1999, Robert F. O'Connor, S.J. Published by OCP Publications, 5536 NE Hassalo, Portland, OR 97213. All rights reserved. Used with permission. "Psalm 25: To You, O Lord," © 1969, 1981, ICEL. All rights reserved. The English translation of the psalm response for Psalm 25 from *Lectionary for Mass* © 1969, 1981, 1997, International Committee on English in the Liturgy, Inc. (ICEL) All rights reserved. "Psalm 23: The Lord Is My Shepherd," © 2000, Carey Landry. Published by OCP Publications, 5536 NE Hassalo, Portland, OR 97213. All rights reserved. Used with permission. The English translation of the psalm response for Psalm 23 from *Lectionary for Mass* © 1969, 1981, 1997, International Committee on English in the Liturgy, Inc. (ICEL) All rights reserved. "Canticle of Mary," © 1993, Owen Alstott and Bernadette Farrell. Published by OCP Publications, 5536 NE Hassalo, Portland, OR 97213. All rights reserved. Used with permission. "Sign Us with Ashes," (Enter the Journey Collection). © 2000, Mark Friedman and Janet Vogt. Published by OCP Publications, 5536 NE Hassalo, Portland, OR 97213. All rights reserved. Used with permission. "God's Greatest Gift," © 1999, Owen Alstott. Published by OCP Publications, 5536 NE Hassalo, Portland, OR 97213. All rights reserved. Used with permission. "Prayer of St. Francis," dedicated to Mrs. Frances Tracy. © 1967, OCP Publications, 5536 NE Hassalo, Portland, OR 97213. All rights reserved. Used with permission. "Love Is Colored Like a Rainbow," Ray Repp, © 1985 by K&R Music Inc. Trumansburg, New York 14886. Used with permission. "Come, Follow Me," © 1992, Barbara Bridge. Published by OCP Publications, 5536 NE Hassalo, Portland, OR 97213. All rights reserved. Used with permission. "Holy Mary," (Enter the Journey Collection). © 2000, Mark Friedman and Janet Vogt. Published by OCP Publications, 5536 NE Hassalo, Portland, OR 97213. All rights reserved. Used with permission.

Copyright © 2015 by William H. Sadlier, Inc. All rights reserved. This book, or any part thereof, may not be reproduced in any form, or by any means, including electronic, photographic, or mechanical, or by any sound recording system, or by any device for storage and retrieval of information, without the written permission of the publisher.
Printed in the United States of America.

ꮪ is a registered trademark of William H. Sadlier, Inc.
WeBelieve™ is a trademark of William H. Sadlier, Inc.

William H. Sadlier, Inc.
9 Pine Street
New York, NY 10005-4700

ISBN: 978-0-8215-3055-9

6 7 8 9 10 WEBC 22 21 20 19

The Subcommittee on the Catechism, United States Conference of Catholic Bishops, has found the doctrinal content of this series, copyright 2015, to be in conformity with the *Catechism of the Catholic Church*.

Photo Credits

Cover: Corbis/Brian Fraunfelter: *water splash*; Getty Images/Greg Pease: *ship sailing*; Ken Karp: *bottle of anointing oil*; Used under license from Shutterstock.com/Nagel Photography: *Basilica of the Sacred Heart on the campus of the University of Notre Dame in South Bend, Indiana*. Interior: age fotostock/AME/a collectionRF: 43 *background*; kroach: 246; KidStock: 33 *left*; David Richardson: 115. Alamy/Nir Alon: R11; Yuri Arcurs: 204 *left*; Olaf Doering: 321 *top*; Peter Horree: 345 *top*; D. Hurst: 264 *top right inset*; Zdenk Malý: R28; Mode Images Ltd/Richard Gleed: 29 *top right*, 153 *center*, 193 *top right*, 204 *right*; Petter Oftedal: 151 *background*; Photo Mere Travel 2: R31. AP Photo/Aaron Favila: 36 *top*, 36 *center right*; Suzanne Plunkett: 195; Emilio Morenatti: 350. The Alexian Brothers: 217 *top*. Art Resource, NY/The Kobal Collection/ITC/RAI: 251; Erich Lessing: R27, 128; Scala/Museo dell'Opera Metropolitana, Siena: 285; Schalkwijk/© 2014 Banco de Mexico Diego Rivera Frida Kahlo Museums Trust, Mexico, D.F./Artists Rights Society (ARS): 153. Lori Berkowitz: 160 *top*. Jane Bernard: 7, 17 *left*, 17 *center right*, 46 *bottom right*, 49 *top*, 51, 70, 71, 74 *bottom*, 75, 93, 123 *top center*, 127, 132, 133, 134, 148 *left*, 186, 274 *left*, 299 *top right*. The Bridgeman Art Library/Giraudon/Musée des Beaux-Arts, Nantes, France: 210; Topham Picturepoint: 126. Karen Callaway: 44 *bottom left*, 44 *bottom right*, 45 *center*, 46 *top right*, 68, 76 *center right*, 80 *inset*, 93 *center right*, 93 *right*, 101, 108, 109, 110, 111, 122 *right*, 148 *right*, 298 *center*, 308. Catholic Relief Services/Daniel Medinger: 260 *left*. Catholic Television of San Antonio: 40. The Claretians: 53. Clipart.com: 52, 77 *bottom*, 312. Comstock Images: 19 *background*, 274 *right*. Corbis/Andy Aitchison: 94; The Art Archive/Alfredo Dagli Orti: 124; Dave Bartruff: 226; Peter Beck: 298 *top left*; Alessandra Benedetti: 293 *top*; Bettmann: 269; Ed Bock: 183; Rolf Bruderer: 267 *center left*; Steve Chenn: 253 *top*; Richard Cummins: 229; Design Pics/David Chapman: 347; Godong/P. Deliss: 104; Godong/Pascal Deloche: 117; Ted Horowitz: 266 *center left*; Wolfgang Kaehler: 303; LWA-Dan Tardiff: 266 *bottom right*; LWA-Stephen Welstead: 252 *bottom*; Tom & Dee Ann McCarthy: 279; Nancy Ney: 266 *center right*; Mark Peterson: 302 *top*; Anthony Redpath: 266 *bottom center*; Reuters: 115; Reuters/Tony Gentile: R12 *top*; Ariel Skelley: 271; Liba Taylor: 88; Kurt-Michael Watermann: 162. The Crosiers/Gene Plaisted, OSC: R1, 17 *center*, R22, 44 *top left*, 46 *bottom left*, 48 *top*, 62, 65 *top*, 69, 89, 116, 123 *top left*, 123 *top right*, 136, 137, 141, 152, 170, 213, 228, 238, 242, 245 *center right*, 260 *center*, 273, 281 *top*, 289 *right*, 290. Courtesy, Daughters of Charity Archives, Emmitsburg, Maryland: 29 *bottom*. Gerald Cubbitt: 234 *left*. Digital Stock Corporation: 321 *top*. Digital Vision: 190–191. Dreamstime.com/Perseomedusa: 351; Valeriya Potapova: 197; Dale Shelton: R29. Octavio Duran, OFM: 264 *bottom right*. Neal Farris: 17 *right*, 19 *bottom*, 25, 31, 38 *top*, 43, 44 *center left*, 48 *bottom*, 55, 67, 95, 102, 103, 107, 119, 131, 143, 146, 147, 149 *right*, 169 *center right*, 171, 184, 187, 189, 190, 191 *left*, 202–203, 207, 209, 219, 241, 245 *center left*, 247, 248–249, 253 *bottom right*, 259, 283, 295, 310, 344. Getty Images/AFP/Musa Al-Shaer: 179 *left*; AFP/Tiziana Fabi: 129; AFP/Tasso Marcelo: R3; AFP/Andreas Solaro: R9; Tony Anderson: 267 *center right*; Christina Angorola: 267 *bottom left*; Dave J. Anthony: 267 *top*; Jason Childs: 69 *background*; Jim Cummins: 156 *left*; Stuart Dee: R19; Digital Vision: 298 *bottom*; Denis Felix: 8, 169 *center left*, 176; Flying Colours Ltd: 32; Leroy Grannis: 68 *background*; Saul Herrera: R17; Russell Illig: 272; Jacobs Stock Photography: 33 *top right*; Spike Mafford: 275 *bottom*, 281 *bottom*; Nancy Ney: 266 *top right*; Kevin Peterson: 60 *top left*, 60 *top center left*, 60 *top center right*, 61 *center left*, 61 *center right*, 61 *right*; Photodisc: 68 *background*, 127 *background*, 252 *top*; John Riley: 139 *top*; David Roth: 266 *bottom right*; Elizabeth Simpson: 165 *top*; Sean Sprague: 37 *bottom*; Stockbyte: 267 *bottom right*; Steve Weinberg: 90; SW Productions: 157 *bottom*, 260 *right*; Arthur Tilley: 266 *top*, 267 *center*; Time & Life Pictures/Cindy Karp: 36 *left*, 36 *center left*. Jeff Greenberg: 138–139 *bottom*. Anne Hamersky: 79 *top left*. The Image Works/Peter Hvizdak: 288 *right*; Jack Kurtz: 289 *left*. Jesuit Volunteer Corp of America: 41. Jupiter Images/Banana Stock: 60 *right*; Burke/Triolo: 21; Corbis: 266 *top left*; Creatas: 43 *background*; Mel Curtis: 267 *center right*; Digital Vision: 267 *top right*; Rubberball Productions: 267 *top*; Stockbyte: 252 *center*, 253 *bottom left*. Ken Karp: 10–11, 12, 13, 14, 44 *center*, 45 *left*, 48–49 *background*, 76 *left*, 85, 86, 161, 201, 245c, 278 *top*, 298 *top right*, 299 *top left*, 307. Eugene Llacuna: 138. Greg Lord: 80 *top*, 227, 351. Masterfile: 323; Gary Black: 143 *background*. Matton/Phovoir: 29 *top left*, 153 *bottom*, 193 *top left*. Lawrence Migdale: 301 *left*. NASA: 304. Odyssey Productions, Inc./Robert Frerck: 234 *right*. Our Lady of the Mississippi Abbey, Dubuque, IA: 36 *bottom*. Mosista Pambudi: 301 *right*. Pauline Books & Media/Thuan Family Archives: 157 *top*. Photodisc: 252–253. PhotoEdit/Robert Brenner: 156 *right*; Cathy Melloan: 165 *bottom*; David Young-Wolff: 349. PhotoZion.com/John Theodor: 309. Polaris Images/Evelyn Hockstein: 38 *bottom*; Allan Tannenbaum: 179, 302 *bottom*. Punchstock/Blend Images: 324 *bottom right*; Photodisc: 324 *bottom left*; Stockbyte: 321 *bottom*. Reuters/Peter Andrews: 146–147; Robert Galbraith: 296–297; Jayanta Shaw: 265. Steve Satushek: 266 *bottom left*. Ellen B. Senisi: 122 *left*. Chris Sheridan: 151. SuperStock/Corbis: R7; DeAgostini: R30; Design Pics: R13; Lisette Le Bon: 275 *top right*; NaturePL: 208–209; Photononstop: 347 *top*; Tetra Images: R14. Susan Spann Photography: 205. St. Joseph's Abbey/Br. Emmanuel Morinelli, OCSO: 264 *top right*. Courtesy of Trinity Stores, www.trinitystores.com, 800.699.4482/St. Dominic Guzman © Br. Robert Lentz, OFM: 181. Used under license from Shutterstock.com/art marta: R18; Donald Joski: R20; Oleksandr Koval: R12 *bottom*; LilKar: 343; V.J. Matthew: 345 *bottom*; medeia: R24; Monkey Business Images: R6, R15 *top*; Dayna More: R26; mtmmarek: 348 *border*; pogonici: R15 *bottom*; Zulhazmi Zabri: 76 *right*. Veer/Image Source: 324 *bottom center*; Photodisc: 76 *center left*. Wikimedia Commons: R4. W.P. Wittman Ltd: 18, 26, 45 *right*, 50, 60 *left*, 60 *center*, 61 *center*, 61 *right*, 63, 74 *top*, 77 *top*, 79 *top right*, 79 *bottom*, 84, 114–115, 149 *left*, 150, 166, 169 *center*, 191 *right*, 193 *bottom*, 212, 217 *bottom*, 220–221, 231, 236, 239, 240 *top*, 278 *bottom*, 288 *left*, 300, 305 *top*, 321 *bottom*, 327. Celebration of Saints by Michael McGrath. Copyright © World Library Publications. www.wlpmusic.com. All rights reserved. Used by permission: 348.

Illustrator Credits

Series Patterned Background Design: Evan Polenghi. Bassino & Guy: 129. Rayne Beaudoin: 40, 140, 170, 216. Diane Bennett: 132–133, 136–137, 291. Tom Boll: 296–297. Chris Butler: 276–277. Lynne Cannoy: 200, 201. Harvey Chan: 146–147, 148–149. Margaret Chodos-Irvine: 101–102. Gwen Connelly: 210–211. Steve Cowden: 145 *top*. Margaret Cusack: 260, 261. David Dean: 22–23, 172–173. Rob Dunlavy: 34, 35. Suzanne Duranceau: 32–33. Luigi Galente: 93 *left*, 98, 125. Stephanie Garcia: 184–185. Janelle Genovese: 245, 262–263. Alex Gross: 254–255. Kate Hosford: 188–189. W. B. Johnston: 50–51, 108–109, 224–225 *background*, 246. Dave Klug: 256, 268. Dave LaFleur: 56–57, 64–65 *bottom*. James Madsen: 180. Diana Magnuson: 229. Angela Martini: 23 *right*. David McGlynn: 44–45, 112–113. Cliff Neilsen: 214–215. Mike Reagan: 286–287. Billy Renkl: 74–75. Zina Saunders: 322 *bottom*. Jane Sterrett: 58–59. Kristina Swarner: 24–25. Amanda Warren: 79–90, 155–159, 161–164, 166, 231, 232, 233 *top*, 234–242, 307–312, 322 *top*. Andrew Wheatcroft: vi, 17, 20, 60, 86 *bottom*, 93 *right*, 96–97, 120–121, 144–145, 169, 174–175, 196, 198–199, 222–223, 224 *top*, *bottom*, 225, 232–233 *bottom*. Linda Wingerter: 72–73.

The Sadlier *We Believe* Program was drawn from the wisdom of the community. It was developed by nationally recognized experts in catechesis, curriculum, and child development. These teachers of the faith and practitioners helped us to frame every lesson to be age-appropriate and appealing. In addition, a team including respected catechetical, liturgical, pastoral, and theological experts shared their insights and inspired the development of the program.

Contributors to the inspiration and development are:

Dr. Gerard F. Baumbach
Professor Emeritus, Institute for Church Life
Director Emeritus of the Echo Program
University of Notre Dame

Carole M. Eipers, D.Min.
Vice President, Executive Director
 of Catechetics
William H. Sadlier, Inc.

Theological Consultants

His Eminence Donald Cardinal Wuerl, M.A., S.T.D.
Archbishop of Washington

Most Reverend Edward K. Braxton, Ph.D., S.T.D.
Official Theological Consultant
Bishop of Belleville

Reverend Joseph A. Komonchak, Ph.D.
Professor Emeritus of Theology and Religious Studies
The Catholic University of America

Most Reverend Richard J. Malone, Th.D.
Bishop of Buffalo

Reverend Monsignor John E. Pollard, S.T.L.
Pastor, Queen of All Saints Basilica
Chicago, IL

Scriptural Consultant

Reverend Donald Senior, CP, Ph.D., S.T.D.
Member, Pontifical Biblical Commission
President Emeritus of Catholic Theological Union
Chicago, IL

Catechetical and Liturgical Consultants

Patricia Andrews
Director of Religious Education
Our Lady of Lourdes Church,
Slidell, LA

Reverend Monsignor John F. Barry, P.A.
Pastor, American Martyrs Parish
Manhattan Beach, CA

Reverend Monsignor John M. Unger
Deputy Superintendent for Catechesis
 and Evangelization
Archdiocese of St. Louis

Thomas S. Quinlan
Director, Religious Education Office
Diocese of Joliet

Curriculum and Child Development Consultants

Brother Robert R. Bimonte, FSC
President, NCEA

Sr. Carol Cimino, SSJ, Ed.D.
Superintendent, Catholic Schools
Diocese of Buffalo

Gini Shimabukuro, Ed.D.
Professor Emeritus
Catholic Educational Leadership Program
School of Education
University of San Francisco

Catholic Social Teaching Consultants

John Carr
Director
Initiative on Catholic Social Thought and Public Life
Georgetown University

Joan Rosenhauer
Executive Vice President, U.S. Operations
Catholic Relief Services
Baltimore, MD

Inculturation Consultants

Allan Figueroa Deck, S.J., Ph.D., S.T.D.
Rector of Jesuit Community
Charles Casassa Chair of Catholic Social Values
Professor
Loyola Marymount University

Kirk P. Gaddy, Ed.D.
Middle School Team Leader/Religion Teacher
St. Francis International School
Silver Spring, MD

Reverend Nguyễn Việt Hưng
Vietnamese Catechetical Committee

Dulce M. Jiménez-Abreu
Director of Bilingual Programs
William H. Sadlier, Inc.

Mariology Consultant

Sister M. Jean Frisk, ISSM, S.T.L.
International Marian Research Institute
Dayton, OH

Media/Technology Consultants

Sister Judith Dieterle, SSL
Past President, National Association of
    Catechetical Media Professionals

Robert Methven
Vice President, Digital Publisher
William H. Sadlier, Inc.

Robert T. Carson
Media Design Director
William H. Sadlier, Inc.

Writing/Development Team

Rosemary K. Calicchio
Executive Vice President, Publisher

Blake Bergen
Director of Publications

Joanne McDonald
Editorial Director

Regina Kelly
Supervising Editor

William M. Ippolito
Director of Corporate Planning

Martin Smith
Planning and Analysis
    Project Director

Dignory Reina
Editor

Peggy O'Neill
Digital Content Manager

Contributing Writers
Christian Garcia
Kathy Hendricks
Shannon Jones
Theresa MacDonald
Gloria Shahin

Suzan Laroquette
Director of Catechetical
    Consultant Services

Judith A. Devine
National Sales Consultant

Victor Valenzuela
National Religion Consultant

Publishing Operations Team

Carole Uettwiller
Vice President of Planning and
    Technology

Vince Gallo
Senior Creative Director

Francesca O'Malley
Art/Design Director

Cheryl Golding
Production Director

Monica Reece
Senior Production Manager

Jovito Pagkalinawan
Electronic Prepress Director

Design/Image Staff
Kevin Butler, Nancy Figueiredo,
Stephen Flanagan, Lorraine Forte,
Debrah Kaiser, Cesar Llacuna,
Bob Schatz, Karen Tully

Production Staff
Monica Bernier, Robin D'Amato,
Rachel Jacobs, Carol Lin,
Vincent McDonough,
Yolanda Miley, Laura Rotondi,
Allison Stearns

We are grateful to our loyal *We Believe* users whose insights and suggestions have inspired *We Believe: Catholic Identity Edition*—the premier faith formation tool built on the six tasks of catechesis.

Contents

UNIT 2

Confirmation and Eucharist Complete Our Initiation

• On Pentecost the Holy Spirit came upon the first disciples. • Laying on of hands and anointing are signs of the Holy Spirit's presence. • In Confirmation we become more like Christ and are strengthened to be his witnesses. • Preparation is an important part of Confirmation.

Ezekiel 37:14; Acts of the Apostles 1:8; 2:1–47

As Catholics .... Symbols of the Holy Spirit

PROJECT DISCIPLE *featuring* Saint John Bosco

Take Home Growing closer to Christ

Chapter Test

• Confirmation leads us from Baptism to the Eucharist. • In the Sacrament of Confirmation, we are sealed with the Gift of the Holy Spirit. • The gifts of the Holy Spirit help those who are confirmed. • Confirmation calls those anointed to live out their Baptism as witnesses of Jesus Christ.

John 14:26; 16:12–13; Galatians 5:22–23
Rite of Confirmation

As Catholics .... Chrismation

PROJECT DISCIPLE *featuring* World Youth Day

Take Home Filling your home with the fruits of the Holy Spirit

Chapter Test

• In the Eucharist we celebrate and receive Jesus Christ. • The Eucharist is a memorial, a meal, and a sacrifice. • We recognize Jesus in the breaking of the bread. • Jesus is the Bread of Life.

John 6:1–14, 27, 35, 51, 55, 56; Luke 22:19–20; 24:13–35; Acts of the Apostles 2:42

As Catholics .... Covenant

PROJECT DISCIPLE *featuring* The Feast of the Body and Blood of Christ

Take Home Offering God thanks and praise

Chapter Test

• The Introductory Rites bring us together as a community. • During the Liturgy of the Word, we listen and respond to the Word of God. • During the Liturgy of the Eucharist, we pray the great prayer of thanksgiving and receive the Body and Blood of Christ. • The Concluding Rites send us out to be the Body of Christ to others.

Luke 22:15–20; The Roman Missal

As Catholics .... Lectionary and *Book of the Gospels*

PROJECT DISCIPLE *featuring* Saint Kateri Tekakwitha

Take Home Taking part in the Mass

Chapter Test

• Jesus teaches us to pray. • We are called to pray daily. • Sacramentals are a part of the Church's prayer life. • Catholics have a rich tradition of special practices and popular devotions.

Psalm 121:1–6; 146:2; Luke 18:13; 23:34; John 11:41; 2 Corinthians 13:13; Philippians 1:9; 1 Thessalonians 5:17; Ephesians 6:18

As Catholics .... Our Lady of Guadalupe

PROJECT DISCIPLE *featuring* Las Posadas

Take Home Taking a "sacramental journey"

Chapter Test

Retreat: LITURGY & SACRAMENTS

• Advent is a season of joyful expectation and preparation for the coming of the Son of God.
John 4:25, 26; The Roman Missal

• The season of Christmas is a time to rejoice in the Incarnation.
Luke 2:1–14; John 1:14; Isaiah 61:10

UNIT 3

The Sacraments of Healing Restore Us....169

SEASONAL CHAPTERS

27 Easter 307
• The Easter season is a special time to rejoice over
the new life we have in Christ.

Mark 16:1–10; 1 Peter 5:4; James 1:12; Luke 1:41–43; The Roman Missal

The *We Believe* program will help us to

learn **share** and **live our Catholic faith.**
celebrate

Throughout the year we will hear about many saints and holy people.

Saint Alexius   Saint Josephine Bakhita
Saint Andrew Kim Taegon   Saint Kateri Tekakwitha
Saint Anthony Claret   Saint Margaret of Scotland
Saint Barbara   Martyrs of Vietnam
Saint Dominic   Mary, Mother of God
Saint Dominic Savio   Our Lady of Guadalupe
Saint Elizabeth Ann Seton   Pope Gregory XIII
Saint John Bosco   Blessed Pope Pius IX
Saint Joseph   Saint John Paul II

Together, let us grow as a community of faith.

Welcome!

✝ We Gather in Prayer

Leader: Welcome, everyone, to Grade 5 *We Believe*. As we begin each chapter, we gather in prayer. We pray to God together. Sometimes, we will read from Scripture, other times we will say the prayers of the Church or sing a song of thanks and praise to God.

Today, let us sing the *We Believe* song!

♫ We Believe, We Believe in God

Refrain:

We believe in God;
We believe, we believe in Jesus;
We believe in the Spirit who gives us life.
We believe, we believe in God.

We believe in the Holy Spirit,
Who renews the face of the earth.
We believe we are part of a living Church,
And forever we will live with God.

(Refrain)

Each day we learn more about God.

In each chapter, we find four main faith statements. They start the day's lesson. They focus us on what we will be learning about in the lesson.

WE GATHER

✝ *Thank you, God, for all our classmates.*

Then we

think about
talk about
act out
draw about
write about

Life

at school
at home
in our parish
in our world
in our neighborhood

Talk about your life right now. What groups, teams, or clubs do you belong to?

Why do you like being a part of these groups?

What does belonging to these groups tell other people about you?

When we see **We Gather** we begin by taking a moment to pray.

When we see **We Believe** we learn more about our Catholic faith.

WE BELIEVE

We learn about:

- the Blessed Trinity—God the Father, God the Son, and God the Holy Spirit

- Jesus, the Son of God, who became one of us

- the Church and its history and teachings

- the Mass and the sacraments

- our call to be a disciple of Jesus.

UNIT 1

Jesus Christ Shares His Life with Us

"As the Father loves me, so I also love you."
(John 15:9)

UNIT 2

Confirmation and Eucharist Complete Our Initiation

"Do this in memory of me."　　(Luke 22:19)

UNIT 3

The Sacraments of Healing Restore Us

"Is anyone among you suffering? He should pray. Is anyone in good spirits? He should sing praise." (James 5:13)

UNIT 4

We Love and Serve as Jesus Did

"So faith, hope, love remain, these three; but the greatest of these is love."　　(1 Corinthians 13:13)

A major theme in your *We Believe* textbook this year is learning more about the Seven Sacraments of the Catholic Church. Your book is divided into four units.

Watch for these special signs:

Whenever we see ✝ we make the Sign of the Cross. We pray and begin our day's lesson.

📖 is an open Bible . When we see it with a blue Scripture reference, what follows is a paraphrase of the Bible. When we see a black reference like this (John 13:34), that passage is directly from the Bible.

When we see 🏃 we do an activity .
We might:

- talk together
- write a story
- draw a picture
- act out a story or situation
- imagine ourselves doing something
- sing a song together, or make up one
- work together on a special project.

There are all kinds of activities! We might see 🏃 in any part of our day's lesson. Be on the lookout!

Can you guess what 🎵 means? That's right, it means it is time to sing, or listen to music . We sing songs we know, make up our own, and sing along with those in our *We Believe* music program.

When we see **Key Words** we review the meanings of important faith words we have learned in the day's lesson.

As Catholics...

Here we discover something special about our faith. We reflect on what we have discovered and try to make it a part of our life. Don't forget to read it!

WE RESPOND

We can respond by:

- thinking about ways our faith affects the things we say and do

- sharing our thoughts and feelings

- praying to God.

Then in our home, neighborhood, school, parish, and world, we say and do the things that show love for God and others.

When we see **We Respond** we reflect and act on what we have learned about God and our Catholic faith.

Draw yourself doing something that shows you are a disciple of Jesus Christ.

We are so happy you are with us!

We sharpen our disciple skills with each chapter's Project Disciple pages!

Show What you Know
We "show what we know" about each chapter's content. A disciple is always learning more about his or her faith.

More to Explore
More to Explore activities develop our comprehension and Internet skills.

Reality Check
Here we can express our ideas and choices.

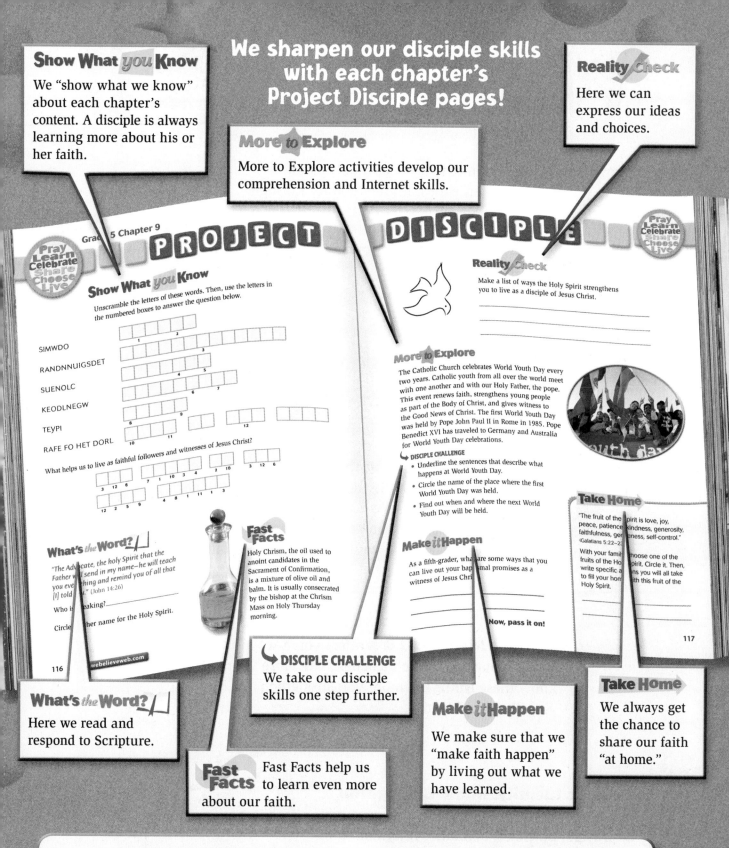

Grade 5 Chapter 9

PROJECT DISCIPLE

Show What you Know
Unscramble the letters of these words. Then, use the letters in the numbered boxes to answer the question below.

SIMWDO

RANDNNUIGSDET

SUENOLC

KEODLNEGW

TEYPI

RAFE FO HET DORL

What helps us to live as faithful followers and witnesses of Jesus Christ?

What's the Word?
"The Advocate, the holy Spirit that the Father will send in my name—he will teach you everything and remind you of all that [I] told you." (John 14:26)

Who is speaking? _____

Circle another name for the Holy Spirit.

116

webelieveweb.com

Fast Facts
Holy Chrism, the oil used to anoint candidates in the Sacrament of Confirmation, is a mixture of olive oil and balm. It is usually consecrated by the bishop at the Chrism Mass on Holy Thursday morning.

Reality Check
Make a list of ways the Holy Spirit strengthens you to live as a disciple of Jesus Christ.

_____
_____
_____

More to Explore
The Catholic Church celebrates World Youth Day every two years. Catholic youth from all over the world meet with one another and with our Holy Father, the pope. This event renews faith, strengthens young people as part of the Body of Christ, and gives witness to the Good News of Christ. The first World Youth Day was held by Pope John Paul II in Rome in 1985. Pope Benedict XVI has traveled to Germany and Australia for World Youth Day celebrations.

DISCIPLE CHALLENGE
- Underline the sentences that describe what happens at World Youth Day.
- Circle the name of the place where the first World Youth Day was held.
- Find out when and where the next World Youth Day will be held.

Make it Happen
As a fifth-grader, what are some ways that you can live out your baptismal promises as a witness of Jesus Christ?

_____
_____
_____

Now, pass it on!

Take Home
"The fruit of the Spirit is love, joy, peace, patience, kindness, generosity, faithfulness, gentleness, self-control." (Galatians 5:22–23)

With your family, choose one of the fruits of the Holy Spirit. Circle it. Then, write specific actions you will take to fill your home with this fruit of the Holy Spirit.

_____
_____

117

DISCIPLE CHALLENGE
We take our disciple skills one step further.

What's the Word?
Here we read and respond to Scripture.

Fast Facts
Fast Facts help us to learn even more about our faith.

Make it Happen
We make sure that we "make faith happen" by living out what we have learned.

Take Home
We always get the chance to share our faith "at home."

There are **LOADS** of **ACTIVITIES** that make us better disciples! Just look at this additional list.

Question Corner—take a quiz

What Would You Do?—making the right choices

Pray Today—talking and listening to God

Celebrate!—all about worshiping God

Saint Stories—finding great role models

Picture This—a great way for us to see and show our disciple skills

Now, Pass It On!—invites us to witness to our faith

And every chapter ends with a Chapter Test!

You are on a journey to continue to grow as a disciple of Jesus Christ. You can strengthen your Catholic Identity through these new features:

Catholic Identity: Retreats provide time for you to reflect on what it means to be a Catholic. There are four retreats in your book.

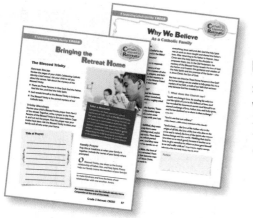

Bringing the Retreat Home helps you to share the theme and highlights of each retreat. **Why We Believe as a Catholic Family** helps you and your family to uphold and explain your Catholic faith to others.

Catholic Identity: Q & A offers you a way to review what the Church teaches. The more you know these truths the more you strengthen your Catholic Identity.

Catholic Identity: Home Companion provides you and your family with a resource of prayers, practices, and other information to enrich your identity as a Catholic family.

Student and Family resources are available at: **religion.sadlierconnect.com**

The Blessed Trinity

Part 1   I Open My Heart

We believe in the Blessed Trinity—God the Father, God the Son, and God the Holy Spirit.

Imagine that you are a famous art critic who has a popular blog. While visiting cathedrals to study religious artwork, you find this stained glass window. It represents the Blessed Trinity. Blog about your reaction below. What does the stained glass image teach you about the Blessed Trinity? How does it portray the following: God the Father, God the Son, and God the Holy Spirit? What do you like about the image? What would you change?

The Blessed Trinity

Part 2   We Come Together for Prayer

Leader: Let us pray.

"After Jesus was baptized, he came up from the water and behold, the heavens were opened [for him], and he saw the Spirit of God descending like a dove [and] coming upon him. And a voice came from the heavens, saying, 'This is my beloved Son, with whom I am well pleased.'" (Matthew 3:16–17)

All: I believe in the Blessed Trinity, One God in Three Persons.

Reader 1: "In the beginning, when God created the heavens and the earth. . . . God said: 'Let us make man in our image, after our likeness.'" (Genesis 1:1, 26)

All: (*Lift arms upwards.*) I believe in God, the Father, the Lord of All Creation.

Reader 2: "No one has ever seen God. The only Son, God, who is at the Father's side, has revealed him." (John 1:18)

All: (*Extend arms outwards.*) I believe in Jesus Christ, the Son, our Lord and Savior.

Reader 3: Jesus said, "I will ask the Father, and he will give you another Advocate to be with you always, the Spirit of truth." (John 14:16–17)

All: (*Fold hands in prayer.*) I believe in the Holy Spirit, the Lord and Giver of Life.

Leader: What words can you use to describe each Person of the Blessed Trinity? Write these words in the interlocking circles.

(*All write and share descriptions.*)

"The mystery of the Most Holy Trinity is the central mystery of the Christian faith and of Christian life. God alone can make it known to us by revealing himself as Father, Son, and Holy Spirit." (*Catechism of the Catholic Church*, 261)

All: Blessed Trinity, may we always continue to grow in our relationship with you. Amen.

Catholic Identity Retreat

The Blessed Trinity

Part 3   I Cherish God's Word

Jesus said, "Go, therefore, and make disciples of all nations, baptizing them in the name of the Father, and of the Son, and of the holy Spirit, teaching them to observe all that I have commanded you. And behold, I am with you always, until the end of the age" (Matthew 28:19–20).

READ the quotation from Scripture. Read slowly. Pay close attention to what you are reading.

REFLECT on:

- What makes a name important and unique? Think about the *name* of the Father, and of the Son, and of the Holy Spirit.

- What help do you need from the Blessed Trinity, Father, Son, and Holy Spirit, today?

- In this reading what are you, as a believer in the Blessed Trinity, asked to do? How will you do that?

SHARE your thoughts and feelings with God in prayer. Let your thoughts and feelings come naturally. Speak to God as a friend.

CONTEMPLATE, or sit quietly and allow your attention to remain focused on God's Word in the Scripture passage from the Gospel of Matthew above.

Pilgrims from around the world gathered for the opening Mass of World Youth Day 2013 in Rio de Janeiro, Brazil

The Blessed Trinity

Part 4   I Value My Catholic Faith

In Baptism you became a child of God, the Father; a member of the Body of Christ, the Church; and you received the Holy Spirit. Through Baptism, Catholics are called to evangelize or to spread the Good News. Teaching the mysteries of our faith, like belief in the Blessed Trinity, is no easy task! Many images and descriptions have been used to explain the Blessed Trinity.

If your group had the opportunity to film a 5-minute podcast that would be streamed worldwide, how would you teach the world about *One* God in *Three* Persons? Plan your podcast in the space below.

Trinity icon, by Andrei Rublev (1360–1430)

The Blessed Trinity

Part 5 I Celebrate Catholic Identity

You are a believer in the Blessed Trinity. How do you show that you believe in this mystery of faith?

In the space below, ask the Blessed Trinity to help you to live your faith. Decorate the space around your prayer. Share this prayer with your family tonight, and pray it together.

The Blessed Trinity

Part 6   I Honor My Catholic Identity

Reader 1: "God is love, and whoever remains in love remains in God and God in him." (1 John 4:16)

Leader: O God, as you reveal yourself to us as Father, Son, and Holy Spirit, you show us that you are love. Through Baptism, you share your love with us. We are joined to you and to one another.

All: God, our Father, let us be one in your love.

Reader 2: "In this way the love of God was revealed to us: God sent his only Son into the world so that we might have life through him." (1 John 4:9)

All: God, the Son, our Lord Jesus Christ, let us be one in your love.

Reader 3: "This is how we know that we remain in him and he in us, that he has given us of his Spirit." (1 John 4:13)

All: God, the Holy Spirit, our Advocate and Guide, let us be one in your love.

Reader 4: "Beloved, let us love one another, because love is of God." (1 John 4:7)

Leader: In closing, let us pray together the Glory Be to the Father. As you pray, think about the love that is God, who is filling your heart and strengthening you. Reflect on how you can love the Blessed Trinity and one another.

All: Glory be to the Father
and to the Son
and the Holy Spirit,
as it was in the beginning
is now, and ever shall be
world without end. Amen.

Bringing the Retreat Home

Catholic Identity Retreat

The Blessed Trinity

Retreat Recap

Review the pages of your child's *Celebrating Catholic Identity: Creed* retreat. Ask your child to tell you about the retreat. Talk about the mystery of the Blessed Trinity:

- There are Three Persons in One God: God the Father, God the Son, and God the Holy Spirit.
- God reveals himself as the Blessed Trinity in Scripture.
- The Blessed Trinity is the central mystery of our Catholic faith.

Trinity Blessings

Review your child's Blessed Trinity prayer from Part 5 of the retreat. Together, write a prayer to the Three Persons of the Blessed Trinity in the space below. Copy it, and cut out the prayer. Post the prayer near your inside front door. Ask the Blessed Trinity to bless your family and all who enter your home.

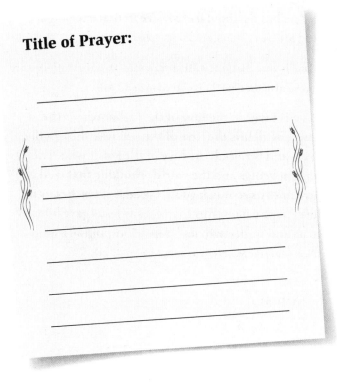

Title of Prayer:

_____

_____

_____

_____

_____

_____

_____

Take a Moment

Sometimes we have questions about mysteries of faith such as the Blessed Trinity. Tell your child that when we pray to God, we are having a conversation with him. We can even ask God our questions of faith. Spend a moment with your child in quiet prayer, asking God your questions and requesting his help to grow in wisdom and understanding as a disciple of Jesus Christ.

Family Prayer

Pray this at mealtime or when your family is together. Include the names of your family where prompted.

O Blessed Trinity, you show us the loving relationship of Father, Son, and Holy Spirit. Please help our family (*name the members of your family*):

_____

to make kindness and love the basis of our relationships with one another. Amen.

For more resources, see the *Catholic Identity Home Companion* at the end of this book.

Why We Believe
As a Catholic Family

What if someone asks us:

- What is the basis of the Catholic belief in the Blessed Trinity? Is this belief found in the Bible?

- How could One God be Three Persons?

The following resources can help us to respond:

The Blessed Trinity is the central mystery of our Catholic faith. That is because it is the mystery of who God is. All the sacraments, liturgies, prayers, and faith of the Church express and celebrate this mystery. In fact, we proclaim it at every Mass in the Nicene Creed and every time we pray the Sign of the Cross!

🌿 What does Scripture say?

"In the beginning, when God created the heavens and the earth, the earth was a formless wasteland, and darkness covered the abyss, while a mighty wind swept over the waters." (Genesis 1:1–2)

When Jesus was baptized by John the Baptist, "heaven was opened and the holy Spirit descended upon him in bodily form like a dove. And a voice came from heaven, 'You are my beloved Son; with you I am well pleased'" (Luke 3:21–22).

"When the time for Pentecost was fulfilled, they were all in one place together. . . . Suddenly there came from the sky a noise like a strong driving wind, and it filled the entire house in which they were. Then there appeared to them tongues as of fire, which parted and came to rest on each one of them. And they were all filled with the holy Spirit." (Acts of the Apostles 2:1–4)

In these and other words from the Bible, the love of God as Father, Son, and Holy Spirit is revealed. From the Gospels we learn that in the Incarnation the Second Divine Person of the Trinity took on a human nature. Thus, Jesus Christ has two natures: divine and human. God the Father, our Creator, was at work in everything Jesus said and did. God the Holy Spirit was at work as Jesus taught and shared the Father's love. After returning to his Father in Heaven, Jesus Christ sent the Holy Spirit to the disciples to empower them, too. In the Old Testament, the mystery of the Blessed Trinity reveals the love of God, the Father and Creator; the guidance and wisdom of the Holy Spirit; and the promise of the Savior—who is Jesus Christ, the Son of God.

But how can there be *Three* Divine Persons in One God? As human beings we are unable to fully grasp this. It is a mystery of our faith, a truth of our faith that we know only because God has revealed it to us.

🌿 What does the Church say?

"God's very being is love. By sending his only Son and the Spirit of Love in the fullness of time, God has revealed his innermost secret: God himself is an eternal exchange of love, Father, Son, and Holy Spirit, and he has destined us to share in that exchange." (CCC, 221; see 1 Corinthians 2:7–16; Ephesians 3:9–12)

"God is one but not solitary." (Fides Damasi, a fifth-century statement of the Church, as quoted in CCC, 254)

"God is love. . . . the love of the Father who is the origin of all life, the love of the Son who dies on the Cross and is raised, the love of the Spirit who renews human beings and the world. Thinking that God is love does us so much good, because it teaches us to love, to give ourselves to others as Jesus gave himself to us and walks with us." (Pope Francis, Angelus message, Solemnity of the Most Holy Trinity, May 26, 2013)

Notes:

Jesus Christ Shares His Life with Us

Seasonal Chapters

DEAR FAMILY

In Unit 1 your child will grow as a disciple of Jesus by:

- understanding that Jesus Christ is God's only Son and that he came to show us God's love
- learning that the Church shares in Jesus' mission and living out the ways to proclaim the Good News
- celebrating Christ's Paschal Mystery in the liturgy and sharing in God's life
- recognizing the meaning of the Sacraments of Initiation, the Sacraments of Healing and the Sacraments at the Service of Communion
- appreciating Baptism as the foundation of Christian life which gives us the hope of Eternal Life.

Saint Stories

In Chapter 4 you will find Saint Paul and some of his story from the Acts of the Apostles. Paul is one of the biblical writers who was inspired by the Holy Spirit. Some of the wonderful images we have for the Church came from Saint Paul's letters. "People of God" and "Body of Christ" are two images that Paul used. Invite your family to complete the sentence:

The Church is like _____

_____.

More to Explore

In Baptism we become members of the Body of Christ, the Church. Check your parish or diocesan Web site to learn more about the local Church to which you belong. You might also go to the Vatican Web site (www.vatican.va).

Reality Check

"Jesus gives us the example of holiness in the daily life of family and work."
(*Catechism of the Catholic Church*, 564)

Picture This

Look at the images of the sacraments on pages 44–45. Talk about what your family can do to support those who are receiving one or more of these. Pray for them.

Show That You Care

One of the Corporal Works of Mercy is to visit the sick. If you have a family friend or neighbor who is ill or elderly, plan a visit. Or, you might make a card together for one of the parish ministers to bring when he or she visits an ill parishioner.

Take Home

Be ready for this unit's Take Home:

Chapter 1: Talking about Jesus' parables

Chapter 2: Choosing one of the Works of Mercy

Chapter 3: Sharing memories of the sacraments

Chapter 4: Choosing a family patron saint

Chapter 5: Discussing the symbols used at Baptism

Jesus Shares God's Life with Us

✝ We Gather in Prayer

Leader: Blessed are you, Lord, God of tenderness and compassion, rich in kindness and faithfulness.
(Cf. Exodus 34:6)

All: Now and for ever.

Leader: Father, you sent your Son to us so that we could know your love and feel your mercy. May all who follow Christ be a sign of your love.

Reader: A reading from the holy Gospel according to Matthew

"Jesus went around to all the towns and villages, teaching in their synagogues, proclaiming the gospel of the kingdom, and curing every disease and illness" (Matthew 9:35).

The Gospel of the Lord.

All: Praise to you, Lord Jesus Christ.

♫ Jesus Is with Us

Refrain:
Jesus is with us today,
beside us to guide us today.
Jesus teaches us, Jesus heals us,
for we are his Church;
we are his chosen;
we are the children of God.

Jesus teaches us to love one another,
to care for our brothers and sisters in need.
For when we show kindness to others,
we are God's children indeed.

(Refrain)

Jesus is the Son of God.

WE GATHER

✝ *Jesus, share your life with us.*

Imagine that an important person is coming to visit your city. What will people do to prepare for this visit?

WE BELIEVE

In the New Testament we read about a person who prepared the people for Jesus. This person was John. Many people knew him as John the Baptist.

John talked to people about repentance and forgiveness. He asked them to change their lives. He told them to show in all that they said and did how important God was to them. John was preparing the people for the Messiah, the Anointed One. *Messiah* is another word for "Christ." Jesus Christ is the Anointed One who would bring new life.

John baptized people with water in the Jordan River. This was a sign of their willingness to change their lives. John said,

"I am baptizing you with water, for repentance, but the one who is coming after me is mightier than I. I am not worthy to carry his sandals. He will baptize you with the holy Spirit and fire" (Matthew 3:11).

In those days Jesus lived in the town of Nazareth in Galilee. He had grown up there with Mary, his mother, Joseph, his foster father and many relatives and friends. When Jesus was about thirty years old, he left Nazareth. He went to the Jordan River where John was preaching.

When Jesus arrived at the Jordan River, he asked John to baptize him. But John said to Jesus, "I need to be baptized by you, and yet you are coming to me?" (Matthew 3:14). However, Jesus convinced John to baptize him. As Jesus came up from the water, the heavens opened. The Holy Spirit, like a dove, descended upon Jesus, and a voice from the heavens said, "This is my beloved Son, with whom I am well pleased" (Matthew 3:17).

Jesus' ministry Jesus Christ is the Son of God. He is the Second Person of the Blessed Trinity who became man. **The Blessed Trinity** is the Three Persons in One God: God the Father, God the Son, and God the Holy Spirit. It was at Jesus' baptism at the Jordan River that the love of God the Father, Son, and Holy Spirit was first made known.

Soon after his baptism Jesus returned to Nazareth. There he "went according to his custom into the synagogue on the sabbath day. He stood up to read and was handed a scroll of the prophet Isaiah. He unrolled the scroll and found the passage where it was written:

'The Spirit of the Lord is upon me,
because he has anointed me
to bring glad tidings to the poor.

He has sent me to proclaim liberty to captives
and recovery of sight to the blind,
to let the oppressed go free,
and to proclaim a year acceptable to the Lord.'

Rolling up the scroll, he handed it back to the attendant and sat down, and the eyes of all in the synagogue looked intently at him. He said to them, 'Today this scripture passage is fulfilled in your hearing.' And all spoke highly of him and were amazed at the gracious words that came from his mouth" (Luke 4:16–22).

This was the beginning of Jesus' ministry, or work to bring people closer to God his Father.

WE RESPOND

With a partner, role-play ways that you can follow Jesus' example and live a life acceptable to the Lord.

Blessed Trinity the Three Persons in One God: God the Father, God the Son, and God the Holy Spirit

Jesus shows us God's love.

WE GATHER

✝ *Dear Jesus, help us to live what we believe.*

If someone were to describe your personality, what words might he or she use? List a few here.

- Sometimes quiet
- annoying
- kind
- funny

WE BELIEVE

In his ministry Jesus brought people closer to God his Father. Jesus:

- taught about the love of God his Father and encouraged all people to have faith

- accepted all people and welcomed them into his life

- fed the hungry and shared meals with people whom others ignored

- forgave the sins of those who were truly sorry

- healed those who were sick.

In all of these ways Jesus showed others God's love.

In the Gospels we read that Jesus traveled from town to town. He met many people. He cared about them and wanted to help them. Jesus ". . . was moved with pity for them because they were troubled and abandoned, like sheep without a shepherd" (Matthew 9:36).

Once a crowd was following Jesus while he taught. He said, "My heart is moved with pity for the crowd, because they have been with me now for three days and have nothing to eat" (Mark 8:2). Jesus then fed the people. Jesus' concern for them shows us that God cares for us.

A religious leader once criticized Jesus for forgiving a sinner who had asked for forgiveness. Jesus told the leader that the one who is forgiven more loves more. Forgiveness heals us and helps us to love.

Another time, a blind beggar on the side of the road was trying to get Jesus' attention. People told the man to be quiet, but he would not. Jesus stopped to talk to him and asked him what he wanted. The man said, "Lord, please let me see." Jesus then said to the man, "Have sight; your faith has saved you" (Luke 18:41, 42). Immediately the man could see. He followed Jesus and gave glory to God.

Jesus' acts of mercy show us that God is merciful. Jesus' fair treatment of people shows that God is just. Jesus was fair to sinners, strangers, those who were ignored, and those who were poor. Jesus challenged those who thought they were better than others. He said, "Stop judging, that you may not be judged. For as you judge, so will you be judged" (Matthew 7:1–2).

In Jesus we see a God who loves us. In Jesus we see a God who cares for us, has mercy on us, and is just to everyone.

WE RESPOND

Read the following situations. In groups role-play what you could do as followers of Jesus.

Mara is your best friend. The popular students in school make fun of her. You are with these students when Mara waves to you.

You received some money for your birthday and had not decided how to spend it. At Mass you hear that a collection will be taken up for earthquake victims.

You need a passing grade on the math final exam or you will go to summer school. Your friend Roberto is an "A" student. He is sitting next to you at the test.

Ask Jesus to help you to be caring, forgiving, and just to others.

Jesus invites people to follow him.

WE GATHER

✝ *Merciful Father, help us to treat others as your Son did.*

Recall a time when you needed someone to help you. What happened?

WE BELIEVE

Jesus invited people to follow him. These people became his disciples. Many disciples traveled with Jesus to towns and villages. They listened to his preaching and witnessed the ways he healed and forgave people.

Jesus wanted his disciples to live as he did. He taught them to obey God's law and live by the commandments. He told them to rely on God, not money, power, or possessions. He invited all people to trust in God and seek God's forgiveness. This was Jesus' mission, to share the life of God with all people and to save them from sin.

Jesus told the people, "The kingdom of God is at hand. Repent, and believe in the gospel" (Mark 1:15). Jesus called people to change the way they lived and to focus on loving God and others.

The Kingdom of God   The Kingdom of God is not a place you can find on a map. The Kingdom of God is the power of God's love active in our lives and in the world. The Kingdom of God is here among us through the life and love of Jesus.

In his teaching Jesus spoke to the people in ways that they could understand. He used short stories about everyday life. These short stories are called parables. In his parables, Jesus used examples from nature, farming, feasts, and everyday work to describe the Kingdom of God. Here is a parable about a mustard seed.

Mustard Seeds

Key Words

Jesus' mission to share the life of God with all people and to save them from sin

Kingdom of God the power of God's love active in our lives and in the world

📖 Matthew 13:31–32

Jesus compared the Kingdom of God to a mustard seed. "It is the smallest of all the seeds, yet when full-grown it is the largest of plants. It becomes a large bush, and the 'birds of the sky come and dwell in its branches'" (Matthew 13:32).

Like the mustard seed, the Kingdom of God can grow and spread. Jesus encouraged his disciples to respond to God's love and to spread the message of the Kingdom of God.

The Kingdom of God is not complete. It will continue to grow until Jesus returns in glory at the end of time.

WE RESPOND

Jesus invites each of us to trust in God and show how important God is to us. What are some ways we can accept this invitation?

_____

_____

_____

Act out some of your ideas.

🎵 Bring Forth the Kingdom

You are a seed of the Word, O people:
bring forth the kingdom of God!
Seeds of mercy and seeds of justice,
grow in the kingdom of God!

Refrain:
Bring forth the kingdom of mercy,
bring forth the kingdom of peace;
bring forth the kingdom of justice,
bring forth the city of God!

25

Jesus' disciples continue his work.

WE GATHER

✞ *Holy Spirit, help us to continue Jesus' work by what we say and do.*

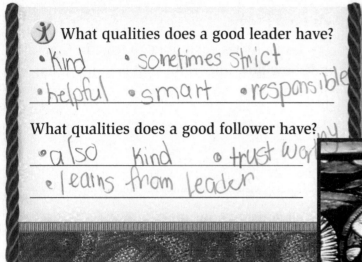

What qualities does a good leader have?
- Kind
- sometimes strict
- helpful
- smart
- responsible

What qualities does a good follower have?
- also kind
- trust worthy
- learns from leader

WE BELIEVE

Jesus asked his disciples to spread the message of his saving work. From among his disciples Jesus chose twelve men to be his Apostles. The **Apostles** shared in Jesus' mission in a special way. They would continue Jesus' saving work when Jesus returned to his Father. Jesus told the Apostles that the Holy Spirit would come to them. Jesus told them that the Holy Spirit would help them remember all that he had said and done.

Jesus gathered his Apostles after his Resurrection. He told them, "All power in heaven and on earth has been given to me. Go, therefore, and make disciples of all nations, baptizing them in the name of the Father, and of the Son, and of the holy Spirit, teaching them to observe all that I have commanded you" (Matthew 28:18–20).

When the Holy Spirit came at Pentecost, the Apostles were strengthened. They went out to share the Good News of Jesus Christ. This was the beginning of the Church. The word *church* means "a group that is called together." The **Church** is all those who believe in Jesus Christ, have been baptized in him, and follow his teachings.

Key Words

Apostles men chosen by Jesus to share in his mission in a special way

Church all those who believe in Jesus Christ, have been baptized in him, and follow his teachings

With Christ as its head, the Church is the seed of the Kingdom of God on earth. Through the Church, the power of God's life in the world increases. Strengthened by the Holy Spirit, ordinary people like us help to spread the Good News of the Kingdom of God. The Kingdom of God grows when we:

- have faith in Jesus Christ and share our belief

- live as Jesus did and follow God's will for us

- seek to build a better community, a more just nation, and a peaceful world.

As Catholics...

We learn about the Apostles from the books of the New Testament. "The names of the twelve apostles are these: first, Simon called Peter, and his brother Andrew; James, the son of Zebedee, and his brother John; Philip and Bartholomew, Thomas and Matthew the tax collector; James, the son of Alphaeus, and Thaddeus; Simon the Cananean, and Judas Iscariot who betrayed him" (Matthew 10: 2–4).

Peter and Andrew were fishermen. Matthew was a tax collector. Thomas was a twin. James was the brother of John and was the first Apostle to die for his faith.

How can you find out more about the Apostles?

WE RESPOND

Think about the Kingdom of God. What are some things that your family, class, or neighborhood can do to help it to grow?

Write your name vertically in the space below. Using the letters of your name, describe the things that you can do to help the Kingdom of God to grow.

apostles
healpful
happiness
grapeVine
Kindness
prayer

27

PROJECT

Show What *you* Know

Complete the crossword puzzle using the 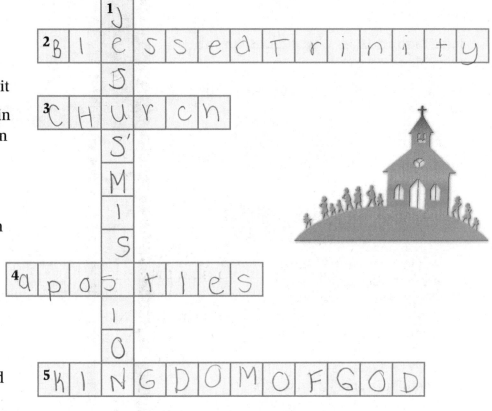 **Key Words**.

Across

2. the Three Persons in One God: God the Father, God the Son, and God the Holy Spirit

3. all those who believe in Jesus Christ, have been baptized in him, and follow his teachings

4. men chosen by Jesus to share in his mission in a special way

5. the power of God's love active in our lives and in the world

Down

1. to share the life of God with all people and to save them from sin

Crossword answers:
1 Down: JESUS' MISSION
2 Across: BLESSED TRINITY
3 Across: CHURCH
4 Across: APOSTLES
5 Across: KINGDOM OF GOD

Picture This

A shamrock is a clover with *three* leaves but just *one* stem. Illustrate a way you think Saint Patrick used the shamrock to teach the Irish people about the Blessed Trinity. (Hint: The Blessed Trinity is the *Three* Persons in *One* God: God the Father, God the Son, and God the Holy Spirit.)

Jesus Shares His Mission with the Church

2

✝ We Gather in Prayer

Leader: Jesus is with us. He said, "For where two or three are gathered together in my name, there am I in the midst of them" (Matthew 18:20).

All: Jesus be with us as we pray in your name.

Reader: A reading from the holy Gospel according to Matthew

All: Glory to you, O Lord.

Reader: "Go, therefore, and make disciples of all nations, baptizing them in the name of the Father, and of the Son, and of the holy Spirit, teaching them to observe all that I have commanded you. And behold, I am with you always, until the end of the age" (Matthew 28:19–20).

The Gospel of the Lord.

All: Praise to you, Lord Jesus Christ.

Leader: Jesus, we are gathered today in your name. Help us share your love and be with us now and forever.

All: Amen.

BE A VOLUNTEER!

1

We are joined to Jesus Christ and to one another.

WE GATHER

✝ *Jesus, be with us always.*

Think of some people whom you trust. How do you show that you trust them?

Think of some people who trust you. How do they show their trust?

WE BELIEVE

Jesus trusted his Father completely and did the work that his Father sent him to do. Jesus healed and forgave in his Father's name. He shared his Father's love.

Jesus often spoke of his relationship with God his Father. He once used the following example to describe that relationship. Jesus said that he was the vine and his Father was the vine grower.

Jesus also told his disciples "Just as a branch cannot bear fruit on its own unless it remains on the vine, so neither can you unless you remain in me. I am the vine, you are the branches. Whoever remains in me and I in him will bear much fruit, because without me you can do nothing" (John 15:4–5).

Jesus Christ is the vine, we are the branches. We are joined to Jesus and to one another. As members of the Church, we need Jesus so that we can grow in faith and love. The Church is connected to Jesus as branches are to a vine. Jesus Christ is the Head of the Church, thus the Church is called the Mystical Body of Christ.

Jesus said, "As the Father loves me, so I also love you. Remain in my love" (John 15:9). We remain in Jesus' love when we follow his example and trust in his Father's will. As disciples of Jesus we love others as he loves us. We tell others of God's great love. With the help of the Holy Spirit, we continue the work of Jesus and remain in his love.

The mission of the Church   The work, or mission, of the Church is to share the Good News of Christ and to spread the Kingdom of God. We are the Church. This is the Good News of Christ that we share:

- God loves and cares for all people because we are created in his image and likeness.

- God so loved the world that he sent his only Son to show us how to live and to save us from sin.

• Jesus shares the very life of God with us and gives us the hope of life forever with God.

• All people are invited to believe in Jesus and to be baptized in the faith of the Church.

The Kingdom of God—the power of God's love active in our lives and in the world—grows as more and more people accept this Good News. As members of the Church, we share the Good News and work for justice and peace in the world and the Kingdom grows.

WE RESPOND

Jesus said, "I am the vine, you are the branches" (John 15:5). Look at the vine with its branch of leaves. On each of the three leaves, write one way that the Church shares the Good News of Christ with others.

We proclaim the Good News of Christ by what we say and do.

WE GATHER

✝ *Holy Spirit, help us to continue the work of Jesus.*

 Think about something you wanted to do that required your time and effort. What was it? What did you do?

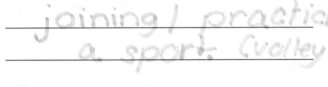

joining / practicing a sport (volley ba

WE BELIEVE

We all share in the mission of the Church. We are called to proclaim the Good News of Christ by what we say and do. This is known as evangelization. Evangelization takes place in our everyday lives. We evangelize those who have not yet heard the message of Jesus Christ. We also evangelize those who have heard the message but need encouragement to live out the gift of faith that is theirs.

Sharing what we believe Proclaiming the Good News is very important. People need to hear the message of Jesus Christ in order to believe it. So we tell others about the wonderful things that Christ has done. We speak to others about the ways that Jesus has changed the world. We encourage them to read the Gospels and find out more about his great love.

We also proclaim the Good News of Jesus Christ through personal and public prayer. We pray by listening and talking to God with our minds and hearts. The liturgy is the official public prayer of the Church. In the liturgy we gather as a community joined to Christ to celebrate what we believe.

> **Key Words**
>
> **evangelization** proclaiming the Good News of Christ by what we say and do
>
> **liturgy** the official public prayer of the Church

Learning about our faith When we proclaim the Good News, we tell others what it means to be a disciple of Jesus. This is one reason why teaching the history and beliefs of the Church is an important part of evangelization. We are involved in this right now as we learn more about Jesus and the Church. As we learn, we grow in faith and can share what we believe. Members of the Church all over the world announce the Good News every day.

Today the Church uses technology to reach people in ways never before imagined. The Church broadcasts the Mass on television stations throughout the world. The pope's words and activities are seen and heard by millions. Parishes from Australia to Zimbabwe have their own Web sites, too. The Bible can even be read using wireless technologies small enough to fit into a pocket.

Giving witness to Christ People from all parts of the world can work together to spread the message of Jesus Christ. It does not matter how old or young we are. Each of us has something to share and bring to the Church and to the world.

Each of us can proclaim the Good News by giving witness to Christ. We give witness when we speak and act based upon the Good News. We give witness when we follow Jesus' example by loving God and others. We give witness when we work for justice and peace. We can do all this by respecting the rights and needs of others, and by treating all people equally. We can help them to see God's love active in their lives and in the world.

WE RESPOND

Name some people you know who proclaim the Good News of Jesus Christ. In what ways do they do this? How can you proclaim the Good News this week?

Design a thirty-second TV commercial to get people interested in the Good News of Jesus Christ. Use this storyboard to plan your commercial.

In the liturgy we celebrate Christ's Paschal Mystery.

WE GATHER

✣ *Let us sing and shout our joy in God!*

Do your family or friends have a certain way to celebrate a birthday or a holiday? If so, what is it?

_____

_____

WE BELIEVE

The Church celebrates the liturgy every day. In the liturgy we gather to praise and worship God: Father, Son, and Holy Spirit. We proclaim the Good News of Jesus Christ and celebrate his Paschal Mystery. The Paschal Mystery is Christ's suffering, Death, Resurrection from the dead, and Ascension into Heaven. It is by his Paschal Mystery that Jesus saves us from sin and gives us new life.

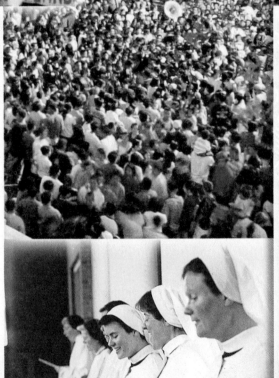

The liturgy includes the celebration of the Eucharist, also called the Mass, and the other sacraments. It also includes prayers called the Liturgy of the Hours. The Church prays the Liturgy of the Hours at different times during the day. In these prayers we celebrate God's work in creation and in our lives.

36

The liturgy is prayer we pray together. It is communal prayer. The community of faith gathers in a special way on Sundays for the celebration of the Mass. In this gathering our relationship with Christ and one another is strengthened by grace, prayer, and love. We are better able to give witness to Christ in our everyday lives.

Work in a group. Describe the different types of liturgy in which you have participated. What do these different celebrations have in common?

_____

_____

_____

Key Word

Paschal Mystery
Christ's suffering, Death, Resurrection from the dead, and Ascension into Heaven

The Body of Christ   The whole Church is united in Christ. We read in the New Testament that "we, though many, are one body in Christ and individually parts of one another" (Romans 12:5). We are joined to Christ who "is the head of the body, the church" (Colossians 1:18).

So we call the Church the Body of Christ. The Body of Christ is all the members of the Church, with Christ as its head. The whole Body of Christ celebrates the liturgy.

We also call the Church the Temple of the Holy Spirit. The Holy Spirit unites the Church as the Body of Christ and joins us to Christ the head. The Holy Spirit gives the Church life. The Church lives and works because of the Holy Spirit's presence and strength.

WE RESPOND

Somos el Cuerpo de Cristo/ We Are the Body of Christ

Somos el cuerpo de Cristo.
We are the body of Christ.
Hemos oído el llamado;
We've answered "Yes," to the call of the Lord.

Somos el cuerpo de Cristo.
We are the body of Christ.
Traemos su santo mensaje.
We come to bring the good news to the world.

What can you do today to say "yes" to the Lord?

When we serve others we give witness to Christ.

✝ *God, our Father, we are your children.*

When we serve others we show our love and care for them. What are some ways you serve others in your family? in your class? in your neighborhood?

WE BELIEVE

During his life Jesus cared for the needs of others. He had a special concern for those who were neglected. He welcomed them and listened to their worries. He made sure that they had what they needed. Jesus prayed for those in need, visited those who were sick, and provided food for the hungry. In all these ways Jesus spent his life serving others. Jesus is our greatest example of service.

Jesus tells us that when we care for other people, we are serving him, too. He tells us that when he comes again in glory at the end of time we will be judged by our works and by the way we cooperate with God's grace. Jesus Christ coming at the end of time to judge all people is called the Last Judgment. At that time all people will be brought before him in their own bodies to give Christ an account of their own deeds. He will say to those who acted justly, "For I was hungry and you gave me food, I was thirsty and you gave me drink, a stranger and you welcomed me, naked and you clothed me, ill and you cared for me, in prison and you visited me" (Matthew 25:35–36).

Then those who were just will ask him when they saw and cared for him like this. And he will say, "Amen, I say to you, whatever you did for one of these least brothers of mine, you did for me" (Matthew 25:40).

As Catholics...

Responding to the needs of others is an important part of our faith. Catholic social teaching reminds us to love and care for others as Jesus did. Jesus' life and teaching are the foundation of Catholic social teaching. This teaching calls us to work for justice and peace as Jesus did. It is the Church's way of putting the Good News of Christ into action.

Catholic social teaching is based on the belief that every person has human dignity. Human dignity is the value and worth that come from being created in God's image and likeness. There are seven themes of Catholic social teaching. These themes are found on page 330.

How does your school promote justice and peace?

What we do for other people, we do for Jesus. He is the one who is hungry. He is the stranger. He is the sick person we care for.

We give witness to Jesus when we perform the Works of Mercy. The Works of Mercy are acts of love that help us care for the needs of others. The Works of Mercy are divided into two groups. The **Corporal Works of Mercy** deal with the physical and material needs of others. The **Spiritual Works of Mercy** deal with the needs of people's hearts, minds, and souls.

Key Words

Last Judgment Jesus Christ coming at the end of time to judge all people

Corporal Works of Mercy acts of love that help us care for the physical and material needs of others

Spiritual Works of Mercy acts of love that help us care for the needs of people's hearts, minds, and souls

Corporal Works of Mercy

Feed the hungry.

Give drink to the thirsty.

Clothe the naked.

Visit the imprisoned.

Shelter the homeless.

Visit the sick.

Bury the dead.

Spiritual Works of Mercy

Admonish the sinner.
  (Give correction to those who need it.)

Instruct the ignorant.
  (Share our knowledge with others.)

Counsel the doubtful.
  (Give advice to those who need it.)

Comfort the sorrowful.
  (Comfort those who suffer.)

Bear wrongs patiently.
  (Be patient with others.)

Forgive all injuries.
  (Forgive those who hurt us.)

Pray for the living and the dead.

WE RESPOND

Work with a partner to list ways your parish and your neighborhood community provide for the needs of others.

	Corporal Works of Mercy	Spiritual Works of Mercy
Parish		
Neighborhood		

What work of mercy can you ask your family to perform this week?

Pray
Learn
Celebrate
Share
Choose
Live

PROJECT

Show What *you* Know

Complete the following using Key Words and definitions.
(Hint: Use the Glossary if you need help!)

1. Corporal Works of Mercy are acts of ___love___ that help us to care for the ___physical___ and ___material___ needs of others.

2. The ___liturgy___ is the official public prayer of the ___church___.

3. Jesus Christ coming at the ___end of ~~the~~___ of time to judge all people is known as the Last ___Judgement___

4. Spiritual Works of Mercy are acts of ___love___ that help us to care for the needs of people's ___hearts___, ___minds___, and souls.

5. The Paschal Mystery is Christ's ___suffering___, Death, ___ressurection___ from the dead, and Ascension into ___heaven___.

6. Evangelization is proclaiming the ___good___ News of Christ by what we ___say___ and ___do___.

Have any of these helped you in learning about the Catholic faith?

Question Corner

Internet	Yes	No
television	Yes	No
whiteboard	Yes	No

Fast Facts

Archbishop Patrick Flores founded CTSA, Catholic Television of San Antonio (Texas), in 1981. It was the first diocesan television station in the United States.

ctsa15
television that inspires

The Church Celebrates Seven Sacraments

✝ We Gather in Prayer

Leader: Let us remember that Jesus is present in our lives.

Reader: A reading from the holy Gospel according to John

"As the Father loves me, so I also love you. Remain in my love. If you keep my commandments, you will remain in my love, just as I have kept my Father's commandments and remain in his love.

I have told you this so that my joy might be in you and your joy might be complete. This is my commandment: love one another as I love you." (John 15:9–12)

The Gospel of the Lord.

All: Praise to you, Lord Jesus Christ.

Leader: As we pray together, let us praise and thank Jesus Christ who is with us always.

All: Jesus, Good Shepherd, thanks and praise to you.

Jesus, Lamb of God, thanks and praise to you.

Jesus, Bread of life and love, thanks and praise to you.

Jesus, Source of strength and joy, thanks and praise to you.

Thank you, Jesus, for your life in mine. Help me live your good news of love and peace.

Amen.

43

Jesus gave the Church Seven Sacraments.

WE GATHER

✝ *Jesus, we praise you as the greatest sign of God's love.*

What are some signs that you see every day? Why are they important to you?

WE BELIEVE

A sign stands for or tells us about something. A sign can be something that we see, such as a stop sign. A sign can be something that we do, such as shaking hands or hugging someone. An event or a person can also be a sign. For example, a police officer in uniform can be a sign of authority and a parade can be a sign of a holiday.

The world is filled with signs of God's love. The beauty of creation, newborn babies, and people caring for one another are just a few of the signs of God's love. But Jesus Christ is the greatest sign of God's love.

Everything that Jesus said or did pointed to God's love for us. Jesus treated all people fairly. He welcomed and spent time with people whom others neglected. He fed those who were hungry and forgave the sins of people who believed in him. Jesus is the greatest sign of God the Father's love because he is the Son of God.

👤 Write a poem about one of the signs of God's love and presence in the world.

_____

_____

_____

_____

_____

Baptism

Penance and Reconciliation

Eucharist

Matrimony

Confirmation

Signs of Jesus' love   After Jesus returned to his Father, the Holy Spirit helped the disciples to be signs of Jesus' love and life. The Holy Spirit helps us to do the same today. By continuing Jesus' work, the Church herself is a sign of God's love and care.

The Church has seven celebrations that are special signs of God's love and presence. We call these special signs sacraments. It is Christ's saving work that we celebrate in the sacraments. Jesus instituted, or began, the sacraments so that his saving work would continue for all time.

All Seven Sacraments are signs of God present in our lives. But they are different from all other signs. Sacraments truly bring about what they represent. For example, in Baptism we not only celebrate being children of God, we actually become children of God. In Penance and Reconciliation we not only celebrate that God forgives, we actually receive God's forgiveness.

This is why we say that a **sacrament** is an effective sign given to us by Jesus through which we share in God's life. The gift of sharing in God's life that we receive in the sacraments is **sanctifying grace**. This grace helps us to trust and believe in God. It strengthens us to live as Jesus did.

The sacraments are the most important celebrations of the Church. The whole Body of Christ celebrates each sacrament. The priest and other members of the Church who participate in the sacraments represent the whole Church. The sacraments join Catholics all over the world with Jesus and with one another. They unite us as the Body of Christ.

WE RESPOND

What sacraments have you received? How have they helped you grow closer to God and other members of the Church?

THE SEVEN SACRAMENTS

Sacraments of Christian Initiation

- Baptism
- Confirmation
- Eucharist

Sacraments at the Service of Communion (of Service to Others)

- Holy Orders
- Matrimony

Sacraments of Healing

- Penance and Reconciliation
- Anointing of the Sick

Key Words

sacrament an effective sign given to us by Jesus through which we share in God's life

sanctifying grace the gift of sharing in God's life that we receive in the sacraments

Holy Orders

Anointing of the Sick

45

The Sacraments of Christian Initiation are Baptism, Confirmation, and Eucharist.

WE GATHER

✝ *Jesus, thank you for your gift of the sacraments.*

What are some of the different clubs, teams, or organizations that you belong to or want to join? What would you need to do to become a member?

WE BELIEVE

Christian initiation is the process of becoming a member of the Church. The Sacraments of Baptism, Confirmation, and Eucharist initiate us into the Church.

Many Catholics are baptized as infants. However, a person can be baptized at any age. In Baptism we are united to Christ and become part of the Body of Christ and the People of God. We become children of God and members of the Church. We are freed from Original Sin and all of our personal sins are forgiven. The celebration of this first Sacrament of Christian Initiation is very important. It is our welcome into the Church.

In the Sacrament of Confirmation we are sealed with the Gift of the Holy Spirit. Confirmation continues what Baptism has begun. Confirmation strengthens us to live as Christ's followers.

The Eucharist is the Sacrament of the Body and Blood of Christ. The Eucharist is connected to our Baptism, too. Each time we receive Holy Communion, our bonds as the Body of Christ are made stronger. As a community of faith, we are nourished by the Eucharist, and God's life in us is strengthened.

Our call to holiness All those who receive the Sacraments of Christian Initiation are called to lives of love for God and service to others. As members of the Church we share a common vocation which is the call to holiness and evangelization. God calls each of us:

- to proclaim the Good News of Christ to all people by what we say and do

- to share and give witness to our faith

- to grow in holiness.

God alone is holy, but he shares his holiness with us. Our holiness comes through grace. Holiness is sharing in God's goodness and responding to his love by the way we live.

Key Words

Christian initiation the process of becoming a member of the Church through the Sacraments of Baptism, Confirmation, and Eucharist

common vocation the call to holiness and evangelization that all Christians share

holiness sharing in God's goodness and responding to his love by the way we live; our holiness comes through grace

Jesus is our model of holiness. He lived his life in perfect love of God the Father and in service to others. Just as Jesus called his first disciples to holiness, he wants us to lead holy lives, too.

To grow in holiness we have to respond to the grace we receive in the sacraments. The Holy Spirit helps us to do this. We become aware of God working in our lives. We follow Jesus' example and his commandment to love others. In all these ways we can grow in holiness.

WE RESPOND

On the computer screen, write or illustrate one way you will respond to God's love today.

Dear Nana,

hi nana. I miss you! I will visit this weekend!

Love,
Olivia

The Sacraments of Healing are Penance and Reconciliation and Anointing of the Sick.

WE GATHER

✝ *God our Father, we are disciples of your Son, Jesus Christ.*

Think about a time when you needed to be forgiven. What did you do?

Think about a time when you forgave someone. What did you do?

WE BELIEVE

We learn from the Gospels that many people believed in Jesus. Jesus often forgave and healed those who believed. By doing this Jesus was showing that God has power over sickness and sin. Jesus' actions were a sign of his saving work. This saving work would be accomplished by Jesus' own suffering, Death, and Resurrection.

Jesus wanted his saving work to continue, so he gave the Apostles the authority to forgive and to heal in his name. This authority continues in the Church today. The Sacraments of Penance and Reconciliation and Anointing of the Sick are two ways that we celebrate Jesus' healing power.

Penance and Reconciliation In this sacrament, which can be called Penance, members of the Church are reconciled with God and with the Church. Those who are truly sorry confess their sins and are forgiven.

Priests forgive sins in the Sacrament of Penance. They do this in the name of Christ and the Church through the power of the Holy Spirit. For those who receive the Sacrament of Penance, their relationship with God and the entire Church is made whole again.

Anointing of the Sick The Church offers this sacrament to those who are very sick. It is also for those who are near death. Family, friends, and parish members gather to pray for God's healing and mercy. This sacrament may be celebrated during a Sunday or a weekday Mass. It can also be celebrated in the home of the sick person, or in a hospital.

During this sacrament the priest and those gathered pray that the person might be healed. The priest anoints the person who is sick and prays for his or her health. Those who receive the sacrament are given the grace to respond to their illness with hope. Their faith in a loving God, who is with them when they are sick or healthy, can be strengthened.

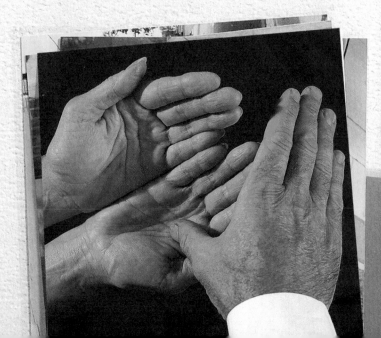

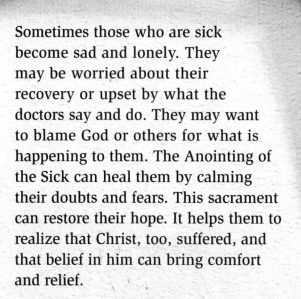

Design a magazine ad that tells about the Sacraments of Healing.

Sometimes those who are sick become sad and lonely. They may be worried about their recovery or upset by what the doctors say and do. They may want to blame God or others for what is happening to them. The Anointing of the Sick can heal them by calming their doubts and fears. This sacrament can restore their hope. It helps them to realize that Christ, too, suffered, and that belief in him can bring comfort and relief.

WE RESPOND

Whenever we can, we need to help those who are sick and in need of our comfort. With hope and faith in God, we can offer prayers for those who are sick. We can visit those who are sick, or we can help an elderly relative or neighbor. Whatever we do, we can try to bring people comfort and peace.

Holy Orders and Matrimony are Sacraments at the Service of Communion.

WE GATHER

✝ *Jesus, strengthen us with your presence here and now.*

Think of a real-life example of people helping others in need. You might recall a story from TV, newspapers, magazines, or the Internet describing someone or a group of people helping others in need.

Write a short summary or dramatic scene of the story. Share it with the class.

WE BELIEVE

The Church celebrates the Sacraments of Holy Orders and Matrimony as Sacraments at the Service of Communion. Those who receive these sacraments are strengthened to serve God and the Church through a particular vocation.

The Sacrament of Holy Orders The mission and the authority that Jesus Christ gave to his Apostles continue in the Church through the Sacrament of Holy Orders. God calls some men to serve him as ordained ministers in the Church. They are ordained as bishops, priests, or deacons in the Sacrament of Holy Orders. However, they have different roles and duties in serving the Church.

The bishops are the successors of the Apostles. They are the leaders and official teachers of the Church. The bishops are called to help the followers of Jesus grow in holiness. They do this through their prayer, preaching, and the celebration of the sacraments.

Priests are coworkers with the bishops. They are called to preach the Good News, celebrate the sacraments with and for us, and guide the members of the Church. Deacons assist the bishops in works of service for the whole Church. They baptize, witness marriages, preside at funerals, proclaim the Good News, and preach.

The Sacrament of Matrimony In the Sacrament of Matrimony, a baptized man and woman pledge to love each other as God loves them. They promise to remain faithful and true to each other. The married couple promise to live lives of service to each other and to their children.

The Sacrament of Matrimony strengthens the couple throughout their lives. It helps them to build a family rooted in a strong faith in God and each other. It enables them to share their faith with their family and to serve the Church and the community.

As Catholics...

A vocation is a calling to a way of life. As baptized Christians we all share a common vocation. God also calls each of us to serve him in a particular way. There are specific ways to follow our vocation: as members of the lay faithful, as religious brothers or sisters, or as priests or deacons.

Discovering our vocation is an exciting part of our lives. The Holy Spirit guides us as we pray and find out more about the different vocations. Family, friends, and teachers also help us to know the ways that God is calling us.

This week pray that you will know what vocation God is calling you to live.

WE RESPOND

Think about your life right now. How is Jesus a part of it? Imagine your life as a young adult. How will Jesus be a part of your life?

Pray Learn Celebrate Share Choose Live

PROJECT

Show What *you* Know

Using the clues, unscramble the Key Words.

Clue	Scrambled Key Word	Your Answer
the process of becoming a member of the Church through the Sacraments of Baptism, Eucharist, and Confirmation	TICNASHRI NTIAITIONI	Christian initiation
the gift of sharing in God's life that we receive in the sacraments	YGNSTAFCNII ERACG	sanctifying Grace
sharing in God's goodness and responding to his love by the way we live	SESILOHN	holiness
an effective sign given to us by Jesus through which we share in God's life	TEMCASRAN	sacrament
the call to holiness and evangelization that all Christians share	NMCOOM CVAINOTO	Common vocation

What's *the* Word?

"And he said to them, 'Thus it is written that the Messiah would suffer and rise from the dead on the third day and that repentance, for the forgiveness of sins, would be preached in his name to all the nations.'" (Luke 24:46–47)

• What did Jesus say would be preached in his name to all the nations?

_____

• Circle the other name for Jesus given in the passage.

DISCIPLE

Celebrate!

The Seven Sacraments are the most important celebrations of the Church. Classify the Seven Sacraments by category.

Healing	Service	Christian Initiation

➥ **DISCIPLE CHALLENGE** Check the sacraments that you have celebrated.

More to Explore

The Claretian Missionaries are a religious community of priests and brothers. They are dedicated to evangelization. They bring the Gospel message to those who are poor or in need throughout the world. The Claretians are involved in issues of justice, peace, and the environment. They minister to immigrants, young people, and families. Saint Anthony Claret founded the Claretians in 1849. Today, there are more than 3,000 Claretians serving in more than 60 countries on five continents.

➥ **DISCIPLE CHALLENGE**

• Underline the sentence that describes how the Claretians evangelize.

• Circle the name of the person who founded the Claretians.

Search the Claretians Web site at www.claretians.org to answer these questions:

• In what country was the Claretians founded?

_____

• What saint did the Claretians honor by opening a national shrine?

_____

Take Home

Make a list of the sacraments that each of your family members have celebrated.

_____

_____

_____

_____

_____

Talk about your experiences.

CHAPTER TEST

Write True or False for the following sentences.
Then change the false sentences to make them true.

1. __F__ _Jesus_ Saint Paul instituted the sacraments so that his saving work would continue.

   Saint

2. __T__ The Church celebrates Holy Orders and Matrimony as Sacraments at the Service of Communion.

3. __T__ The Sacraments of Penance and Anointing of the Sick are two ways that the Church celebrates Jesus' healing power.

4. __F__ The Sacraments of Christian Initiation are Baptism, Eucharist, and Matrimony.

   the sacraments of Christian initiation are baptism Eucharist & confirmation

Write the letter of the definition that matches each term.

5. __b__ holiness

6. __a__ sanctifying grace

7. __e__ common vocation

8. __d__ sacrament

a. the gift of sharing in God's life that we receive in the sacraments

b. sharing God's goodness and responding to his love by the way we live; this comes through grace

c. the process of being a member of the Church through the Sacraments of Baptism, Confirmation, and Eucharist

d. an effective sign given to us by Jesus through which we share God's life

e. the call to holiness and evangelization that all Christians share

Write a sentence to answer each question.

9. Why are the sacraments the most important celebrations of the Church?

   because it brings you closer to god

10. How can we grow in holiness?

   Serve to others, help others.

New Life in Christ

4

✝ We Gather in Prayer

Leader: Let us pray to God as one family.

Reader: A reading from the Book of the Prophet Isaiah

"Hear then, O Jacob, my servant,
  Israel, whom I have chosen.
I will pour out water upon the
    thirsty ground,
  and streams upon the dry land;
I will pour out my spirit upon your offspring,
  and my blessing upon your
    descendants." (Isaiah 44:1, 3)

The word of the Lord.

All: Thanks be to God.

🎵 We Belong to God's Family

Refrain:
  We belong to God's family.
  Brothers and sisters are we,
  singing together in unity about
  one Lord and one faith,
  one family.

  We are one in the water,
  the fountain of rebirth.
  We are God's new creation
  and our song will cover the earth.
  (Refrain)

Baptism is the foundation of Christian life.

WE GATHER

✞ *Jesus, you bring us new life. Alleluia!*

Right now you are in fifth grade. To be a happy and healthy person in the future, what must you do now?

WE BELIEVE

Jesus wanted everyone to know him and to share his life and love. Before he returned to his Father in Heaven, Jesus asked his disciples to tell others about him. He even sent his Apostles out to all nations. He told them to go out and baptize people in the name of the Father, and of the Son, and of the Holy Spirit. With the coming of the Holy Spirit on Pentecost, Jesus' disciples were strengthened to do as he asked.

On Pentecost the Apostles began to preach the Good News. They told the crowds the amazing things Jesus had done. The Apostles told them that Jesus Christ had died and risen to new life. They shared their belief that Christ is the Son of God. Peter told them, "Repent and be baptized, every one of you, in the name of Jesus Christ for the forgiveness of your sins; and you will receive the gift of the holy Spirit" (Acts of the Apostles 2:38).

Many people who heard the Good News of Christ were baptized and became disciples. Even whole families were baptized because of their belief.

SAINT PAUL

Saint Paul lived nearly two thousand years ago. He traveled many miles and preached to many people about the Good News of Jesus Christ. Paul's preaching excited the crowds who heard him. Many listeners began to believe in Christ and were baptized.

In the early years of the Church, Christians were persecuted for their belief in Christ. Because of his success in spewading the Gospel, Roman officials threw Paul and a fellow disciple named Silas into prison. They were sent to the darkest cell and their feet were chained. While Paul was praying with another prisoner "there was suddenly such a severe earthquake that the foundations of the jail shook; all the doors flew open, and the chains of all were pulled loose" (Acts of the Apostles 16:26)

Their jailer recognized that God was with Paul and his companion. He asked, "'Sirs, what must I do to be saved?' And they said, 'Believe in the Lord Jesus and you and your household will be saved'" (Acts of the Apostles 16:30–31). Paul immediately baptized the jailer and all of his family.

We see that Baptism was a part of the Church from its very beginning. Baptism is the foundation of Christian life. It is upon Baptism that we build our lives as followers of Christ.

The importance of Baptism

Baptism is the sacrament in which we are freed from sin, become children of God, and are welcomed into the Church. Through this sacrament:

- We are joined to Christ and rise to new life in him.

- We become members of the Church, the Body of Christ and the People of God.

- We are united with all others who have been baptized.

- Justification is conferred on us. It has been won for us

by the Passion of Christ. It conforms us more closely to the justice of God.

Baptism is the very first sacrament that we celebrate. In fact, we are unable to receive any other sacrament until we first have been baptized. Baptism is our welcome into the Church. It leads us to the other two sacraments of Christian initiation Confirmation and Eucharist.

Baptism the sacrament in which we are freed from sin, become children of God, and are welcomed into the Church

fold

WE RESPOND

The Sacrament of Baptism is the foundation of Christian life. Trace this pattern using a separate sheet of paper. Follow the directions on the pattern to create a "baptismal building block."

fold

fold

fold

On each side write or illustrate an example that shows you are a baptized follower of Jesus Christ.

What are some ways that you can show that you are united to other members of the Church?

fold

fold

fold

fold

fold

fold

In Baptism we are freed from sin and become children of God.

WE GATHER

✝ *Loving Father, thank you for our new life in Baptism.*

Have you ever seen something that has been restored, or made new again? What was it? How was it made to seem new again?

WE BELIEVE

God created human beings to know him in a way that none of his other creation could. He created human beings to be close to him, to share in his life and love forever. However, we learn from the Old Testament that the first human beings turned away from God and from the freedom and happiness that they shared. They disobeyed God. Because of their sin, called Original Sin, they lost the closeness with God that they had enjoyed.

We all are born with Original Sin. Because of it, human beings suffer. We are affected by Original Sin throughout our lives. We are tempted to turn away from God and to commit personal sin.

But God did not turn away from his people. He promised to save us from sin. Out of his great love, God sent his Son to restore our relationship with God. The truth that the Son of God became man is called the **Incarnation**.

Jesus is the Son of God. By his Death and Resurrection, Jesus Christ saves us from sin. Jesus' victory over sin and death offers us salvation. **Salvation** is the forgiveness of sins and the restoring of friendship with God.

Key Words

Incarnation the truth that the Son of God became man

salvation the forgiveness of sins and the restoring of friendship with God

Like faith, Baptism is necessary for salvation. Baptism frees us from Original Sin and all of our personal sins are forgiven.

When we are baptized we become children of God. We become sisters and brothers with everyone else who has been baptized. Baptism makes us members of one family. In this family, there are no boundaries or preferences. God sees us all as his children. He loves each of us.

When we are baptized we share in God's own life. Our share in God's life is called grace. The grace of Baptism helps us to believe in God the Father and to love him. It gives us the power to live and act as disciples of Christ in the world. It draws us into a community of believers led by the Holy Spirit. We are able to live lives of goodness and love for God and others.

Make a "word search." List the following terms horizontally, vertically, or diagonally in the space below.

Original Sin
Incarnation
salvation
Baptism
forgiveness
grace
restore
sacrament
initiation
rebirth

Exchange your puzzle with a classmate. As each term is found and circled, talk about its meaning.

WE RESPOND

What will you do this week to live as a disciple of Christ?

We are a priestly, prophetic, and royal people.

WE GATHER

✝ *Holy Spirit, help us to show that we belong to Jesus.*

All of us have many roles. For example, one person can be a daughter, sister, coach, friend, writer, dancer, leader, and more.

What are some of the different roles you have?

WE BELIEVE

At Jesus' baptism at the Jordan River the Holy Spirit came upon him. A voice was heard saying, "You are my beloved Son; with you I am well pleased" (Mark 1:11). This anointing by the Holy Spirit established Jesus as priest, prophet, and king.

We call Jesus a priest because he gave the sacrifice that no one else could. Jesus offered himself to save us. Jesus was a prophet because he delivered God's message of love and forgiveness. He spoke out for truth and justice. Jesus showed himself to be a king by the care he gave to all his people.

In Baptism we are anointed and sealed forever in Christ. To be anointed is to be blessed with holy oil. The seal of Baptism marks us as belonging to Christ. Because of this seal we receive Baptism only once.

This baptismal anointing recalls the anointing of Jesus. As members of the Church, the Body of Christ, we share in Jesus' role of priest, prophet, and king.

A priestly people   We know that Jesus is the only one, true priest. However, he calls all the baptized to share in his priesthood. This is the priesthood of the faithful. We can live out our priesthood in many ways. We can pray daily. We can participate in the liturgy, especially the Eucharist. We can offer our lives to God. However, our sharing in Jesus' priesthood does not make us ordained priests who have received the Sacrament of Holy Orders.

A prophetic people A prophet is someone who speaks on behalf of God, defends the truth, and works for justice. We are called to be prophets like the men and women in the Old Testament, like John the Baptist and like Christ. The preaching of John the Baptist connects the words of the prophets of the Old Testament to the life of Jesus. John the Baptist prepared the people for the coming of the Messiah, the Anointed One of God. When John baptized Jesus at the Jordan River, John knew that Jesus was the Messiah.

We are prophets when we proclaim the Good News and give witness to the truth of Christ. We can be prophets in the corridors of our schools, in our communities, with our friends, and even in our families. The Holy Spirit strengthens us to speak truthfully about Christ and to live as we should.

A royal people Jesus' reign, or rule, is not that of a king of a country. Jesus' reign makes God's love present and active in the world. As the Anointed King and Messiah Jesus came to serve not to be served. He leads his people as a servant-king.

Jesus calls us to be servants, too. He wants us to care for others, especially those who are poor or suffering in any way. He wants us to encourage others to respond to God's love in their lives. Jesus asks us to bring about the reign of God's love in the world by what we say and do.

> **Key Word**
> **prophet** someone who speaks on behalf of God, defends the truth, and works for justice

WE RESPOND

You share in Jesus' role of priest, prophet, and king. What tasks would you assign yourself as a priest, as a prophet, and as a servant-king? On this work sheet, write down these tasks in the appropriate columns.

Priest	Prophet	Servant-King
• Speaks in mass	• speaks be half on god	

Take a moment to pray silently.

Jesus, help me to speak the truth about you!

Because of our Baptism, we have hope of eternal life.

WE GATHER

✝ *Christ, lead us to holiness.*

What are some things that unite you with members of your family? your classmates? people in your neighborhood?

WE BELIEVE

The Church is a world-wide community of believers with different languages, traditions, customs, governments, and ways of life. However, we are all part of the Body of Christ. We are united by our Baptism.

Because of our Baptism we have the hope of eternal life. **Eternal life** is living in happiness with God forever. As part of the Body of Christ, we follow Christ's teachings and try to live as he did. People who have responded to God's grace and have remained in his friendship will have eternal life when they die. Those who have lived lives of holiness on earth will immediately share in the joy of Heaven and eternal life. Others whose hearts need to be made perfectly pure will prepare for Heaven in Purgatory. Through certain good works and prayers, we can obtain indulgences for ourselves or souls in Purgatory. An indulgence is the remission of punishment due to sin.

St. Joseph

St. Dominic

St. Kateri Tekakwitha

St. Frances Cabrini

St. Francis of Assisi

As Catholics...

The Body of Christ unites us to all who have been baptized. The union of the baptized members of the Church on earth with those who are in Heaven and in Purgatory is called the Communion of Saints.

When are some times that your parish prays for those who have died?

Unfortunately, there are those who have chosen to completely break their friendship with God. They have continually turned away from God's mercy and refused his forgiveness. They remain forever separated from God and do not share in eternal life. This eternal separation is called Hell.

However, God wants all of his children to respond to his grace in their lives. He calls those who have turned away from him to return to his love and receive his forgiveness.

Lives of holiness Through Baptism and throughout our lives, God gives each of us the grace to grow in holiness. Sharing in God's goodness makes it possible for us to respond to his love. We show our love by the way we live our lives. We give witness to Christ as active members of the Church. Together we participate in the celebration of the sacraments and work for justice and peace. We help each other live as Christ calls us to live.

Saints are followers of Christ who lived lives of holiness on earth and now share in eternal life with God in Heaven. Because the saints are closely united to Christ, they help the Church to grow in holiness.

Discuss some saints that you know about. How did they live lives of holiness?

We ask the saints to pray to God for us and for those who have died. Those of us on earth pray, especially during the celebration of the Eucharist, for all who have died. We pray that they may know God's love and mercy and may one day share in eternal life.

Key Words

eternal life living in happiness with God forever

saints followers of Christ who lived lives of holiness on earth and now share in eternal life with God in Heaven

WE RESPOND

Write a prayer for those who have died that they may have eternal life.

_____

_____

_____

_____

_____

_____

PROJECT

Show What *you* Know

Make a memory game using the Key Words. Write the remaining Key Words and definitions in different squares. Then, cover each square with a sticky note or scrap paper. Play the game by asking a partner to choose squares to find matching pairs of Key Words and definitions.

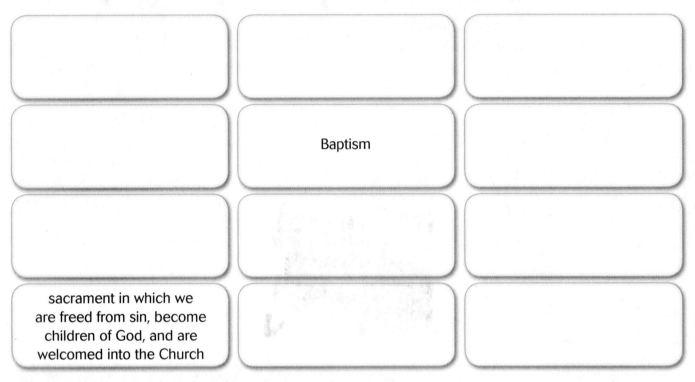

Baptism

sacrament in which we are freed from sin, become children of God, and are welcomed into the Church

What's *the* Word?

"Peter said to them, 'Repent and be baptized, every one of you, in the name of Jesus Christ for the forgiveness of your sins; and you will receive the gift of the holy Spirit.'" (Acts of the Apostles 2:38)

• In whose name did Peter say the people should be baptized? _____

• Why should the people be baptized? _____

• Underline the gift received through Baptism.

↳ **DISCIPLE CHALLENGE** You are asked about the importance of Baptism by someone who is not Catholic. What will you say?

_____

The Celebration of Baptism

5

✝ We Gather in Prayer

Leader: Do you believe in God,
the Father almighty,
creator of heaven and earth?

All: I do.

Leader: Do you believe in Jesus Christ,
his only Son, our Lord,
who was born of the Virgin Mary,
was crucified, died, and was buried,
rose from the dead,
and is now seated at the right
hand of the Father?

All: I do.

Leader: Do you believe in the Holy Spirit,
the holy catholic Church, the
communion of saints,
the forgiveness of sins,
the resurrection of the body,
and the life everlasting?

All: I do.

Leader: This is our faith. This is the faith
of the Church. We are proud to profess it,
in Christ Jesus our Lord.

All: Amen.

The Church welcomes all to be baptized.

WE GATHER

✝ *Jesus, be with us as we follow your way.*

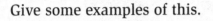 Sometimes taking a trip can be as much fun as arriving at your destination.

Give some examples of this.

_____

_____

_____

WE BELIEVE

Baptism, Confirmation, and Eucharist are the Sacraments of Christian Initiation. Not everyone begins or completes Christian initiation at the same time. Many people are baptized as infants or young children. Others are baptized as older children, adolescents, or adults. The important thing to remember is that no one is ever too old or too young to begin their new life in Christ.

Christian Initiation of Adults From her very beginning the Church has initiated adults. In fact, whole families have been baptized and welcomed into the Church. Today the Church baptizes adults and older children in a way very similar to that of the early Church. We call this the Rite of Christian Initiation of Adults (RCIA). Those who participate in the RCIA celebrate the three Sacraments of Christian Initiation in one celebration, usually at the Easter Vigil.

Adults and older children who have come to believe in Jesus Christ are welcomed to prepare for and celebrate the Sacraments of Christian Initiation. These adults and older children enter the catechumenate. The **catechumenate** is a period of formation for Christian initiation. It includes prayer and liturgy, religious instruction, and service to others. Those who enter this formation are called catechumens.

> **Key Word**
> **catechumenate** a period of formation for Christian initiation that includes prayer and liturgy, religious instruction, and service to others

The entire parish takes part in the formation of the catechumens. Some parish members serve as sponsors, and others teach the catechumens about the Catholic faith. The catechumens participate in prayer celebrations that introduce them to the symbols of the sacraments. And the catechumens usually join the assembly for the Liturgy of the Word during the Sunday celebration of the Eucharist.

Baptism of children When infants or very young children are baptized, they are baptized in the faith of the Church. The parents choose a godmother and godfather for the child. The godparents are to be a Christian example and promise to support the child as he or she grows in faith. The parents, godparents, and the entire parish community agree to help the children grow in faith. They promise to be good examples to the children.

If baptized as infants, children celebrate the remaining Sacraments of Christian Initiation when they are older. Some children celebrate Confirmation and Eucharist together. Others celebrate Eucharist first followed by Confirmation at a later time.

An ideal day to celebrate Baptism is on Sunday. Sunday is the Lord's Day. It is the day of Jesus' Resurrection. The celebration of Baptism on Sunday highlights the fact that we rise to new life like Jesus did. It also allows the parish to welcome the newly baptized. It is important for the members of the parish to know the new members of their faith family.

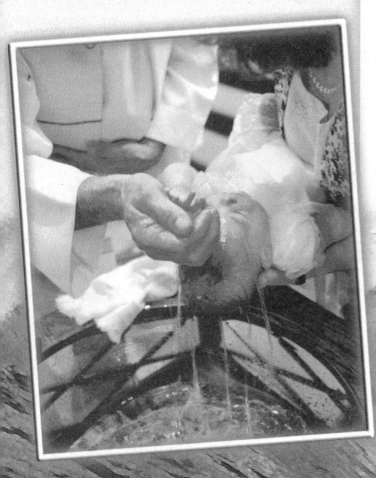

WE RESPOND

Imagine that you have been asked to be a godparent. What do you think you will have to do as a godparent?

Write a prayer for or a letter to your future godchild.

hey (name)! do you want to go ~~to~~ to church on Sunday? Let me know. Anyways, how is school? What are you learning? Religon? ~~anyway~~ bye for now—

Love,
OLIVIA

69

The parish community participates in the celebration of Baptism.

WE GATHER

✝ *We have put on Christ, in him we have been baptized. Alleluia, alleluia!*

How does your family welcome people who come to your home?

WE BELIEVE

We can learn more about the Sacrament of Baptism by looking at the way it is celebrated. Here is the way the Church celebrates the Baptism of infants and very young children.

As Catholics...

Did you know that in an emergency, anyone can baptize? The person baptizes by pouring water over the head of the one to be baptized while saying, "N., I baptize you in the name of the Father, and of the Son, and of the Holy Spirit." It is important for parents, nurses, and doctors to know how to baptize since they are more likely to be present in emergencies.

Who else may need to baptize in an emergency?

Reception of those to be baptized   A celebrant is the bishop, priest, or deacon who celebrates the sacrament for and with the community. At Baptism the celebrant greets the family at the entrance to the church. This place of greeting is very important, because Baptism is the "entrance" sacrament. The parents and godparents present the child to the Church for Baptism. The celebrant traces the sign of the cross on the child's forehead. He invites the parents and godparents to do the same. This tracing of the cross is a sign of the new life Christ has won for us on the cross.

Liturgy of the Word Readings from the Bible are proclaimed to remind those gathered that God is present. Two or three readings may be proclaimed. A psalm or song is often sung between the readings. Then the celebrant gives a homily to explain the readings and the meaning of the sacrament.

Intercessions, or the Prayer of the Faithful, are offered by the people. The community prays for the infant or the child who is about to be baptized, for the whole Church, and for the world.

Then, the celebrant prays asking God to free the child from Original Sin. He asks God to send the Holy Spirit to dwell in the child's heart.

The child is then anointed on the chest with the oil of catechumens. The purpose of this anointing is to cleanse and strengthen the child about to be baptized.

WE RESPOND

What are some times that you make the Sign of the Cross? Why do you think people make the Sign of the Cross?

Water is an important sign of Baptism.

WE GATHER

✝ *We have been washed by the waters of Baptism.*

Water is often referred to as the "source of life." Why is water so important?

WE BELIEVE

In the Sacrament of Baptism the water is blessed with a prayer.

Father,
you give us grace through sacramental signs,
which tell us of the wonders of your unseen
    power.

In baptism we use your gift of water,
which you have made a rich symbol of the
    grace
you give us in this sacrament.

At the very dawn of creation
your Spirit breathed on the waters,
making them the wellspring of all holiness.

> We learn about water in the Old Testament. From the beginning of the world, God has made water special. In the story of creation (Genesis 1:1—2:4) God swept the water with a mighty wind. By this action, water becomes a source of holiness.

The waters of the great flood
you made a sign of the waters of baptism
that make an end of sin
and a new beginning of goodness.

> The story of the great flood and Noah's ark (Genesis 6:5—8:19) also shows the power of water. We read in this story that the rains came down heavily on Noah, his family, and the animals. They had to pass through water to find safety.

Through the waters of the Red Sea
you led Israel out of slavery
to be an image of God's holy people
set free from sin by baptism.

> In the life of Moses, we once again see that passing through water is the way to freedom and safety. Moses and the chosen people were fleeing Egypt with Pharaoh's army in pursuit. With a strong wind, God parted the Red Sea for Moses and his people to escape. (Exodus 14:19–31)

In the waters of the Jordan
your Son was baptized by John
and anointed with the Spirit.

Your Son willed that water and blood should
    flow from his side
as he hung upon the cross.

> The Old Testament examples of life-saving water prepare for the new life given to all by Jesus. Because of Jesus' dying and rising to new life, each of us can have eternal life.

After his Resurrection he told his disciples:
"Go out and teach all nations,
baptizing them in the name of the Father,
    and of the Son, and of the Holy Spirit."

This is the beginning of the second part of the prayer. The celebrant calls upon God for help and support. This is called an invocation of God.

At this point the celebrant touches the water with his right hand.

Father,
look now with love upon your Church
and unseal for it the fountain of baptism.

By the power of the Holy Spirit
give to this water the grace of your Son,
so that in the sacrament of baptism
all those whom you have created in your
 likeness
may be cleansed from sin
and rise to a new birth of innocence
by water and the Holy Spirit.

We ask you, Father, with your Son
to send the Holy Spirit upon the waters of
 this font.
May all who are buried with Christ in the
 death of baptism
rise also with him to newness of life.

We ask this through Christ our Lord.

Amen.

Next the celebrant asks the parents and godparents some questions. The parents and godparents reject, or say no to, sin. Then they state what they believe. This is called a profession of faith.

WE RESPOND

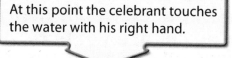

Make a map for the journey of faith begun in Baptism. Include in this map the starting point, the challenges, who might be traveling with you, the people who help you on the journey, the things that you are called to do on this journey, and the destination.

Take a moment to thank God for the people who help you on your journey of faith.

The baptized begin their new life as children of God.

WE GATHER

✝ *O Father, we are your children forever.*

What is one of the most important decisions that you have made in your life?

Was it an easy decision? How has it changed your life?

WE BELIEVE

We have now arrived at the heart of the sacrament. Those being baptized will die to sin and rise up from the water into their new life as children of God.

Baptism The actual baptism can take place in two ways. The celebrant can immerse, or plunge, the child in water three times. Or the celebrant can pour water over the child three times. While immersing or pouring, the celebrant says,

"N., I baptize you in the
name of the Father,
and of the Son,
and of the Holy Spirit."
(*Rite of Baptism for Children*, 60)

Anointing Sacred Chrism is perfumed oil blessed by the bishop. The celebrant anoints the newly baptized on the crown of the head with Sacred Chrism. This anointing is a sign of the Gift of the Holy Spirit. It shows that the newly baptized share in the mission of Christ. They are to be priest, prophet, and king. This anointing also connects Baptism to the Sacrament of Confirmation. In Confirmation another anointing with Sacred Chrism will take place.

Key Word

Sacred Chrism perfumed oil blessed by the bishop

74

List three things you can do today to let the light of Christ shine through you. Pray silently: Jesus, you are the light of the world.

A white garment is placed on the newly baptized, symbolizing new life in Christ. The celebrant says, "See in this white garment the outward sign of your Christian dignity." The celebrant, taking the Easter candle, says "Receive the light of Christ." One of the parents or godparents then lights the child's candle from the Easter candle. This symbolizes that Christ has enlightened the newly baptized.

Baptism imprints on our soul a character, a permanent spiritual sign. Thus, we are only baptized once.

Then the celebrant and the family gather by the altar to pray the Our Father. This connects the Sacrament of Baptism to the Eucharist. The celebrant then offers a final blessing. Those gathered are dismissed.

75

PROJECT

Pray Learn Celebrate Share Choose Live

Show What *you* Know

Write the  Key Words by following the code. Then, write a sentence for each. (Hint: use your Glossary if you need help!)

A	B	C	D	E	F	G	H	I	J	K	L	M	N	O	P	Q	R	S	T	U	V	W	X	Y	Z
1	2	3	4	5	6	7	8	9	10	11	12	13	14	15	16	17	18	19	20	21	22	23	24	25	26

1. ___ ___ ___ ___ ___ ___   ___ ___ ___ ___ ___
   19   1   3   18   5   4   3   8   18   9   19   13

   _____

2. ___ ___ ___ ___ ___ ___ ___ ___ ___ ___ ___ ___
   3   1   20   5   3   8   21   13   5   14   1   20   5

   _____

Picture This

Water, a baptismal candle, a white garment, and Sacred Chrism are used at Baptism. Next to its picture, write what each symbolizes in the sacrament.

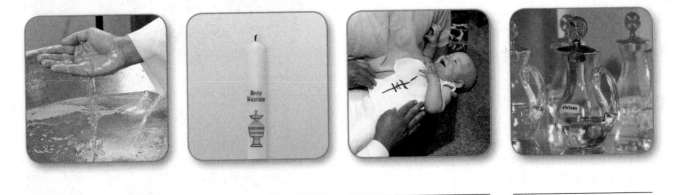

_____   _____

Pray Today

Who are your godparents? Write a prayer for them. Say it often.

_____

_____

"All things are of your making,
all times and seasons obey your laws."
Preface for Sunday in Ordinary Time V

SEASONAL

This chapter presents an overview of the
Liturgical Year.

CHAPTER 6

Throughout the liturgical year we remember and celebrate the life of Christ.

WE GATHER

✝ *Lord, you create all things to give you glory.*

How do you keep track of the day, the month, the year, or the season? How does knowing these things help you?

WE BELIEVE

The Church year is based on the life of Christ and the celebration of his life in the liturgy. So, the Church's year is called the liturgical year. The Church has its own way of marking the passing of time and the liturgical seasons of the year. In one liturgical year we recall and celebrate the whole life of Jesus Christ. We celebrate his birth, younger years, his later years of teaching and ministry, and most especially his Paschal Mystery— his suffering, Death, Resurrection, and Ascension into Heaven. During the year we also venerate, or show devotion to, Mary the Mother of God, and all the saints.

The liturgical year begins with the season of Advent in late November or early December. The Easter Triduum is the center of our year, and the dates of all the other liturgical seasons are based upon the dates of the Easter Triduum. This is why the seasons begin and end at slightly different times each year.

Around the border, following the curved track:

Advent

Christmas

Ordinary Time

Ordinary Time

Lent

Triduum

Easter

Advent   The season of Advent is a time of joyful preparation. We look forward to Christ's second coming at the end of time. We celebrate that Christ comes into our lives every day. We await the celebration on Christmas of the first coming of the Son of God.

Christmas   The Christmas season begins on Christmas Day with the celebration of the birth of the Son of God. During this season we celebrate that God is with us.

Lent   The season of Lent begins on Ash Wednesday. Lent is a special time to live out our baptismal promises and to grow closer to Jesus through prayer, fasting, and penance. In these ways we prepare for the Church's greatest celebration.

Triduum   The Easter Triduum is the Church's greatest and most important celebration. The word *triduum* means "three days." Each year we celebrate these three days sometime in March or April. During these three days, from Holy Thursday evening until Easter Sunday evening, we remember the Death of Jesus and celebrate his Resurrection.

Easter   The season of Easter begins on Easter Sunday evening and continues until Pentecost Sunday. During this season we rejoice in Jesus' Resurrection and the new life we have in Christ.

Ordinary Time   The season of Ordinary Time is celebrated in two parts: the first part is between Christmas and Lent, and the second part is between Easter and Advent. During this time we celebrate the whole life of Christ and learn the meaning of living as his disciples.

THE LITURGICAL YEAR

The Civil Calendar

The civil calendar was once very different from what it is today. It did not always begin in January. The early Greeks and Romans began their year in the spring, when they planted their crops. Later, the Romans, for military reasons, ordered the year and the calendar so that it began in January.

However, the calendar often did not match the season. People would look at a calendar that said it was spring, then look outside to see that it was really still winter! The Roman calendar constantly had to be revised.

In 1582, Pope Gregory XIII formed a group to revise the calendar. He even founded the Vatican Observatory so that astronomers could check their calculations against the movement of the sun and the stars.

These experts gave some months thirty days, others thirty-one. They made February a month of twenty-eight days, with an extra day every four years. This is the system we still have today for our civil calendar. It is called the Gregorian calendar. It was named after Pope Gregory XIII who started the revision.

Do you know this rhyme?

Thirty days hath September,
April, June, and November.
All the rest have thirty-one,
Save February, which has twenty-eight,
And in leap-year, twenty-nine.

This rhyme helps us to remember how many days there are in each month of the year.

WE RESPOND

As Catholics we not only follow the civil calendar year but also the liturgical year. In groups list some ways that your parish helps you to know which liturgical season you are celebrating. What are some signs of that season? Make plans to prepare your prayer space for each of the seasons in the liturgical year.

"Every day I will bless you;
I will praise your name forever."

Psalm 145:2

SEASONAL

CHAPTER 7

This chapter helps us to understand
the season of Ordinary Time.

Ordinary Time is a special season to learn about the life of Christ and to grow as his followers.

WE GATHER

✝ *Jesus, be with us all the days of our lives.*

If someone asked you to describe an ordinary day, what would you say? In groups discuss what might make a day ordinary.

WE BELIEVE

We often use the word *ordinary* when we want to describe something as "normal," "common," or "average." In some ways we could describe the season of Ordinary Time in these ways. As the longest season of the liturgical year, Ordinary Time is a time to learn and follow the teachings of Christ in our daily lives. It is a time to grow as his followers and to become better able to give witness to his Good News in our "normal" or everyday lives.

However, in the name of this season, the word *ordinary* means "in number order." The season is called Ordinary Time because the weeks are "ordered." This means they are named in number order. For example, the First Sunday in Ordinary Time is followed by the Second Sunday in Ordinary Time, and so on.

The season of Ordinary Time lasts thirty-three to thirty-four weeks, and it is celebrated twice during the liturgical year. The first part is short. It takes place between the seasons of Christmas and Lent. The second part lasts for several months between the seasons of Easter and Advent. This part begins in late May or June and ends in late November or early December. Ordinary Time is a season of life and hope. We use the color green during its many weeks to remind us of the life and hope that come from Christ.

Other seasons during the liturgical year focus on a particular event or period in Jesus' life. During the season of Ordinary Time, we remember all of the events and teachings of the life of Jesus Christ. We celebrate all that he gave us through his birth, life, Death, Resurrection, and Ascension.

During the season of Ordinary Time, we can concentrate in a special way on the Word of God. On the Sundays and weekdays of Ordinary Time, we read from one of the Gospels of the New Testament in number order, chapter by chapter. In this way we learn about the whole life of Jesus Christ. We hear his teachings on God his Father, love and forgiveness, and the meaning of being his disciples. Jesus is our great teacher, and during this season we say, "Teach me, O Lord, and I will follow your way."

The witness of the saints

This season is a time to grow as followers of Christ. It is a time to look to the example of the holy women and men who have given witness to Christ in their daily lives. The Church has special days in memory of Mary and the saints. These days are special because they help us to thank God for the lives of the saints and to ask the saints to remember and pray for us. The Church celebrates these days all year long, but it is especially during the many weeks of Ordinary Time that we honor the saints.

These special days to celebrate the lives of Mary, the saints, and events in the life of Jesus, are divided into three categories: memorials, feasts, and solemnities.

Memorials are usually celebrated in honor of the saints. A memorial for a saint is usually celebrated on or near the day he or she died. On these days we rejoice because the saint now lives in happiness with God forever.

Feasts are celebrations that recall some of the events in the lives of Jesus and Mary. On feasts we celebrate the Apostles, angels, and great martyrs, the followers of Christ who died for their faith.

Solemnities are the most important celebrations of all. Solemnity comes from the word *solemn*, and these feasts are great celebrations for the Church.

Some solemnities we celebrate are:

Christmas Day (December 25)
Mary, the Mother of God (January 1)
Easter Sunday (changes every year)
Pentecost Sunday (changes every year)
Body and Blood of Christ (changes every year)
Saints Peter and Paul, Apostles (June 29)
All Saints' Day (November 1)
Immaculate Conception (December 8)

What practices or devotions to the saints are you most familiar with? Do you have a saint that you remember in a special way?

What are some ways your family, parish, or school remember and celebrate the lives of the saints? Work in groups to list some of these ways.

Family _____

Parish _____

School _____

An important solemnity during Ordinary Time is All Saints' Day, November 1. On this day we remember and honor all those who were faithful followers of Christ and now share in eternal life. We know the stories of the lives of some of the saints. Other saints are known only to God. On this day we celebrate all of the saints. We are especially mindful of our patron saints—the saints whose names we share, the saints for whom schools and parishes are often named, and the saints that our families honor.

On November 2 the Church celebrates All Souls' Day. On this day we remember all those who have died, especially those in our own families and parishes. This day is usually a day for visiting the graves of family members and friends.

We pray that they may know God's love and share in his life forever.

All Souls' Day in Mexico   All Souls' Day is one of the great celebrations in Mexico. There are different prayer practices and celebrations to celebrate "El Día de los Muertos," or Day of the Dead. In some parts of Mexico the celebration actually starts on October 31 with the welcoming of the souls of children who have died and ends on November 2 with the farewell of the souls of adults.

Besides the celebration of the Masses in honor of all souls, many people in Mexico set up a prayer altar in their homes for family members who have died. Another tradition is to visit the graves of their loved ones. They clean and decorate the area with flowers and candles, and sometimes even bring the favorite foods of those who have died and spend time there celebrating their lives.

WE RESPOND

What are some ways families in your parish and neighborhood remember those who have died?

Families gather in a cemetery on the Day of the Dead in Acatlan, Mexico

✠ We Respond in Prayer

Leader: Praise be to God our Father, who raised Jesus Christ from the dead. Blessed be God for ever.

All: Blessed be God for ever.

Reader: "I am the resurrection and the life; whoever believes in me, even if he dies, will live, and everyone who lives and believes in me will never die." (John 11:25–26)

All: Lord, we believe in you.

Reader: Let us be silent as we remember all those who have died, especially those among our families and friends.

Leader: Let us now ask the saints to pray for us and for all of our loved ones who are no longer with us in this life.

🎵 Saints of God

Saints of God, we stand before you.
This we ask you, pray for us.
Holy men and holy women,
in your goodness, pray for us.

St. Mary, God's mother, our mother, pray for us.
All angels in heaven, so holy, pray for us.
St. Joseph, St. Peter, St. Andrew, pray for us.
St. Stephen, St. Paul, St. Lawrence, pray for us.

Save us, Lord, from sin and every evil.
Be merciful, O Lord,
we ask you, hear our prayer.

Grade 5 Ordinary Time
PROJECT DISCIPLE

Show What you Know

Feast days celebrate events in the lives of Jesus and Mary. Feast days also honor the Apostles, angels, and saints. Use the letters in the word *feast* to tell others about Ordinary Time.

F _____

E _____

A _____

S _____

T _____

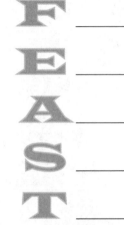

Pray Today

Dear God, Thank you for all the days in Ordinary Time. Help me to follow Jesus in my daily life. Amen.

Take Home

Encourage your family to concentrate on the Word of God during Ordinary Time. Invite them to visit, *This Week's Liturgy* which can be found on www.webelieveweb.com. This feature includes the Sunday readings and holy day liturgies, as well as activities for the whole family.

Reality Check

Make a list of specific ways you will follow Jesus in thought, word, and action during Ordinary Time.

_____

_____

_____

_____

Now, pass it on!

90    www.webelieveweb.com

UNIT TEST

Fill in the circle beside the correct answer.

1. The _____ is the power of God's love active in our lives and in the world.

   ○ Kingdom of God   ○ liturgy   ○ Incarnation

2. The _____ is all those who believe in Jesus Christ, have been baptized in him, and follow his teachings.

   ○ common vocation   ○ Church   ○ catechumenate

3. The gift of sharing in God's life that we receive in the sacraments is _____.

   ○ Sacred Chrism   ○ Christian initiation   ○ sanctifying grace

4. All Christians share _____, a call to holiness and evangelization.

   ○ the catechumenate   ○ a common vocation   ○ Original Sin

5. Acts of love that help us care for the needs of people's hearts, minds, and souls are _____.

   ○ sacraments   ○ Corporal Works of Mercy   ○ Spiritual Works of Mercy

6. The _____ is the Three Persons in One God: God the Father, God the Son, and God the Holy Spirit.

   ○ Kingdom of God   ○ Blessed Trinity   ○ Christian initiation

7. _____ is Christ's suffering, Death, Resurrection from the dead, and Ascension into Heaven.

   ○ Jesus' mission   ○ The Incarnation   ○ The Paschal Mystery

8. _____ is the forgiveness of sins and the restoring of friendship with God.

   ○ Salvation   ○ Evangelization   ○ Eternal life

continued on next page   **91**

Choose a word from the box to complete each sentence.

9. Proclaiming the Good News of Christ by what we say and do

   is _____.

10. Sharing in God's goodness and responding to his love by the way

    we live is _____.

11. The period of formation for Christian initiation that includes prayer
    and liturgy, religious instruction, and service to others is the

    _____.

12. The official public prayer of the Church is the _____.

13. The truth that the Son of God became man is the

    _____.

14. An effective sign given to us by Jesus through which we share God's

    life is a _____.

15. _____ is perfumed oil blessed by the bishop.

16. _____ is the sacrament in which we are freed from sin,
    become children of God, and are welcomed into the Church.

liturgy
Baptism
Sacred Chrism
vocation
Incarnation
holiness
sacrament
evangelization
Eucharist
catechumenate

Answer the questions.

17–18. How can a fifth grader proclaim the Good News to those who have not yet
       heard Jesus' message, or help those who have heard but who need
       encouragement to live out their gift of faith?

19–20. How would you explain to a young child the importance of water, the
       significance of Sacred Chrism, the wearing of a white garment, and the lighting
       of a candle at Baptism?

Confirmation and Eucharist Complete Our Initiation

DEAR FAMILY

Pray Learn Celebrate Share Choose Live

In Unit 2 your child will grow as a disciple of Jesus by:

- understanding the story of Pentecost and the sign of the laying on of hands as the origin of the Sacrament of Confirmation
- becoming aware of the rite, or celebration, of the Sacrament of Confirmation
- recognizing that in the Sacrament of the Eucharist Jesus is truly present under the appearances of bread and wine
- appreciating that through the celebration of the Eucharist, the Mass, we are strengthened to answer our call to discipleship
- exploring the importance of prayer.

What's the Word?

In Chapter 10, the children hear the story of Jesus' appearance on the road to Emmaus (Luke 24:13–35). Read the story on page 124. The disciples finally recognized this was the risen Jesus! We, too, recognize the risen Jesus in the breaking of the bread at Eucharist. Do you and your family recognize him as you walk through the events of your day?

Pray Today At your next family meal, pray together:

Jesus, never be a stranger,
always be a friend,
present with our family,
now and forever.
Amen.

Reality Check

"The Christian family is a communion of persons, a sign and image of the communion of the Father and the Son in the Holy Spirit."

(Catechism of the Catholic Church, 2205)

Question Corner

Check the definition of prayer that means the most in your life today:

- ❏ Prayer is asking God for help.
- ❏ Prayer is offering my thoughts and feelings to God.
- ❏ Prayer is having a conversation with God.
- ❏ (other) _____

Show That You Care

As a family celebrate the Eucharist together. Write one thing your family can do to live out the meaning of the Eucharist.

_____

_____

Take Home

Be ready for this unit's Take Home:

Chapter 8: Growing closer to Christ

Chapter 9: Filling your home with the fruits of the Holy Spirit

Chapter 10: Offering God thanks and praise

Chapter 11: Taking part in the Mass

Chapter 12: Taking a "sacramental journey"

The Coming of the Holy Spirit

✝ We Gather in Prayer

Leader: Let us pray as one family filled with the Holy Spirit.

Reader: A reading from the Book of Ezekiel

"I will put my spirit in you that you may live, and I will settle you upon your land; thus you shall know that I am the LORD. I have promised, and I will do it, says the LORD." (Ezekiel 37:14)

The word of the Lord.

All: Thanks be to God.

♫ We Belong to God's Family

Refrain:

We belong to God's family.
Brothers and sisters are we,
singing together in unity about
one Lord and one faith, one family.

We are one in the Spirit,
the gift from God above.
We are sent to proclaim God's word
and live together in love. (Refrain)

On Pentecost the Holy Spirit came upon the first disciples.

WE GATHER

✝ *Holy Spirit, come to live among us.*

Has anyone ever helped you to change something about yourself, for example, the things you eat or the way you play sports? If so, who was it and how did you change?

WE BELIEVE

Jesus called all of his disciples to be his witnesses. He wanted them to spread the message of God's Kingdom. After his Resurrection, Jesus sent his Apostles to preach in his name and to baptize those who believed in him.

Jesus told his Apostles that they would not be alone in this work. He promised to send the Holy Spirit to guide and help them. They would be changed by the presence of the Holy Spirit in their lives. Jesus promised, "you will receive power when the holy Spirit comes upon you, and you will be my witnesses in Jerusalem, throughout Judea and Samaria, and to the ends of the earth" (Acts of the Apostles 1:8).

After Christ ascended to his Father, the Apostles returned to Jerusalem. Mary, the mother of Jesus, and some other disciples were there, too. While they were gathered in Jerusalem the Jewish feast of Pentecost was celebrated. The word *Pentecost* comes from a Greek word *pente*, meaning "the fiftieth day." This fiftieth day after Passover was a harvest festival for the Jews. On this day, the Jewish People thanked God for all their blessings, especially for the fruits of the earth.

It was during this time that the Holy Spirit came as Jesus had promised. This is the way the coming of the Holy Spirit is described in the Acts of the Apostles.

📖 Acts of the Apostles 2:1–47

"When the time for Pentecost was fulfilled, they were all in one place together. And suddenly there came from the sky a noise like a strong driving wind, and it filled the entire house in which they were. Then there appeared to them tongues as of fire, which parted and came to rest on each one of them. And they were all filled with the holy Spirit and began to speak in different tongues, as the Spirit enabled them to proclaim." (Acts of the Apostles 2:1–4)

The people outside heard all of this, but they did not know what was happening. The Apostles went out into the crowd. Peter told the people that God the Father had indeed raised Jesus. He said that what they had just seen and heard had been the coming of the Holy Spirit.

Each person heard this Good News of Christ in his or her own language. The people in the crowd were amazed. They asked Peter and the others what they should do. Peter told them to be sorry for their sins and to repent. He told them to be baptized and receive the Gift of the Holy Spirit. About three thousand people believed and became disciples that day.

Each year on Pentecost we celebrate in a special way the coming of the Holy Spirit. Pentecost is also a feast of gratitude for the gifts and fruits of the Holy Spirit. On Pentecost, the Apostles began to go into the world as Jesus had asked.

Jesus calls all people to follow him and share his Good News with others. Strengthened by the Holy Spirit, we are all God's workers in the world.

WE RESPOND

How can the Holy Spirit help you to be a witness to Christ today?

🏃 In groups role-play the story of Pentecost as if it were happening today. Where would the disciples be? Who would be among the crowd? How would you give witness to Christ and help others to believe?

Laying on of hands and anointing are signs of the Holy Spirit's presence.

WE GATHER

✝ *Holy Spirit, we welcome you.*

In a classroom you often see students raising their hands. What might this action be a sign of? What are some other actions that we use as signs?

WE BELIEVE

After Pentecost the Apostles were strengthened and guided by the Holy Spirit. They began to spread the message of God's Kingdom throughout the world. They gave witness to Jesus Christ by what they said and did. They baptized many believers.

The newly baptized received the strengthening power of the Holy Spirit when the Apostles placed their hands on them. These early Church members understood the importance of the laying on of hands. This ancient action is a powerful sign of God's blessing. By the laying on of hands, authority and grace were given in God's name. By the Apostles' laying on of hands, the Holy Spirit came upon those who believed in Jesus Christ.

From the very beginning of the Church there was a connection between Baptism and this laying on of hands by the Apostles. The laying on of hands was the beginning of the Sacrament of Confirmation.

As the Church grew and spread, eventually an anointing was joined to the laying on of hands. The word *anoint* means to apply oil to someone as a sign that God has chosen that person for a special mission. Like the laying on of hands, anointing is an ancient practice. Anointing was an important part of Jewish life during Jesus' time.

The early Church continued anointing with oil as a sign of God's presence in the life of the person anointed. The anointing that took place with the laying on of hands was a sign of the Holy Spirit's presence and of the receiving of the Holy Spirit.

In time the anointing became the essential sign of the Gift of the Holy Spirit. Sacred Chrism, oil blessed by a bishop, was used in this anointing. Today in the Sacrament of Confirmation, the anointing with oil is done as the celebrant anoints the forehead of the one being confirmed.

As Catholics...

There are many symbols that remind us of the Holy Spirit. Two of them can be found in the Pentecost story: wind and fire. Each symbol helps us to understand the ways the Holy Spirit acts in our lives.

The word *spirit* comes from a Hebrew word that means "wind," "air," and "breath." The presence of the Holy Spirit is often symbolized as wind. Wind travels everywhere. It surrounds us. The Holy Spirit does the same.

The symbol of fire suggests warmth, energy, power, and change. Fire changes whatever it touches. So does the Holy Spirit. We are changed by the power of the Holy Spirit.

Talk about other symbols or images of the Holy Spirit.

WE RESPOND

With a partner talk about the different actions that are part of our worship. What do we do, or see others doing, to praise God? How are these actions signs that we believe in God the Father, Son, and Holy Spirit? Illustrate one of these actions.

In Confirmation we become more like Christ and are strengthened to be his witnesses.

WE GATHER

✝ *Holy Spirit, be at our side always.*

When you are in school, at camp, and are away from your family and friends, how can you still feel close to them?

WE BELIEVE

God loves us and wants us to be close to him. He sent his own Son so that we could know and love him. He sent the Holy Spirit to help us to grow in our love for him. God the Holy Spirit is always close to us. We can turn to the Holy Spirit for comfort and guidance, for strength and peace. The Holy Spirit is always with the Church.

In the Sacrament of **Confirmation** we receive the Gift of the Holy Spirit in a special way. We become more like Christ and are strengthened to be his witnesses.

Confirmation is a Sacrament of Christian Initiation. The first Sacrament of Christian Initiation is Baptism. Confirmation completes Baptism and, like Baptism, imprints on our souls a character, an indelible spiritual seal. Thus, we only receive Confirmation once. The Eucharist fully initiates us into the Church.

The importance of the sacrament

The Sacrament of Confirmation deepens the grace we first received at Baptism. In Confirmation:

- We are sealed with the Gift of God the Holy Spirit.

- We become more like Jesus the Son of God and are strengthened to be active witnesses of Jesus.

- Our friendship with God the Father is deepened.

- Our relationship with the Church is strengthened.

- We are sent forth to live our faith in the world.

Key Word

Confirmation the sacrament in which we receive the Gift of the Holy Spirit in a special way

All baptized members of the Church are called to receive the Sacrament of Confirmation. Those who have been baptized as infants usually celebrate the Sacrament of Confirmation between the ages of seven and sixteen.

Confirmation most often takes place in the parish community. The bishop usually visits parishes or groups of parishes at various times during the year and confirms all those who have prepared to receive the sacrament.

In some places adults and older children may participate in the catechumenate. Together the catechumens, those who are preparing to be initiated into the Church, pray, study, and grow in faith. They receive the Sacraments of Baptism, Confirmation, and Eucharist at one celebration, usually the Easter Vigil.

WE RESPOND

🎵 **We Belong to God's Family**

Refrain:

We belong to God's family.
Brothers and sisters are we, singing
together in unity about one Lord
and one faith, one family.

We are one in the Spirit,
the gift from God above.
We are sent to proclaim God's
word and live together in love.
(Refrain)

Preparation is an important part of Confirmation.

WE GATHER

✝ *Holy Spirit, Giver of Life, guide our way.*

Both at home and in our neighborhoods, we prepare for important events. Think of one. How and why do you prepare for it?

WE BELIEVE

Preparation for the Sacrament of Confirmation is very important. Those preparing for this sacrament are called *candidates*. Candidates who have reached the age of reason must profess the faith and be in the state of grace. They must want to receive Confirmation and to take on the role of disciple and witness within the Church and the world.

Candidates prepare for Confirmation by praying and reflecting on the life of Jesus Christ and on the mission of the Church. During this time candidates learn about the Gift of the Holy Spirit.

During this preparation candidates grow closer to Christ. The relationship with Christ that began at their Baptism is strengthened. The candidates begin to see how they can better live out the promises made at Baptism. Through their preparation, candidates can feel a greater sense of belonging to the Church. They learn to share more completely in the mission of the Church. They learn to give witness to the Good News of Christ through their lives.

The whole parish can participate in this preparation. People in a parish:

- pray with and for the candidates
- meet with the candidates to talk about their faith
- help the candidates to find ways to serve together in the parish.

Connections to Baptism   If we were baptized as infants, our parents made some choices regarding our Baptism. They selected a name for us. Our name is often that of a saint or someone whom our parents admire. In fact, one of the first questions asked during the celebration of Baptism is "What name do you give your child?"

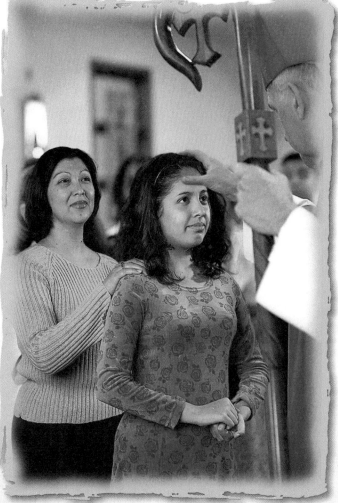

Sponsors can be involved in our preparation for Confirmation. They can share their own experiences with us and answer any questions we may have about our faith. Sponsors also play an important role in the celebration of Confirmation. They present us to the bishop for anointing.

At Confirmation we choose a name, usually that of a saint whose example we can follow in becoming closer to Jesus. Although we can choose the name of any saint, we are encouraged to take the name given to us at Baptism. This highlights the link between the Sacraments of Baptism and Confirmation.

If we were baptized as infants, our parents also chose godparents for us. Godmothers and godfathers are people who help us to grow in faith. When we are preparing for Confirmation, we also choose someone to help us grow in our faith. We choose a sponsor. A sponsor needs to be a Catholic who has received the Sacraments of Christian Initiation and is a person we respect and trust. Our sponsor can be a family member other than a parent, a friend, or someone from our parish. Selecting one of our godparents to be our sponsor again shows the link between Baptism and Confirmation. But whomever we choose, our sponsor should be an example of Christian living so that he or she can continue to encourage us to follow Jesus.

WE RESPOND

Think of people in your neighborhood, parish, or school who are examples of Christian living. In what ways do they encourage others to follow Jesus? How can the way you live encourage others to follow Jesus?

PROJECT

Pray
Learn
Celebrate
Share
Choose
Live

Show What *you* Know

Complete the word web by writing words or phrases that relate
to the Sacrament of Confirmation.

CONFIRMATION

Fast Facts

Red, as the color of fire,
symbolizes the Holy
Spirit and is the
liturgical color used
on Pentecost and
for the Sacrament
of Confirmation.

Pray Today

Jesus had asked the first disciples to
share his Good News with others.
Write a short prayer to the Holy Spirit
for the courage to do this.

_____

_____

_____

_____

Question Corner

What is the average age of the candidates in
the Sacrament of Confirmation in your parish?

❑ 10   ❑ 12   ❑ 14   ❑ other _____

The Celebration of Confirmation

9

Counsel

Knowledge

Understanding

Piety

Fear of the LORD

Wisdom

Fortitude

✝ We Gather in Prayer

Leader: Lord, send out your Spirit.

All: And renew the face of the earth!

🎵 Envía Tu Espíritu

Refrain:

Envía tu Espíritu,
envía tu Espíritu,
envía tu Espíritu,
sea renovada la faz de la tierra.
Sea renovada la faz de la tierra.

Leader: Come, Holy Spirit, fill the hearts of your faithful.

All: And kindle in them the fire of your love.

Leader: Send forth your Spirit and they shall be created.

All: And you will renew the face of the earth.

Leader: Let us pray.
Lord,
by the light of the Holy Spirit
you have taught the hearts of your
    faithful.
In the same Spirit
help us to relish what is right
and always rejoice in your consolation.

We ask this through Christ our Lord.

All: Amen.

Confirmation leads us from Baptism to the Eucharist.

WE GATHER

✝ *We believe in the Holy Spirit, the Lord and giver of life.*

Have you ever attended a Confirmation? If so, share your experiences with the class.

If you have not, what questions would you like to ask about your parish's celebration of Confirmation?

WE BELIEVE

Baptism, Confirmation, and the Eucharist are the three Sacraments of Christian Initiation. In the celebration of Confirmation, we gather with our parish community and express our belief in Jesus Christ. We are nourished by Jesus himself in Holy Communion. Because Confirmation leads us to the Eucharist and full initiation into the Church, we usually celebrate Confirmation within Mass.

Confirmation Overview
Celebrated within Mass

Liturgy of the Word

Sacrament of Confirmation
Presentation of the Candidates

Homily

Renewal of Baptismal Promises

Laying on of Hands

Anointing with Chrism

Prayer of the Faithful

Liturgy of the Eucharist

Here is some of what happens during the celebration of Confirmation.

Liturgy of the Word   As in all the other sacraments, the Word of God is proclaimed. The first reading is usually from the Old Testament. The second reading is usually from the New Testament. The third reading is from one of the four Gospels. From the Gospel reading we may hear different titles for the Holy Spirit. These titles describe who the Holy Spirit is and the Holy Spirit's role and power in our lives.

Presentation of the Candidates
The pastor or a parish leader presents those to be confirmed. These candidates may be called by name as they stand with their sponsors.

Homily   After the presentation of candidates, the bishop gives a brief homily to help everyone understand the readings. He talks about the Sacrament of Confirmation that is being celebrated. He reminds us of our gift of faith, and of the power of the Holy Spirit in our lives. The bishop may ask the candidates about their faith.

ADVOCATE

Jesus spoke to his Apostles about the coming of the Holy Spirit. He said, "The Advocate, the holy Spirit that the Father will send in my name—he will teach you everything and remind you of all that [I] told you" (John 14:26).

An advocate is someone who intercedes on our behalf, someone who speaks for us, someone who even defends us. An advocate comforts and teaches. The Holy Spirit is our Advocate.

Jesus also called the Holy Spirit "the Spirit of truth." Jesus said to his Apostles, "I have much more to tell you, but you cannot bear it now. But when he comes, the Spirit of truth, he will guide you to all truth" (John 16:12–13). The Holy Spirit guides us as we learn the truths of our faith, the truths that Jesus and the Church teach us.

The titles of Advocate and Spirit of Truth are important to our understanding of the Holy Spirit and the Sacrament of Confirmation. These titles are prayed in the prayers during the celebration of the sacrament.

Renewal of Baptismal Promises The candidates stand and renew their baptismal promises. They answer each of the questions about their belief in the Blessed Trinity and the Church with the words *I do.*

The renewal of the baptismal promises at Confirmation is very important. This is a good time for those who were baptized as infants to profess their faith for themselves.

SPIRIT OF TRUTH

WE RESPOND

One great part of being Catholic is that we all share the same beliefs! Sit quietly and think about what you believe as a Catholic. Then work in groups and list some of these beliefs.

We Believe

- We Believe in God
- _____

_____

_____

How do you show that you live by these beliefs?

In the Sacrament of Confirmation, we are sealed with the Gift of the Holy Spirit.

WE GATHER

✝ *Holy Spirit, strengthen us.*

Think about the different kinds of oil that you and your family use. List them here and describe how these oils help us.

- olive oil
- coconut oil
- essential oil
- ~~deen~~ oil for heat

WE BELIEVE

In the celebration of Confirmation, after the candidates have renewed their baptismal promises, the bishop reminds all assembled of their Baptism. He invites everyone to pray for the outpouring of the Holy Spirit on those to be confirmed. In the liturgy of Confirmation, the whole Church prays for all those who are being confirmed. The special presence of the Holy Spirit in Confirmation is brought about through the words and actions used in the sacrament.

Laying on of Hands The bishop and priests celebrating with him extend their hands over the whole group of candidates. This reminds us of the laying on of hands by the Apostles and early Church. The bishop prays to God the Father, "Send your Holy Spirit upon them to be their Helper and Guide." He continues by praying that they receive the gifts of the Holy Spirit.

Anointing with Sacred Chrism The sponsor stands near the candidate and places a hand on the candidate's shoulder. This shows the support and guidance of the sponsor and the ongoing care of the whole parish for those who are being confirmed.

The bishop confirms each candidate by the anointing with Sacred Chrism on the forehead, and through the words, "N., be sealed with the Gift of the Holy Spirit." The one confirmed responds, "Amen."

The bishop then shares a sign of peace with the newly confirmed. Each person also offers peace to the bishop. This important action reminds us of the union of the whole Church with the bishop, our leader and guide.

Helper

Prayer of the Faithful Although only a few people read these intercessions aloud, this is a prayer of the whole Church. We remember the newly confirmed, their families and sponsors, and the whole Church. After each prayer those gathered offer their responses. We might respond, "Lord, hear our prayer."

Liturgy of the Eucharist The newly confirmed now join with all assembled to continue to worship God by sharing in the gift of Jesus in the Eucharist.

Holy Spirit

WE RESPOND

Sing this song asking God's blessing on all candidates for Confirmation.

🎵 **Envía Tu Espíritu**

Refrain:
    Envía tu Espíritu,
    envía tu Espíritu,
    envía tu Espíritu,
    sea renovada la faz de la tierra.
    Sea renovada la faz de la tierra.

    Spirit of the living God, burn in
        our hearts,
    and make us a people of hope and
        compassion. (Refrain)

111

The gifts of the Holy Spirit help those who are confirmed.

WE GATHER

✝ *Holy Spirit, be with me and all whom you give me to love.*

Have you ever seen a birth certificate, passport, or diploma? Documents like these are marked with an official seal. Discuss why this seal is important.

WE BELIEVE

In Confirmation, the bishop uses chrism, blessed oil, to anoint each candidate. By this anointing, we receive the seal of the Holy Spirit. We are marked as people who share fully in Jesus' mission. This anointing confirms and completes our baptismal anointing. The Holy Spirit is with us to strengthen us to share in the mission of Jesus Christ and to be his witnesses to others. This seal of the Holy Spirit identifies us as belonging to Jesus Christ. Like the seal of Baptism, it is with us always. Because of this we receive Confirmation only once.

The Holy Spirit guides the Church and all of its members. The Holy Spirit gives us the desire to be disciples. When we receive the Sacrament of Confirmation, the Holy Spirit strengthens us with special gifts. The **gifts of the Holy Spirit** are wisdom, understanding, counsel, fortitude, knowledge, piety, and fear of the Lord. These seven gifts of the Holy Spirit have an effect on us. They help us to live as faithful followers and witnesses of Jesus Christ.

Key Word

gifts of the Holy Spirit wisdom, understanding, counsel, fortitude, knowledge, piety, and fear of the Lord

How the Gifts of the Holy Spirit Help Us

Wisdom
helps us to see and follow God's will in our lives.

Understanding
helps us to love others as Jesus calls us to do.

Counsel
(Right Judgment)
aids us in making good choices.

Fortitude
(Courage)
strengthens us to give witness to our faith in Jesus Christ.

Knowledge
brings us to learn more about God and his plan, and leads us to wisdom and understanding.

Piety
(Reverence)
makes it possible for us to love and respect all that God has created.

Fear of the Lord
(Wonder and Awe)
helps us to see God's presence and love filling all creation.

Think about people who are faithful followers and witnesses of Jesus Christ. In groups complete the following:

When someone has the gift of wisdom he or she

helps us to see and follow God's will in our lives

When someone has the gift of understanding he or she

helps us to love others as Jesus calls us to do

When someone has the gift of counsel he or she

aids us in making good choices

When someone has the gift of fortitude he or she

strengthens us to give witness to our faith in Jesus Christ

When someone has the gift of knowledge he or she

Brings us to learn more about God & his plan, & leads us to wisdom & understanding

When someone has the gift of piety he or she

makes it possible for us to love & respect all that God has created

When someone has the gift of fear of the Lord he or she

helps us to see God's presence and love filling all creation

These gifts of the Holy Spirit strengthen all of us to do what Christ asks of us.

Role-play some ways you can respond to the gifts of the Holy Spirit in your lives.

WE RESPOND

Think about the ways the world would be changed if everyone was filled with the gifts of the Holy Spirit. How can these gifts help you as a disciple of Jesus?

As Catholics...

The Eastern Catholic Churches celebrate the Sacrament of Chrismation. *Chrismation* is another name for Confirmation. Chrismation and the first celebration of the Eucharist take place right after Baptism. So all three Sacraments of Christian Initiation are celebrated in one ceremony.

In Chrismation, various parts of the body are anointed with myron. *Myron* is another name for the Sacred Chrism. The forehead, eyes, ears, nose, lips, chest, back, hands, and feet are all anointed with myron. Each anointing is accompanied by the words "the seal of the Gift of the Holy Spirit."

Find out if there is an Eastern Catholic Church in your city or town.

113

Confirmation calls those anointed to live out their Baptism as witnesses of Jesus Christ.

WE GATHER

✝ *Guide us, Spirit of God, on the way of Jesus Christ.*

When you are traveling someplace that you have never been before, how do you find your way? What actions or signs might someone use to direct you?

WE BELIEVE

Each day as we grow in faith, we are strengthened by the Holy Spirit to follow God's call to holiness. When we respond to the gifts of the Holy Spirit, our lives are filled with the fruits of the Holy Spirit. "The fruit of the Spirit is love, joy, peace, patience, kindness, generosity, faithfulness, gentleness, self-control." (Galatians 5:22–23)

The fruits of the Holy Spirit are the good things that people can see in us when we respond to the gifts of the Holy Spirit.

God's grace that was first given at Baptism lives within each one of us. As a Church we gather each week with our parish to celebrate that God is with us and to receive the great gift of Jesus Christ himself in the Eucharist.

With the help and guidance of the Holy Spirit, we commit ourselves to the work of Jesus. With the strength and nourishment of Jesus in the Eucharist we are filled with love of God and others. We grow in holiness.

We continue Jesus' work of spreading the message of the Reign of God, a kingdom of justice and peace. We become witnesses of Jesus Christ. We can do this by becoming people who:

- show kindness to those who are poor
- help a new person in our class feel welcome
- share with others the joy of our Catholic faith
- stand up against injustice and hatred
- work for a better community and world.

Add some other ways that we can be witnesses of Jesus Christ.

- _____
- _____
- _____

WE RESPOND

Which fruits of the Holy Spirit do you see in the people around you? What fruits can others see in the way you live as a disciple?

PROJECT

Show What *you* Know

Unscramble the letters of these words. Then, use the letters in the numbered boxes to answer the question below.

SIMWDO   w i s d o m
(1) (2)

RANDNNUIGSDET   u n d e r s t a n d i n g
(3)

SUENOLC   c o u n s e l
(4) (5)

KEODLNEGW   k n o w l e d g e
(6) (7)

TEYPI   P i e t y
(8) (9)

RAFE FO HET DORL   F . _ _ of the L o r d
(10) (11) (12)

What helps us to live as faithful followers and witnesses of Jesus Christ?

t h e   g i f t s   o f   t h e
(3)(12)(6) (7)(1)(10)(3)(4) (2)(10) (3)(12)(6)

h o l y   s p i r i t
(12)(2)(5)(9) (4)(8)(1)(11)(1)(3)

What's *the* Word?

"The Advocate, the holy Spirit that the Father will send in my name—he will teach you everything and remind you of all that [I] told you." (John 14:26)

Who is speaking?_____

Circle another name for the Holy Spirit.

Fast Facts

Sacred Chrism, the oil used to anoint candidates in the Sacrament of Confirmation, is a mixture of olive oil and balm. It is usually consecrated by the bishop at the Chrism Mass on Holy Thursday morning.

Jesus Christ, the Bread of Life

10

✝ We Gather in Prayer

Leader: Jesus said, "Do not work for food that perishes but for the food that endures for eternal life, which the Son of Man will give you" (John 6:27).

All: Give us life today and forever.

Leader: Jesus said, "I am the bread of life; whoever comes to me will never hunger, and whoever believes in me will never thirst" (John 6:35).

All: Give us life today and forever.

Leader: Jesus said, "I am the living bread that came down from heaven; whoever eats this bread will live forever; and the bread that I will give is my flesh for the life of the world" (John 6:51).

All: Give us life today and forever.

Leader: Jesus said, "Whoever eats my flesh and drinks my blood remains in me and I in him" (John 6:56).

All: Give us life today and forever.

Leader: Jesus, help us stay close to you always. May the food you give strengthen us always.

All: Amen.

In the Eucharist we celebrate and receive Jesus Christ.

WE GATHER

✝ *Jesus, open our minds and our hearts to you.*

Name some ways that people we love remain close to us even when they are not with us.

WE BELIEVE

God is always present to his people. He acts in their lives, guiding and protecting them. Throughout history, the Jewish People have remembered and celebrated God's great love for them. On a feast called **Passover** they remember the miraculous way that God saved them from death and slavery in ancient Egypt. God "passed over" the houses of his people, protecting them from the suffering that came to the Egyptians. God then helped Moses and his people escape Egypt by crossing the Red Sea.

Every year the Jewish People gather to celebrate this feast. Jesus did the same with his family and friends. On the night before he was to die, Jesus and the Apostles celebrated the feast of Passover in Jerusalem. The Apostles did not know that this Passover meal would be different from all others. They did not know that Jesus would die the next day.

Jesus wanted to remain present with his disciples. So he gave them a special way to remember him and to be with him. Jesus took his place among the Apostles. "Then he took the bread, said the blessing, broke it, and gave it to them, saying, 'This is my body, which will be given for you; do this in memory of me.'

And likewise the cup after they had eaten, saying, 'This cup is the new covenant in my blood, which will be shed for you.'" (Luke 22:19–20)

Jesus often broke bread and ate with his disciples. It was not until this Last Supper, on the night before Jesus died, that this simple act took on a special meaning. At the Last Supper, Jesus' breaking of the bread and sharing of the cup was an offering of himself for our salvation.

At the Last Supper Jesus gave us the gift of himself and instituted the Eucharist. Through the Eucharist Jesus remains with us forever.

The importance of the Eucharist Jesus truly becomes present to us in the Sacrament of the Eucharist. The **Eucharist** is the Sacrament of the Body and Blood of Christ.

Jesus is truly present under the appearances of bread and wine. In the Sacrament of the Eucharist:

- We are nourished by the Word of God and receive Jesus Christ in Holy Communion.

- We are made into the Body of Christ, the Church, and joined more closely to Christ and one another.

- The grace first received in Baptism grows in us.

- We are strengthened to love and serve others, especially those who are poor or in need.

As Catholics...

A covenant is an agreement made between God and his people. God made a covenant with Moses and his people after their escape from Egypt. God promised to be their God and to protect and provide for them. The people promised to be his people. They would worship the one true God and live by his laws. Jewish People today still live by this covenant.

Christians believe that a new covenant was made by Jesus' Death and Resurrection. Through this new covenant we are saved, and it is possible for us to share in God's life again. As we celebrate the Eucharist this week remember that we are celebrating the new covenant.

Key Words

Passover the feast on which Jewish People remember the miraculous way that God saved them from death and slavery in ancient Egypt

Eucharist the Sacrament of the Body and Blood of Christ; Jesus is truly present under the appearances of bread and wine

WE RESPOND

Design an invitation for your parish Web site or newsletter that tells people about the importance of the Eucharist.

We celebrate the Eucharist every week.

"Do this in memory of me." (Luke 22:19)

The Eucharist is a memorial, a meal, and a sacrifice.

WE GATHER

✝ *Lord Jesus Christ, we are nourished by your Body and Blood.*

Think about an important event that has happened in your life or in the life of your family. What are some things that we do to remember these events from the past?

WE BELIEVE

The Eucharist is so important to the Church that we are called to participate in its celebration every Sunday or Saturday evening. It is the only Sacrament of Christian Initiation that we receive again and again. The Eucharist nourishes us to be faithful members of the Church.

When we celebrate the Eucharist, we are really doing three things all at once. We are:

- honoring Jesus by remembering what he did for us

- sharing in a meal

- participating in a sacrifice.

The Eucharist as memorial   Jesus told his Apostles to "do this in memory of me" (Luke 22:19). By gathering and breaking bread, we are remembering Jesus. We are remembering the new life we have because of Jesus' Death and Resurrection. A memorial is something that helps us to remember a person or an event. Buildings and holidays are examples of memorials. The Eucharist is a memorial, too.

The Eucharist is different from other memorials, however. It is much more than just remembering past events. In the Eucharist, Christ is really present. By the power of the Holy Spirit, the Paschal Mystery of Christ's suffering, Death, Resurrection, and Ascension is made present to us. It is present to us today just as Jesus himself is present.

The Eucharist as meal   When Jesus gave us the Eucharist, he and his friends were eating and celebrating together. In the Eucharist we share in a meal. We are nourished by the Body and Blood of Christ. When we receive Holy Communion, Jesus lives in us and we live in him. Jesus tells us: "For my flesh is true food, and my blood is true drink. Whoever eats my flesh and drinks my blood remains in me and I in him" (John 6:55–56).

The Eucharist is a meal.

We are nourished by the Body and Blood of Jesus Christ.

The Eucharist is a sacrifice.

The Eucharist as sacrifice During the celebration of the Eucharist, Jesus acts through the priest. A sacrifice is a gift offered to God by a priest in the name of all the people. At each celebration of the Eucharist, Jesus' sacrifice on the cross, his Resurrection, and his Ascension into Heaven are made present again. Through this sacrifice we are saved. We are reconciled with God and one another.

In the Eucharist Jesus also offers his Father the gifts of praise and thanksgiving. This thanks and praise is for all the gifts that God has given us in creation. In every celebration of the Eucharist, the whole Church offers thanks and praise. We join Jesus in offering ourselves to God the Father. We offer to God all of the joys and concerns that we have. We offer our willingness to continue to live as Jesus' disciples.

Key Word

sacrifice a gift offered to God by a priest in the name of all the people

Design a photo essay on the Eucharist as a meal, sacrifice, and a memorial. What pictures would you include? What captions would you give to those pictures? Name and plan your photo essay here.

meal

WE RESPOND

Name some ways that you can remember Jesus this week.

We recognize Jesus in the breaking of the bread.

WE GATHER

✛ *Jesus, walk with us always.*

Imagine a friend or a family member is next to you. How could you describe this person so that someone else would recognize him or her?

Master of Santo Domingo de Silos (late 11th–mid 12th Century), *Journey to Emmaus*

WE BELIEVE

Three days after Jesus' Death on the cross, Mary Magdalene, Joanna, and Mary the mother of James discovered the empty tomb of Jesus. Two men in shining robes told them that Jesus had been raised from the dead. Jesus' disciples were afraid and did not know what to think or believe.

📖 Luke 24:13–35

On that very same day, two disciples were walking to the village of Emmaus, which was seven miles outside of Jerusalem. They were very sad about Jesus' Death. They had heard about the empty tomb and were concerned about what had happened. As the two disciples were talking, a man joined them. It was the risen Jesus. However, the disciples did not recognize him.

Jesus asked them what they had been discussing. The disciples told him about the Death of Jesus and the empty tomb and they were amazed that this stranger had not heard about this.

Finally, Jesus asked them, "Was it not necessary that the Messiah should suffer these things and enter into his glory?" (Luke 24:26). Then Jesus continued to teach them about Scripture as they walked. When they got to Emmaus, the disciples invited Jesus to have dinner with them.

At this meal Jesus took bread and blessed it. He then broke the bread and gave it to them. Suddenly, the disciples recognized that this was the risen Jesus. Then instantly, Jesus was gone.

The two disciples returned to Jerusalem immediately. They told the others what had happened and how Jesus " . . . was made known to them in the breaking of the bread" (Luke 24:35).

The first Christians used the words "breaking of the bread" to describe their celebrations of the Eucharist. We read in the Acts of the Apostles that the small Christian community that formed the Church "devoted themselves to the teaching of the apostles and to the communal life, to the breaking of the bread and to the prayers" (Acts of the Apostles 2:42).

These Christians gathered together as one community. They listened to stories about God. They broke bread together sharing in Christ's Body as he commanded. They drank from the cup and shared the very life of Jesus. They said and did what Jesus told them to do at the Last Supper.

We learn from the Acts of the Apostles that from the very start of the Church, the followers of Jesus Christ celebrated the Eucharist.

The Real Presence Today we are like the disciples on the road to Emmaus. We journey with one another and gather together every Sunday for the celebration of the Eucharist. We, too, listen to God's Word proclaimed. And like those first disciples we share a meal. The bread and wine are blessed and become the Body and Blood of Christ.

What looks and tastes like bread and wine is truly Jesus' Body and Blood. Every time we receive the Eucharist, Jesus is truly with us. In the Eucharist, the Body and Blood of Christ are actually present under the appearances of bread and wine. Jesus is really and truly present in the Eucharist. This is called the **Real Presence**.

When we receive the Eucharist, we are receiving Jesus himself. He nourishes us with his life. He gives us his own strength to help us lead loving and holy lives.

Real Presence Jesus really and truly present in the Eucharist

WE RESPOND

Imagine that you are one of the disciples from Emmaus. Get a sense of the sights, sounds, and smells that surround you. What does Jesus look like? Write four words that describe your feelings when you recognize Jesus in the breaking of the bread.

_____   _____

_____   _____

Let us pray,

Jesus, never be a stranger,
always be a friend,
present with me,
now and forever.

Amen.

Christ feeding the multitude,
Ethiopia, 1664–1665

Jesus is the Bread of Life.

WE GATHER

✝ *Jesus, you spread a banquet before us.*

What are some things that you need to stay healthy and happy? What happens when people cannot have the things they need in life?

WE BELIEVE

Many people followed Jesus as he went from village to village. These people felt Jesus' power and presence. They looked to him for help and guidance. Sometimes on these journeys there was not enough food for everyone to eat. So Jesus tried to help feed his hungry disciples.

📖 John 6:1–14

Once about five thousand people had followed Jesus up a mountain. Miraculously Jesus was able to feed all of them with only five loaves of bread and two fish. Even after everyone ate, some food was still left!

People were amazed when Jesus did this. The next day they asked Jesus about what he had done. Jesus told them, "I am the bread of life; whoever comes to me will never hunger, and whoever believes in me will never thirst" (John 6:35).

Jesus' followers knew that they needed bread to live. But Jesus wanted them to know something more. He wanted them to know that belief in him is needed to have life with God. So Jesus continued, "I am the living bread that came down from heaven; whoever eats this bread will live forever; and the bread that I will give is my flesh for the life of the world" (John 6:51).

By Jesus calling himself the Bread of Life and the Living Bread, Jesus helped his disciples to understand that he was the Son of God sent to bring God's life to them. Jesus brings life with God forever. Whoever truly believes that Jesus is the Son of God and lives as his disciple will have eternal life.

Strengthened to be disciples As members of the Church, we are Jesus' disciples, too. Jesus wants all of us to believe in him. He wants us to be nourished by his life so that we can help others in his name. He wants us to have life with God forever. So he gives himself to us in the Eucharist. Jesus is our Bread of Life.

When we receive the Eucharist, we share in God's own life—the life of the Father, the Son, and the Holy Spirit. The Eucharist nourishes us so that we can respond to the gifts of the Holy Spirit. Through the grace of the sacrament we can live as Jesus did.

When we receive the Body and Blood of Christ in Holy Communion, our relationship with Christ and one another is strengthened. We become the Body of Christ, the Church. We are joined to all believers everywhere. The Eucharist unites our parish community. We become Christ to one another. We share his love with one another and grow as a community of believers. We are better able to live as children of God and to live our faith in the world. We can do this by protecting life, respecting the rights of others, and helping people to meet their needs.

WE RESPOND

Work with a partner. Role-play ways that your parish community shows that Jesus lives in them.

🎵 I Am the Bread of Life

I am the Bread of life.
You who come to me shall not hunger;
and who believe in me shall not thirst.
No one can come to me unless the Father
    beckons.

The bread that I will give
Is my flesh for the life of the world.
And if you eat of this bread,
you shall live for ever,
you shall live for ever.

Pray Learn Celebrate Share Choose Live

PROJECT

Show What *you* Know

Complete the following using the Key Words and definitions.

1. On a feast called ___passover___, Jewish People remember the miraculous way that ___God___ saved them from death and slavery in ancient ___egypt___

2. The ___Eucharist___ is the Sacrament of the ___Body___ and Blood of ___Christ___. Jesus is truly ~~becomes~~ *present* under the appearances of ___bread___ and ___wine___.

3. A ___sacrifice___ is a gift offered to God by a ___priest___ in the name of all the _____.

4. Jesus is really and truly ___present___ in the Eucharist. This is called the Real ___Eucharist___.

Fast Facts

The most well known image of the Last Supper is Leonardo da Vinci's painting. The huge painting (15 feet by 29 feet) covers an entire wall in the dining room of a convent in Italy. Art historians consider it one of the world's finest examples of one-point perspective. The attention of viewers is drawn to the center and subject of the work—Jesus Christ. Da Vinci completed the work in 1498. A major restoration was completed in 1999.

The Celebration of the Eucharist

11

✝ We Gather in Prayer

Leader: Let us listen to the story of Jesus and his Apostles as they gathered for the Last Supper.

Reader 1: Jesus said to the Apostles, "'I have eagerly desired to eat this Passover with you before I suffer, for, I tell you, I shall not eat it [again] until there is fulfillment in the kingdom of God.' Then he took a cup, gave thanks, and said, 'Take this and share it among yourselves; for I tell you [that] from this time on I shall not drink of the fruit of the vine until the kingdom of God comes.'"
(Luke 22:15–18)

All: Jesus, you have given your life for us.

Reader 2: "Then he took the bread, said the blessing, broke it, and gave it to them, saying, 'This is my body, which will be given for you; do this in memory of me.' And likewise the cup after they had eaten, saying, 'This cup is the new covenant in my blood, which will be shed for you.'" (Luke 22:19–20)

All: Jesus, you have given your life for us.

🎵 We Belong to God's Family

Refrain:
We belong to God's family.
Brothers and sisters are we,
singing together in unity
about one Lord and one faith,
one family.

We are one in the body of
Jesus Christ the Lord.
We are one in the blood of him
whom earth and heaven adore.

(Refrain)

The Introductory Rites bring us together as a community.

WE GATHER

✝ *God our Father, let us gather together in your name.*

Name a time when everyone in your school gathers together as one community. Why is this an important time?

WE BELIEVE

Sunday is the day that Jesus Christ rose from the dead. It is a very special day for the Church, the People of God. It is the Lord's Day. Every Sunday Catholics all over the world gather to celebrate the Eucharist.

The Mass is another name for the celebration of the Eucharist. In the Mass the Church gathers as the Body of Christ. The assembly, or community of people gathered to worship in the name of Jesus, participates in many ways throughout the Mass. Some of the things we do are sing, listen and respond to the readings, pray for all people, and receive Holy Communion.

Jesus is among us offering himself so that we can grow in God's friendship and love. Jesus is present to us in the Word of God, in the assembly gathered in his name, in the priest celebrant, and most importantly in his very Body and Blood which we receive in Holy Communion.

There are four parts to the Mass: the Introductory Rites, the Liturgy of the Word, the Liturgy of the Eucharist, and the Concluding Rites. The **Introductory Rites** is the part of the Mass that unites us as a community. It prepares us to hear God's Word and to celebrate the Eucharist.

CELEBRATING THE EUCHARIST

Key Word

Introductory Rites the part of the Mass that unites us as a community; it prepares us to hear God's Word and to celebrate the Eucharist

Introductory Rites

Procession/Opening Song Altar servers, readers, the deacon, and the priest celebrant process forward to the altar. The assembly sings as this takes place. The priest and deacon kiss the altar and bow out of reverence.

Greeting The priest and assembly make the Sign of the Cross, and the priest reminds us that we are in the presence of Jesus.

Penitential Rite Gathered in God's presence the assembly sees its sinfulness and proclaims the mystery of God's love. We ask for God's mercy in our lives.

Gloria On most Sundays we sing or say this ancient hymn. (p. 325)

Opening Prayer This prayer expresses the theme of the celebration and the needs and hopes of the assembly.

We, the Church, are the Body of Christ on earth. Different members of the Church have different roles and responsibilities. Each of us is important and needed. We all have abilities and interests, and we share them in different ways. This is true in the celebration of the liturgy, too. We may participate in different ways, but we all participate in the celebration of the Mass, our greatest act of worship.

Liturgical ministries There are many people who help us during the celebration of the liturgy. The different ways that people serve the Church in worship are called liturgical ministries.

Reader

Celebrant

The celebrant is the priest who celebrates the Eucharist for and with the People of God. He does and says the things Jesus did at the Last Supper. The deacon has a special role in proclaiming the Gospel and in the preaching. He assists at the altar and leads the assembly in certain prayers. Altar servers assist in many ways before, during, and after Mass. They light the candles, lead the procession carrying the cross, and help the priest and deacon near the altar.

Altar Servers

Readers proclaim the Word of God and extraordinary ministers of Holy Communion help to distribute Holy Communion. Greeters or ushers often welcome us before Mass begins. They may help us to find a seat, take up the collection during Mass, and distribute parish bulletins. Musicians help the whole assembly participate through song. Some parishes have organists, musicians, cantors (lead singers), and adult and children's choirs.

Musicians

In many parishes the parish director of liturgy, the liturgy committee, and the pastor prepare for the celebration. They work to make the celebration as prayerful as possible. Sacristans are responsible for all of the sacred vessels and objects that are used during the celebration. They prepare the chalices, containers of wine and water, candles and cloths, vestments, and other objects.

Sacristans

WE RESPOND

Illustrate ways you can take part in your parish's Sunday celebration of the Mass. How can you help others to participate, too?

During the Liturgy of the Word, we listen and respond to the Word of God.

WE GATHER

✝ *Loving God, you have the words of everlasting life.*

Telling stories about important events helps us to remember them. What are some stories that tell of events that are important to you and your family? Where can we find stories about the events of God's people?

WE BELIEVE

After the opening prayer, we listen to the living Word of God proclaimed from Scripture. The **Liturgy of the Word** is the part of the Mass in which we listen and respond to God's Word. We hear about God's great love for his people. We hear about the life and teaching of Christ. We profess our faith and pray for all people in need.

Proclamation of the Word   During the Liturgy of the Word, the Word of God is proclaimed for all to hear. To proclaim something is to announce it loudly, clearly, and from the heart. To proclaim during the liturgy is to announce with faith. Our response to the readings proclaims our belief in God's Word. After the first and second reading we respond "Thanks be to God." After the

Gospel we respond "Praise to you, Lord Jesus Christ." The homily is a proclamation, too. The words of the deacon or priest are a call to live the Good News and to be witnesses to Christ.

Praying for all of God's people   The entire assembly prays for the needs of all God's people. One or several members of the assembly read the prayers aloud, and we all respond "Lord, hear our prayer" or another suitable response.

As the Body of Christ united for worship, we pray for the needs of the whole Church, for the pope, and all Church leaders. We pray for our local community and all of our needs. We ask God to guide world leaders and be with all those in public positions. We call on God to be with those who suffer from sickness and to help us care for those who are in need. We pray that those who have died may experience God's love and mercy.

As Catholics...

The readers proclaim the Word of God from the Lectionary, and the deacon or priest proclaims the Gospel from the *Book of the Gospels*. The Lectionary is a collection of Scripture readings that have been assigned to the various days of the Church year. We treat the Lectionary with respect because it contains the Word of God. We treat the *Book of the Gospels* with special reverence because it contains the Good News of Jesus Christ. The deacon usually carries the *Book of the Gospels* in the opening procession and places it on the altar. The deacon or priest kisses the *Book of the Gospels* after proclaiming the reading.

Find out where your parish keeps the Lectionary and the *Book of the Gospels*.

Liturgy of the Word

First Reading This reading is usually from the Old Testament. We hear of God's love and mercy for his people before the time of Christ. We hear stories of hope and courage, wonder and might. We learn of God's covenant with his people and of the ways they lived his law.

Responsorial Psalm After reflecting in silence as God's Word enters our hearts, we thank God for the Word just heard.

Second Reading This reading is usually from the New Testament letters, the Acts of the Apostles, or the Book of Revelation. We hear about the first disciples, the teachings of the Apostles, and the beginning of the Church.

Gospel Acclamation We stand to sing the Alleluia or other words of praise. This shows we are ready to hear the Good News of Jesus Christ.

Gospel This reading is always from the Gospel of Matthew, Mark, Luke, or John. Proclaimed by the deacon or priest, this reading is about the mission and ministry of Jesus. Jesus' words and actions speak to us today and help us know how to live as his disciples.

Homily The priest or deacon talks to us about the readings. His words help us understand what God's Word means to us today. We learn what it means to believe and be members of the Church. We grow closer to God and one another.

Profession of Faith The whole assembly prays together the Nicene Creed (p. 326) or the Apostles' Creed (p. 325). We are stating aloud what we believe as members of the Church.

Prayer of the Faithful We pray for the needs of all God's people.

WE RESPOND

Key Word

Liturgy of the Word the part of the Mass in which we listen and respond to God's Word; we profess our faith and pray for all people in need

Answer each question. Then using your answer write your own prayer for the needs of God's people.

What are some of the needs of your parish community?

> they collect for different situations!

What is happening in the nation and the world? What situations are our leaders facing?

> Austrailian wildfire.

Do you know of someone who is sick? Do you know someone suffering from injustice because his or her basic human rights are not being met?

> - yes for someone who is sick (rylie) ~~ot~~
> no one for second one

Who in your family, parish, and neighborhood might need your prayers?

> my mom because she is stressed

Now pray them together.

135

During the Liturgy of the Eucharist, we pray the great prayer of thanksgiving and receive the Body and Blood of Christ.

WE GATHER

✝ *Lord Jesus, we worship you.*

The gifts we give those we love are not always things. What other kinds of gifts might they be?

WE BELIEVE

The proclamation of the Word of God leads us to the celebration around the altar, the Liturgy of the Eucharist.

The **Liturgy of the Eucharist** is the part of the Mass in which the Death and Resurrection of Christ are made present again. In this part of the Mass our gifts of bread and wine become the Body and Blood of Christ, which we receive in Holy Communion. The Liturgy of the Eucharist is made up of three parts: the Preparation of the Gifts, the Eucharistic Prayer, and the Communion Rite.

Liturgy of the Eucharist

During the *Preparation of the Gifts* the altar is prepared by the deacon and the altar servers. We offer gifts. These gifts include the bread and wine and the collection for the Church and for those in need. As members of the assembly carry the bread and wine in a procession to the altar, we sing. The bread and wine are placed on the altar, and the priest asks God to bless and accept our gifts. We respond "Blessed be God for ever."

The *Eucharistic Prayer* is truly the most important prayer of the Church. It is our greatest prayer of praise and thanksgiving. It joins us to Christ and to one another. This prayer consists of

- offering God thanksgiving and praise. We lift up our hearts to the Lord. We praise and thank God for the good work of salvation by singing "Holy, Holy, Holy."

- calling on the Holy Spirit to bless the gifts of bread and wine. The priest prays that the gifts of bread and wine will be changed into the Body and Blood of Christ. This is called transubstantiation. We pray that we, too, will be changed into the Body of Christ on earth.

- recalling Jesus' words and actions at the Last Supper. By the power of the Holy Spirit and through the words and actions of the priest, the bread and wine become the Body and Blood of Christ. This part of the prayer is called the **Consecration**.

- recalling Jesus' suffering, Death, Resurrection, and Ascension.

God has blessed us with the gift of his Son. We receive this gift in order to give it to others. We do this by the way we live, speak, and act at home, in our school, and in our neighborhood.

WE RESPOND

Every day we are called to give God thanks and praise and to offer ourselves to him. For what will you give thanks and praise today? What will you do this week to offer your love and service to God?

Key Words

Liturgy of the Eucharist the part of the Mass in which the Death and Resurrection of Christ are made present again; our gifts of bread and wine become the Body and Blood of Christ, which we receive in Holy Communion

Consecration the part of the Eucharistic Prayer when, by the power of the Holy Spirit and through the words and actions of the priest, the bread and wine become the Body and Blood of Christ

- remembering that the Eucharist is offered by the Church in Heaven and on earth. We pray for the needs of the Church. We pray that all who receive the Body and Blood of Christ will be united.

- praising God and praying a great "Amen" in love of God: Father, Son, and Holy Spirit. We unite ourselves to this great prayer of thanksgiving which is prayed by the priest in our name and in the name of Christ.

The **Communion Rite** is the third part of the Liturgy of the Eucharist. We pray aloud or sing the Lord's Prayer. We pray that Christ's peace be with us always. We offer one another a sign of peace to show that we are united in Christ.

We say aloud or sing the Lamb of God, asking Jesus for his mercy, forgiveness, and peace. The priest breaks apart the Host, and we are invited to share in the Eucharist. We are shown the Host and hear "The Body of Christ." We are shown the cup and hear "The Blood of Christ." Each person responds "Amen" and receives Holy Communion.

While people are receiving Holy Communion, we sing as one. After this we silently reflect on the gift of Jesus and God's presence with us. The priest then prays that the gift of Jesus will help us live as Jesus' disciples.

The Concluding Rites send us out to be the Body of Christ to others.

WE GATHER

✠ *Heavenly Father, strengthen us by your Son's sacrifice.*

Who or what helps to keep you focused on your responsibilities and working toward your goals?

WE BELIEVE

After those gathered have received Communion, the Mass is coming to an end. The last part of the Mass is called the Concluding Rites. In these rites we are blessed and sent forth to be Christ's servants in the world and to love others as he has loved us.

The Concluding Rites begin with a greeting by the priest. He says, "The Lord be with you." We answer, "And with your spirit."

The priest then blesses everyone. After the blessing, the deacon or priest says, "Go forth, the Mass is ended." He might also dismiss the assembly with the words "Go and announce the Gospel of the Lord" or "Go in peace."

These words may sound like a way to bring the eucharistic celebration to an end. But it is much more than that. Jesus sends us out to make the world a better place to live. So we say, "Thanks be to God."

We say these words to show that we are thankful and willing to do all that we can to live as the People of God. We say these words together to show that we will work at being the Body of Christ to the world.

Growing in holiness and acting with justice
In Holy Communion we receive the gift of Jesus Christ himself and are joined more deeply to him. All who have received him in the Eucharist are strengthened as the Body of Christ. The Holy Spirit unites us in our love for Christ.

In this way the celebration of the Eucharist brings together people of all ages and all cultures. Together we are the Body of Christ, the Church. We use our traditions and customs to express our faith. We join one another in praising God and bringing his love to others.

Concluding Rites the last part of the Mass in which we are blessed and sent forth to be Christ's servants in the world and to love others as he has loved us

The Eucharist is nourishment. It renews our Baptism. Like healthy food, it restores our strength. We can be weakened by sin. We can find ourselves wandering off the path and away from God. Yet when we worship God each week at Mass, we are really saying "Yes, we are with you, Lord. Be with us each day."

The Eucharist commits us to caring for the needs of others. It helps us recognize their needs and to reach out to them. Jesus gives himself freely to us in Holy Communion. He asks us to do the same. He sends us out from Mass to give ourselves freely to help others. When we help those who cannot feed or clothe themselves, we are really caring for Jesus who lives in them.

When we work to change the things that keep people from having what they need, we show the power of God's life in our lives and in the Church.

Concluding Rites

Greeting The priest offers the final prayer. His words serve as a farewell promise that Jesus will be with us all.

Blessing The priest blesses us in the name of the Father, Son, and Holy Spirit. We make the Sign of the Cross as he blesses us.

Dismissal The deacon or priest sends us out to announce the Gospel of the Lord.

Closing Song The priest and deacon kiss the altar. They, along with others serving at the Mass, bow to the altar, and process out as we sing.

Work with a partner.
Look back at the Prayer of the Faithful you wrote earlier in this chapter. What can your family and your parish community do to show God's love and care to the people named in your prayers? Complete the chart. Then share your ideas with the class.

We prayed for	We show them God's love by
_____	_____
_____	_____
_____	_____
_____	_____

WE RESPOND

What are some times that you can act as Jesus did to bring about justice and peace?

PROJECT

Show What *you* Know

Complete the crossword puzzle using **Key Words**.

Across

5. In the _____ Rites we prepare to hear God's Word and celebrate the Eucharist.

Down

1. The _____ is the part of the Eucharistic Prayer when, by the power of the Holy Spirit and through the words and actions of the priest, the bread and wine become the Body and Blood of Christ.

2. The Liturgy of the _____ is the part of the Mass in which we listen and respond to God's Word.

3. The Liturgy of the _____ is the part of the Mass in which the Death and Resurrection of Christ are made present again.

4. In the _____ Rites we are blessed and sent forth to be Christ's servants in the world and to love others as he has loved us.

Crossword answers:
1 Down: consecration
2 Down: word
3 Down: Eucharist
4 Down: concluding
5 Across: introductory

www.webelieveweb.com

Living As Prayerful People

12

✝ We Gather in Prayer

Leader: O God, come to my assistance.

All: Lord, make haste to help me.

Side 1: Glory to the Father, and to the Son, and to the Holy Spirit:

Side 2: as it was in the beginning, is now, and will be for ever. Amen.

Leader: "My help comes from the LORD,

All: the maker of heaven and earth."
    (Psalm 121:2)

Side 1: "I raise my eyes toward the
        mountains.
        From where will my help come?

Side 2: My help comes from the LORD,
        the maker of heaven and earth.

Side 1: God will not allow your foot to slip;
        your guardian does not sleep.

Side 2: Truly, the guardian of Israel
        never slumbers nor sleeps.

Side 1: The LORD is your guardian;
        the LORD is your shade
        at your right hand.

Side 2: By day the sun cannot harm you,
        nor the moon by night."
    (Psalm 121:1–6)

Side 1: Glory to the Father, and to the Son, and to the Holy Spirit:

Side 2: as it was in the beginning, is now, and will be for ever. Amen.

All: "My help comes from the LORD."
    (Psalm 121:2)

Jesus teaches us to pray.

WE GATHER

✝ *Jesus, we lift our hearts and minds to you.*

In what ways would you describe a good conversation between two friends? between two family members? How does conversation help your relationships with family and friends?

WE BELIEVE

Prayer is like a conversation. God calls to us in prayer, and we respond. Our prayer is a response to God's constant love for us. We listen to what God has to say to us, and we trust in him. We share our thoughts, dreams, and needs with God. We can tell God what is happening in our lives and know that he is listening.

In prayer we open our hearts and minds to God. We can pray in the silence of our hearts, or we can pray aloud. We can pray alone or with others. We can even sing our prayer. Sometimes we do not use words to pray, but sit quietly trying to focus only on God. But however we pray, we turn to God with hope and faith in his love for us. We rely on him for guidance and direction. We trust that he will help us to know his will for us. We ask him to help us to follow his will. Trust in God and reliance on God are very important in our prayer.

Jesus taught us to pray with patience and with complete trust in God. He taught us to pray by showing us how he prayed. Jesus prayed in many circumstances and in many ways. Jesus praised God and thanked him for his blessings. Jesus asked God to be with him and act on his behalf. Jesus prayed for the needs of others. Jesus forgave sinners in the name of his Father. Even as he was dying Jesus prayed "Father, forgive them, they know not what they do" (Luke 23:34). From the example and words of Jesus, most especially the Lord's Prayer, we learn to pray.

The Holy Spirit guides the Church to pray. Urged by the Holy Spirit, we pray these basic forms of prayer: blessing, petition, intercession, thanksgiving, and praise. However we pray, we are showing God our love.

Blessing

"The grace of the Lord Jesus Christ and the love of God and the fellowship of the holy Spirit be with all of you." (2 Corinthians 13:13)

To bless is to dedicate someone or something to God or to make something holy in God's name. God continually blesses us with many gifts. Because God first blessed us, we, too, can pray for his blessings on people and things.

Petition

"O God, be merciful to me, a sinner." (Luke 18:13)

Prayers of petition are prayers in which we ask something of God. Asking for forgiveness is the most important type of petition.

Intercession

"And this is my prayer: that your love may increase ever more and more in knowledge." (Philippians 1:9)

Intercession is a type of petition. When we pray a prayer of intercession, we are asking for something on behalf of another person or a group of people.

Thanksgiving

"Father, I thank you for hearing me." (John 11:41)

Prayers of thanksgiving show our gratitude to God for all he has given us. We show our gratitude most especially for the life, Death, and Resurrection of Jesus. We do this when we pray the greatest prayer of the Church, the Eucharist.

Praise

"I shall praise the LORD all my life, sing praise to my God while I live." (Psalm 146:2)

Prayers of praise give glory to God for being God. Prayers of praise do not involve our needs or our gratitude. We praise God simply because he is God.

WE RESPOND

 Think about what is happening in your life right now. Think about what is going on in the world around you. Write your own prayer.

Pray that everyone stays healthy during the coronavirus outbreak.

What kind of prayer did you write? Pray this prayer throughout the week.

145

We are called to pray daily.

WE GATHER

✝ *Jesus, you invite us to be with you always.*

Think of some things that you do every day. Why do you do them?

WE BELIEVE

Saint Paul knew the importance of prayer. He wrote to the early Christian communities "Pray without ceasing" and "Pray at every opportunity" (1 Thessalonians 5:17; Ephesians 6:18).

By praying throughout the day, we respond to God's desire to know us. We welcome Jesus into our lives. Both personal prayer and communal prayer—prayer we pray as a community—help us to feel and remember God's presence. God is with us each day of our lives.

The habit of daily prayer grows by making special times for prayer. We can pray in the morning and offer our entire day to God including our study, our play, and our work. Before and after meals we can give thanks to God for his many gifts. At night we can think about what we have said and done during the day. We can see the ways God has been acting in our lives. We can reflect on the ways we have or have not shown love for God and for others. Each day we can pray prayers of the Church, for example,

the Our Father or the Hail Mary. We can also use our own words or silently reflect on God's love and presence in our lives.

The habit of daily prayer also grows by joining in prayer with other members of the Church. We do this when we gather with the People of God for the celebration of the Mass. Another way is through the Liturgy of the Hours. The Liturgy of the Hours is a public prayer of the Church. It is made up of psalms, readings from Scripture and Church teachings, prayers and hymns, and is celebrated at various times during the day.

Sunday, the Lord's Day, holy. We celebrate Christ's Death and Resurrection in a special way on this day. On Sundays we worship God in a public way. We gather with our parishes to celebrate the Eucharist. This Sunday celebration is at the very heart of our life in the Church. In fact, it is so important that we are obliged, or required, to participate in Sunday Mass. Sunday Mass may be celebrated any time from Saturday evening to Sunday evening.

In addition to Sunday, we are also obliged to participate in the Mass on holy days of obligation. A holy day of obligation is a day set apart to celebrate a special event in the life of Jesus, Mary, or the saints. As in every celebration of the Mass, we join together to praise God for the salvation he has given us through his Son.

The Liturgy of the Hours helps us to praise God throughout the entire day. Morning prayer and evening prayer are the two most important prayers of the Liturgy of the Hours. Many parish communities gather for morning prayer and evening prayer. There is also daytime prayer and night prayer. All these prayers remind us that God is active and present in our lives all the time. Sometimes it is difficult to pray. We get distracted. We need to focus our hearts and turn to God for help.

Sunday and holy days   All around the world, Catholics pray together and keep

Key Words

Liturgy of the Hours
a public prayer of the Church made up of psalms, readings from Scripture and Church teachings, prayers and hymns and celebrated at various times during the day

holy day of obligation
a day we are obliged to participate in the Mass to celebrate a special event in the life of Jesus, Mary, or the saints

Here are the holy days of obligation that the Church in the United States celebrates:

Solemnity of Mary, Mother of God
(January 1)

Ascension
(when celebrated on Thursday during the Easter season)*

Assumption of Mary
(August 15)

All Saints' Day
(November 1)

Immaculate Conception
(December 8)

Christmas
(December 25)

*(Some dioceses celebrate the Ascension on the following Sunday.)

WE RESPOND

What are some times that you can pray each day?

Think of a place that you find peaceful and calm. Imagine that you are there now. Remember that you are in the presence of God. Open your heart to God. Listen to what he is saying to you.

Sacramentals are a part of the Church's prayer life.

WE GATHER

✝ *God, bless all our classmates.*

🧎 Think about the ways you use your senses to hear, see, smell, touch, and taste. How can your senses help you to understand the world around you? the things you study? your family and friends?

_____

_____

_____

_____

WE BELIEVE

Our prayer not only involves our thoughts and words, it involves our feelings and our senses, too.

Think about the ways that we use our senses when we pray. Think about the many gestures, actions, and objects that are an important part of the Church's liturgy and of our personal prayer.

Blessings, actions, and objects that help us respond to God's grace received in the sacraments are **sacramentals**. Blessings are the most important sacramentals. Not only is the blessing itself a sacramental, but what is blessed can also become a sacramental.

Sacramentals are used in the liturgy and in personal prayer. Here are some examples of sacramentals:

- blessings of people, places, foods, and objects

- objects such as rosaries, medals, crucifixes, blessed ashes, and blessed palms

- actions such as making the Sign of the Cross and sprinkling blessed water.

148

Sacraments are effective signs given to us by Jesus through which we share in God's life, grace. Many sacramentals remind us of the sacraments and of what God does for us through the sacraments. Sacramentals help us respond to the grace we receive in the sacraments.

Sacramentals make us more aware of God's presence in our lives. Sacramentals keep us focused on God and help us to grow in holiness. Blessing the food we eat, making the Sign of the Cross as we enter or leave a church, and seeing a crucifix in our home are all reminders of our faith and trust in God.

sacramentals blessings, actions, and objects that help us respond to God's grace received in the sacraments

WE RESPOND

Work in groups. Discuss the different sacramentals that you may have seen or used. What are some sacramentals that your family or parish may have used or celebrated? After your discussion, write down some sacramentals that can help you to pray at home and at school.

Blessings	Objects	Actions

Catholics have a rich tradition of special practices and popular devotions.

WE GATHER

✝ *Almighty God, our faith in you continues to grow.*

🧍 Work with a partner. Make a list of the ways the word *popular* is used.

WE BELIEVE

The Mass is the Church's greatest act of worship. Eucharistic adoration, which takes place outside the celebration of the Mass, is also part of the liturgy of the Church. Jesus' presence in the Eucharist is honored in various ways. After Holy Communion, the remaining consecrated Bread, or Hosts, are put aside, or reserved, in the tabernacle. This reserved Eucharist is called the Blessed Sacrament. The Blessed Sacrament can be brought to those who are sick and unable to participate in the Mass. It is also reserved for worship. We can pray before the Blessed Sacrament that is reserved in the tabernacle in our church. Our prayer shows Jesus our love and devotion for him. It continues the thanksgiving that was begun at Mass.

Many parishes have an Exposition of the Blessed Sacrament. In this ceremony the Blessed Sacrament, placed in a special holder called a *monstrance*, is presented for all to see. In a ceremony called Benediction, the community gathers to pray and to worship Jesus in the Blessed Sacrament. All gathered are blessed by the presence of Christ in the Eucharist.

Simon helps Jesus carry his cross.
(The fifth Station of the Cross)

Popular devotions Benediction of the Blessed Sacrament is sometimes a part of popular devotions. Popular devotions are prayer practices that are not part of the Church's official public prayer, or liturgy. Popular devotions have grown from the practices of different groups of people. Catholics have a rich and diverse tradition of these prayer practices.

There are many popular devotions. Some are practiced by Catholics in specific areas of the world. Others are used more widely throughout all the Church. What makes these devotions so special is the way people of different cultures and traditions celebrate them. Some of the popular devotions include novenas, Stations of the Cross, and pilgrimages.

Novenas include special prayers and are often followed by Benediction. The word *novena* comes from the Latin word meaning "nine." Novenas are special prayers or prayer services that occur nine times. They can occur nine days in a row, on the same day of the week for nine weeks in a row, or on any schedule of nine times.

A special novena honoring the Blessed Sacrament occurs on the first Fridays of nine months in a row. Other novenas can accompany popular devotions to Jesus, Mary, or the saints. They can also be part of preparing for major feasts like Christmas.

Another popular devotion is the Stations of the Cross. Stations of the Cross focus our attention on the suffering and Death of Jesus. In most churches, the fourteen Stations of the Cross are paintings or sculptures that are placed throughout the Church. The Stations of the Cross are found on page 327.

By moving from one station to the next and praying the appropriate prayers, those gathered for this devotion join Jesus as he makes his way to his Death on the cross. Each station usually ends with this prayer:

We adore you, O Christ,
  and we bless you.

Because by your holy cross,
  you have redeemed the world.

Pilgrimages, or prayer journeys, to holy places or shrines, and processions to honor Mary and the saints are also forms of devotion. Many parishes have processions on special feast days. Often the priest leads the procession carrying the Blessed Sacrament in a monstrance. Benediction of the Blessed Sacrament often takes place at the end of the procession.

Devotions that come from our different cultures and traditions have great meaning. They draw us into the mystery of Christ. These popular devotions help us to express our faith and the faith of our communities.

As Catholics...

Some devotions to Mary, the Blessed Mother, came about after her appearances to people in various countries. She appeared at Lourdes, France in 1858 and Fatima, Portugal in 1917.

Mary's appearances outside Mexico City are very important to Catholics living in the Americas. In 1531 the Blessed Mother came to an Aztec man named Juan Diego. She appeared to him on a hill. Speaking in his native language, she told him, "Do not be afraid, you have nothing to fear. Am I not here, your compassionate mother?" Her image miraculously appeared on Juan Diego's cloak. Her face was that of a Native American. This image proved so powerful that the people, including Church leaders, believed that Mary had truly been there. She became known by this image as Our Lady of Guadalupe.

Every year we celebrate the feast of Saint Juan Diego on December 9 and of Our Lady of Guadalupe on December 12. How does your parish celebrate these special feasts?

WE RESPOND

What are some popular devotions in your community? When have you participated in them? What were they like?

Procession for the Feast of the Assumption.

聖母升天

Parade in honor of Our Lady of Guadalupe.

151

PROJECT

Show What you Know

Use the code to find each  . Then, write a sentence using the word.

A	B	C	D	E	F	G	H	I	J	K	L	M	N	O	P	Q	R	S	T	U	V	W	X	Y	Z
26	25	24	23	22	21	20	19	18	17	16	15	14	13	12	11	10	9	8	7	6	5	4	3	2	1

1. S A C R A M E N T A L S
   8 26 24 9 26 14 22 13 7 26 15 8

   They have sacramental prayers at that church

2. H O L Y D A Y O F
   19 12 15 2 23 26 2 12 21

   O B L I G A T I O N
   12 25 15 18 20 26 7 18 12 13

   They go to mass on the holy days of obligation.

3. L I T U R G Y
   15 18 7 6 9 20 2

   O F T H E H O U R S
   12 21 7 19 22 19 12 6 9 8

Question Corner

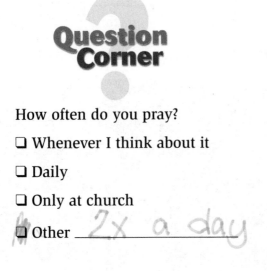

How often do you pray?

❏ Whenever I think about it

❏ Daily

❏ Only at church

❏ Other ___2x a day___

Pray Today

Saint Teresa of Avila calls silent prayer "a close sharing between friends." She writes, "it means taking time frequently to be alone with him who we know loves us." Take a moment now to pray silently to God.

O Radiant Dawn, splendor of eternal light,
sun of justice.

This chapter prepares us to celebrate
the season of Advent.

SEASONAL
CHAPTER 13

Advent is a season of joyful expectation and preparation for the coming of the Son of God.

WE GATHER

✝ *O Radiant Dawn, Jesus, come and shine on us!*

Have you ever seen an exciting movie clip that ended with the words "Coming soon"? How did these words make you feel?

WE BELIEVE

The word *Advent* means "coming." Jesus Christ, the Son of God who became one of us, is coming into our lives. During the four weeks of Advent, we prepare to celebrate Christ's coming.

- We hope for Christ's coming in the future, and we prepare by being his faithful followers today.

- We celebrate Christ's presence in the world today. He comes to us every day in the celebration of the Eucharist, in all the sacraments, and in the love we have for one another.

- We wait with joyful expectation to celebrate that Jesus first came to us over two thousand years ago in Bethlehem. We prepare to celebrate that coming of the Savior, the Son of God.

We use the color violet during Advent as a sign of waiting and joyful expectation. This color is also a sign of penance. So in Advent celebrating the Sacrament of Penance is an important way to prepare for the celebration of the coming of Christ.

During the weeks of Advent, we wait as the people did before Jesus' birth. They had waited many, many years for the Savior to come. During those years of waiting, God spoke to his people through the prophets.

Faithful followers of Jesus, working together and showing the love we have for one another

The prophets encouraged the people to live by the covenant. They told them that their God was loving and merciful, that he had not forgotten them. The prophets spoke of a Messiah who would be an anointed king, a just ruler, and a Savior. He would bring about a kingdom of peace and justice.

We believe that Jesus is the Messiah for whom they waited, but he is more. Jesus Christ is the Son of God who became one of us.

From December 17 through December 23, our hope and expectation grow. We are eager to celebrate the coming of the Messiah into the world. So during this time the Church prays the "O Antiphons." An antiphon is a short prayer. They are called the "O Antiphons" because they all begin with the one-letter word "O."

In each of the seven antiphons, we call on Jesus by different titles that come from the Old Testament prophets. In each of these short prayers we praise Christ for what he has done for us and call on him to come to all of God's people.

157

Today the O Antiphons are most familiar to us in the hymn "O Come, O Come Emmanuel." Each verse of the hymn parallels one of the antiphons.

From December 17 to December 23 the O Antiphons are recited or sung during Evening Prayer and sung at Mass before the Gospel reading.

Look at the list of signs for each O Antiphon in this chart.

	Old Testament Title	What it means to us	Sign of title
Dec. 17	O Wisdom!	Jesus is our wise teacher.	oil lamp open book
Dec. 18	O Lord of Israel!	Jesus is our leader.	burning bush stone tablet
Dec. 19	O Flower of Jesse's Stem!	Jesse was the father of King David and the ancestor of Jesus. Jesus is the "flower" on the family tree.	vine or plant with flower
Dec. 20	O Key of David!	Jesus opens the gates of God's Kingdom to us.	key broken chain
Dec. 21	O Radiant Dawn!	Jesus is our light.	rising sun
Dec. 22	O King of All Nations!	Jesus is the king who unites us all.	crown, scepter
Dec. 23	O Emmanuel!	Emmanuel means "God with us." Jesus is with us always.	chalice and host

For centuries these signs have been pictured in artwork. Check to see if your parish newsletter or Web site gives examples of these signs.

WE RESPOND

The O Antiphons can help us get ready for the coming of Christ. Use one of these seven titles of Jesus to write a short prayer. You may want to thank Jesus or ask him to help you give witness to the Good News in your daily life.

✝ We Respond in Prayer

Leader: Our help is in the name of the Lord.

All: Who made heaven and earth.

Reader: Once a woman said to Jesus, "I know that the Messiah is coming, the one called the Anointed; when he comes, he will tell us everything." Jesus told her in reply, "I am he" (John 4:25, 26).

All: Jesus, you are the Messiah.

Leader: O Wisdom! You guide creation with your strong yet tender care.

All: Come, show your people the way to salvation.

Leader: O Lord of Israel! You gave Moses the Law on Mount Sinai.

All: Come, stretch out your mighty hand to set us free.

Leader: O Flower of Jesse's Stem! You have been raised up as a sign for all people.

All: Come, let nothing keep you from coming to our aid.

Leader: O Key of David! You control the gates of heaven.

All: Come, lead your captive people to freedom.

Leader: O Radiant Dawn! You are the splendor of eternal light and the sun of justice.

All: Come, shine on those who dwell in darkness.

Leader: O King of All Nations! You are the only joy of every heart.

All: Come, save the creature you fashioned from the dust.

Leader: O Emmanuel! You are the desire of all nations and the Savior of all people!

All: Come, set us free, Lord our God.

Grade 5 Advent

PROJECT DISCIPLE

Pray Learn Celebrate Share Choose Live

Show What you Know

Find these words of the season in the puzzle below.

Advent
hope
antiphon
joyful
birth
Messiah
Christ
preparation
Emmanuel
~~prophet~~
expectation
violet

L	E	Y	C	Y	T	M	N	W	D	Y	P	R
U	R	M	R	J	E	S	L	H	F	E	E	A
F	U	L	M	S	O	H	I	T	O	N	N	S
Y	W	J	S	A	T	X	J	R	O	C	O	P
O	D	I	I	E	N	A	M	I	H	E	I	R
J	A	V	L	U	K	U	T	Y	K	C	T	O
H	X	O	C	D	C	A	E	C	A	B	A	P
N	I	B	I	R	T	H	Q	L	H	V	R	H
V	L	F	N	C	H	I	S	M	T	Y	A	E
I	K	S	E	J	P	O	H	M	U	H	P	T
S	B	P	A	N	T	I	P	H	O	N	E	S
Y	X	T	N	E	V	D	A	E	J	X	R	M
E	V	I	J	E	X	B	Q	G	F	R	P	K

Fast Facts

The Third Sunday of Advent is called Gaudete Sunday. *Gaudete* means "rejoice." The rose-colored candle of the Advent wreath is lit on Gaudete Sunday. Rose-colored vestments may be worn by the priest to celebrate the Mass on Gaudete Sunday.

More to Explore

The following are some of the saints that are celebrated during Advent: Mary (as the Immaculate Conception and Our Lady of Guadalupe), Saint Nicholas, Saint Juan Diego, Saint Lucy, and Saint John of the Cross.

Search the Internet (such as *Lives of the Saints* on www.webelieveweb.com) or books about the saints to find out more about these holy people.

Take Home

With your family write your own O Antiphon praising Jesus for what he has done for us. Ask him to come to all of God's People.

_____

_____

Then prepare an Advent wreath to use at home. At dinner after the blessing of the food, take turns lighting the candle for the week of Advent. Say your family O Antiphon prayer as the candle is lit.

"A light will shine on us this day,
the Lord is born for us."

Mass at Dawn, Introductory Rites

SEASONAL

CHAPTER 14

This chapter addresses the entire
Christmas season.

The season of Christmas is a time to rejoice in the Incarnation.

WE GATHER

✝ *Jesus, fill us with your light.*

Sometimes people may celebrate different events for different periods of time. For example, they may celebrate Valentine's Day for a day, birthdays for a whole weekend, and a family reunion for a whole week. How does your family celebrate different events?

WE BELIEVE

What we celebrate on Christmas Day, and during the whole Christmas season, is the wonderful gift of God with us. During Advent and Christmas we hear Jesus called by the name Emmanuel. The name *Emmanuel* means "God with us." During Christmas we celebrate in a special way that God is with us today, now, and forever.

The season of Christmas is a time to rejoice in the Incarnation, the truth that the Son of God became man. We celebrate Christ's presence among us now as well as his first coming into the world over two thousand years ago. We recall that God so loved the world that he sent his only Son to be our Savior.

Many people do not know that we celebrate Christmas Day with three Masses: the Mass at Midnight, the Mass at Dawn, and the Mass during the Day. Each Mass helps us to celebrate the light of Christ in the world today.

Mass at Midnight For the celebration of this Christmas Mass, all is dark and peaceful, and maybe even cold. The church is lit with candles. The priest opens with the words, "Father, you make this holy night radiant with the splendor of Jesus Christ our light." The Gospel reading is the story of the birth of Jesus.

Christmas Mass, Mittersill, Austria

Joseph and Mary had traveled to Bethlehem, the city of David, to be enrolled and counted in a census. "While they were there, the time came for her to have her child, and she gave birth to her firstborn son. She wrapped him in swaddling clothes and laid him in a manger, because there was no room for them in the inn." (Luke 2:6–7)

There were shepherds in the fields nearby. The angel of the Lord came to them and said:

"Do not be afraid; for behold, I proclaim to you good news of great joy that will be for all the people. For today in the city of David a savior has been born for you who is Messiah and Lord. And this will be a sign for you: you will find an infant wrapped in swaddling clothes and lying in a manger."

Suddenly there were many voices singing with the angel:

"Glory to God in the highest
and on earth peace to those
on whom his favor rests"
(Luke 2:10–12, 14).

Our great hymn the *Gloria*, or the Glory to God, is based on this song of the angels. We say or sing the Glory to God in Mass on Sundays all during the year, except during Advent and Lent. In the Masses of Christmas we sing this hymn with great joy. The light of Christ has come into the world and remained with us!

Mass at Dawn   For the celebration of this Christmas Mass, the sun is rising in the east. Just as the shepherds hurried to the stable, the faithful hurry to their parish churches. The priest opens with the words, "Father, we are filled with the new light by the coming of your Word among us."

You have heard many titles of Jesus. Messiah, Christ, Anointed One, Savior, and Lord are just a few. These titles are all ways to speak about the Son of God, the Second Person of the Blessed Trinity who became one of us. "The Word among us" and "the Word made flesh" are also titles for Christ, but there are more. They are actually ways of explaining the Incarnation. In fact, the word *Incarnation* means "becoming flesh."

During the Christmas season we rejoice that the Word is among us, today and always.

Mass During the Day   For the celebration of this Christmas Mass people greet each other with joy. The priest begins, "God of love, Father of all, the darkness that covered the earth has given way to the bright dawn of your Word made flesh."

The Gospel reading for this Mass is the beginning of the Gospel of John. Here is part of that reading.

"And the Word became flesh
   and made his dwelling among us,
   and we saw his glory,
   the glory as of the Father's only Son,
   full of grace and truth." (John 1:14)

Christmas does not end once these three Masses have been celebrated. The season of Christmas lasts until the Feast of the Baptism of the Lord, which is usually in the second week in January.

The days after Christmas are often called "The Twelve Days of Christmas" because the Feast of Epiphany was originally celebrated on this twelfth day, January 6. Today, in the United States, Epiphany is celebrated on the second Sunday after Christmas.

People in all parts of the world celebrate Christmas and the feasts of the Christmas season. They celebrate using local customs and traditions. But however different the celebrations may be, they all help us to remember that Christ is our Light today, he is God-with-us today, the Word among us today and always.

WE RESPOND

Work in groups to make a chart of the many ways people celebrate Christmas Day and the whole season of Christmas. Talk about whether or not these ways help us to remember the real meaning of Christmas.

UNIT TEST

**Write True or False for the following sentences.
Then change the false sentences to make them true.**

1. _____ In the Sacrament of Confirmation we are sealed with the Gift of the Apostles.

   _____

2. _____ Wisdom, understanding, counsel, fortitude, knowledge, piety, and fear of the Lord are fruits of the Holy Spirit.

   _____

3. _____ The Stations of the Cross is a memorial, a meal, and a sacrifice.

   _____

4. _____ There are four parts to the Mass: the Introductory Rites, the Liturgy of the Word, the Liturgy of the Eucharist, and the Concluding Rites.

   _____

5. _____ During Confirmation we renew our baptismal promises.

   _____

6. _____ In the Mass, the Church gathers as the Bread of Life.

   _____

7. _____ After his Resurrection, the risen Jesus was made known to his disciples when he broke bread with them.

   _____

8. _____ Consecration is a day we are obliged to participate in the Mass to celebrate a special event in the life of Jesus, Mary, or the saints.

   _____

continued on next page

Grade 5 Unit 2

Write the letter that best defines each term.

9. _____ Consecration

10. _____ sacramental

11. _____ Introductory Rites

12. _____ Confirmation

13. _____ Real Presence

14. _____ Liturgy of the Word

15. _____ sacrifice

16. _____ Liturgy of the Hours

a. a gift offered to God by the priest in the name of all the people

b. Jesus really and truly present in the Eucharist

c. the part of the Mass in which we listen and respond to God's Word; we profess our faith and pray for all people in need

d. public prayer of the Church made up of psalms, readings from Scripture and Church teaching, prayers and hymns

e. the part of the Eucharistic Prayer when, by the power of the Holy Spirit and through the words and actions of the priest, the bread and wine become the Body and Blood of Christ

f. a blessing, action, or object that helps us respond to God's grace received in the sacraments

g. the sacrament in which we are sealed with the Gift of the Holy Spirit

h. the part of the Mass that unites us as a community and prepares us to hear God's Word and celebrate the Eucharist

Answer the questions.

17–18. Why is preparation an important part of Confirmation?

19–20. Name three sacramentals. How do these sacramentals help us grow in holiness?

Sacraments at the Service of Communion

Part 1   I Open My Heart

Pope Francis has challenged young people: "Go, do not be afraid, and serve" (Pope Francis, homily for World Youth Day Mass, July 28, 2013). Imagine Pope Francis sitting before you today, telling you the same. What does this mean for you? How does God call you to go, without fear, and serve others? In the space below, write a list of ways you can serve others.

Pope Francis greeting the faithful gathered for prayer

Sacraments at the Service of Communion

Part 2 We Come Together for Prayer

Leader: Lord, you call people to the Sacraments of Holy Orders and Matrimony. In these sacraments, you give them "a particular mission in the Church and serve to build up the People of God" (*CCC*, 1534).

All: Lord, give bishops, priests, deacons, and married couples the courage to live what they have celebrated in these sacraments.

Leader: Lord, you call us to turn the focus of our lives toward others. We pray that those who celebrate these sacraments may be strengthened by your love. Pope Francis encourages the faithful:

Reader 1: "Dear young people, don't be afraid to marry. A faithful and fruitful marriage will bring you happiness." (Pope Francis, Twitter, February 14, 2014)

Reader 2: "Let us pray for seminarians, that they may listen to the voice of the Lord and follow it with courage and joy." (Pope Francis, Twitter, February 13, 2014)

Reader 3: "The life of Jesus is a life for others. It is a life of service. . . . Go, do not be afraid, and serve." (Pope Francis, homily for World Youth Day Mass, July 28, 2013)

Leader: What words of encouragement would you give to priests, deacons, or married couples? *(Write and share responses.)*

_____

_____

_____

_____

_____

_____

_____

All: Lord, give me the courage to serve you and our community with joy. Amen.

Sacraments at the Service of Communion

Part 3 I Cherish God's Word

"As he passed by the Sea of Galilee, he saw Simon and his brother Andrew casting their nets into the sea; they were fishermen. Jesus said to them, 'Come after me, and I will make you fishers of men.' Then they abandoned their nets and followed him." (Mark 1:16–18)

READ the quotation from Scripture. Read slowly. Pay close attention to what you are reading.

REFLECT on what you read. Think about:

- Imagine you are Simon. Jesus calls to you, "Come after me." How would you react?

- The fishermen left their nets to follow Jesus. What sacrifices do deacons, priests, and bishops make to follow Jesus? What sacrifices do married couples make to follow Jesus?

- Read the words of Jesus again. What sacrifices might you have to make in your life to follow Jesus?

SHARE your thoughts and feelings with God in prayer. Let your thoughts and feelings come naturally. Speak to God as a friend.

CONTEMPLATE, or sit quietly and allow your attention to remain focused on God's Word in the Scripture passage from the Gospel of Mark above.

Sacraments at the Service of Communion

Part 4   I Value My Catholic Faith

Through the Sacrament of Holy Orders, the mission and the authority that Jesus Christ gave to his Apostles continue in the Church. In Holy Orders, baptized men are ordained as bishops, priests, or deacons. They all have different roles and duties in serving the Church.

Through the Sacrament of Matrimony, a man and a woman make a life-long commitment to live as faithful and loving partners. They promise to live lives of service to each other and to their children.

The Sacraments of Holy Orders and Matrimony have much in common. Both require total faithfulness, commitment, love, and sacrifice. These qualities are so valuable, but they are not always valued in our society today. You can change that trend by appreciating, respecting, and living out these qualities. Create a mural that celebrates the Sacraments at the Service of Communion and the people who live them faithfully. Sketch a scene for your mural below.

Sacraments at the Service of Communion

Part 5   I Celebrate Catholic Identity

In every stage of life, we are called to serve one another. One form of service is praying for others who are preparing to receive one of the Sacraments at the Service of Communion. Write a letter of support to a seminarian or an engaged couple in your family, parish, or diocese.

Promise to pray for this individual or couple every day. Invite your family to pray with you!

I promise to pray for

_____

_____

_____

on the sacramental journey.

Sacraments at the Service of Communion

Part 6   I Honor My Catholic Identity

Leader: As you go forth from this retreat, remember how important the Sacraments at the Service of Communion are to our Church and to our world.

Reader 1: For the ordained, that they may build up the People of God with their love and commitment,

All: Lord, hear our prayer.

Reader 2: For married couples, that they may build up the Church with their love and faithfulness,

All: Lord, hear our prayer.

Reader 3: For us, that we may recognize the way that God is calling us to serve him, we pray:

All: Lord, I know that you love me and that you have great plans for me.
But sometimes I am overwhelmed by the thought of my future.
Show me how to walk forward one day at a time.

As I explore the various options which lie before me,
help me to listen openly to others,
and to pay attention to what is in the depth of my
    own heart.
In this way, may I hear your call to a way
    of life
which will allow me to love as only I can,
and allow me to serve others with the special
    gifts you have given me.

("Prayer for Discernment: Walking One Day at a Time,"
by the Salesian Sisters of St. John Bosco)

Leader: May we use our gifts today to serve and teach others. In doing so, we will bring glory to God!

All: Amen.

Bringing the Retreat Home

Catholic Identity Retreat

Sacraments at the Service of Communion

Retreat Recap

Review the pages of your child's *Celebrating Catholic Identity: Liturgy & Sacraments* retreat. Ask your child to tell you about the retreat. Talk about the following:

■ In the Sacrament of Holy Orders, baptized men respond to God's call to service by being ordained as bishops, priests, or deacons, who have different roles and duties in serving the Church.

■ In the Sacrament of Matrimony, a man and a woman make a life-long commitment to live as faithful and loving partners. They promise to love and serve each other and their children.

■ God calls each of us to serve him and our community with joy.

Letters of Love and Support

Review the letter your child wrote to support a seminarian or an engaged couple in Part 5 of the retreat. Now, write short letters or notes to one another in your family. Say how much you love one another and how you will show your love and support. Perhaps leave your letter in the other person's lunch box, workbag, or backpack as a nice surprise. Loving and supporting one another are ways to live out your call to be a domestic Church, or a "Church in the home." Family love and support are also your child's foundation for a future call to a vocation. You can read more about the domestic Church in the *Catholic Identity Home Companion* at the end of your child's book.

Take a Moment

Sit down together and view photos of important family events or milestones, such as marriage, Baptism, First Communion, holiday gatherings, or vacations. Spend time appreciating these moments in your family. Say a simple prayer of thanksgiving to God for all the people in your family.

Family Prayer

Pray these words together at mealtime or another convenient time for your family.

We ask you, Lord,
to protect and watch over this family,
so that in the strength of your grace
its members may enjoy prosperity,
possess the priceless gift of your peace,
and, as the Church alive in the home,
bear witness in this world to your glory.

We ask this through Christ our Lord. Amen.
(From *Book of Blessings*)

For more resources, see the *Catholic Identity Home Companion* at the end of this book.

Why We Believe
As a Catholic Family

What if someone asks us:

- Why is the Catholic Church led by the pope?
- Why do we follow bishops?

The following resources can help us to respond:

The baptized men who receive the Sacrament of Holy Orders take on a mission to lead and serve the Catholic Church. In Holy Orders, men are ordained as bishops, priests, or deacons. They all have different roles and duties in serving the Church. The pope is the Bishop of Rome, the leader of the Catholic Church. The bishops, with the pope as their head, work with the pope to lead and guide the Church.

🌿 What does Scripture say?

Jesus said, "You are Peter, and upon this rock I will build my church, and the gates of the netherworld shall not prevail against it" (Matthew 16:18).

"Go, therefore, and make disciples of all nations," said Jesus, "baptizing them in the name of the Father, and of the Son, and of the holy Spirit, teaching them to observe all that I have commanded you. And behold, I am with you always, until the end of the age." (Matthew 28:19–20)

Jesus said to his Apostles, "Peace be with you. As the Father has sent me, so I send you" (John 20:21).

Jesus appointed his Apostle Peter to lead his Church. The pope is the successor of the Apostle Peter, who was the first leader of the Church of Rome. As the Bishop of Rome, the pope has a special responsibility to care for and lead the Church.

After his Resurrection, Jesus gave his Apostles a special mission when he said, "Go therefore, and make disciples of all nations" (Matthew 28:19). The Apostles appointed bishops as their successors to continue this mission of teaching and guiding God's People. (We can read about this in the Acts of the Apostles.) The bishops are the successors of the Apostles. They are the leaders and official teachers of the Church. The bishops are called to help the followers of Jesus grow in holiness. The pope and the bishops form the Magisterium, the teaching authority of the Church.

🌿 What does the Church say?

"The Lord made St. Peter the visible foundation of his Church. He entrusted the keys of the Church to him. The bishop of the Church of Rome, successor to St. Peter, is 'head of the college of bishops, the Vicar of Christ and Pastor of the universal Church on earth' (CIC, can. 331)." (CCC, 936)

The Church founded by Christ, "constituted and organized in the world as a society, subsists in the Catholic Church, which is governed by the successor of Peter and by the Bishops in communion with him" (Pope Paul VI, *Lumen Gentium*, 8, November 21, 1964).

"It is possible . . . to contemplate the tradition of the apostles which has been made known to us throughout the whole world. And we are in a position to enumerate those who were instituted bishops by the apostles and their successors down to our own times." (Irenaeus, one of the Church Fathers, A.D. 189)

Notes:

The Sacraments of Healing Restore Us

Seasonal Chapters

Pray Learn Celebrate Share Choose Live

In Unit 3 your child will grow as a disciple of Jesus by:

- hearing Jesus' call to conversion and being reconciled to God and the Church through the Sacrament of Penance and Reconciliation
- learning the ways the Church celebrates the Sacrament of Penance
- recognizing that Jesus healed people and the Church continues Jesus' healing ministry
- appreciating that the Sacrament of the Anointing of the Sick offers comfort and strength to those who are elderly or seriously ill
- honoring Mary for her role in God's plan of salvation and her place as the greatest of all the saints.

Make it Happen

When sin leads to unjust situations or conditions in society, it is called social sin. Discuss together any examples of injustice you know of in your neighborhood, or city, or in the world. Identify one thing you can do as a family to work for peace and justice as Jesus did. Then do it!

Pray Today

God of compassion,
you take every family under your care
and know our physical and spiritual needs.

Transform our weakness by the strength
of your grace
and confirm us in your covenant
so that we may grow in faith and love.

We ask this through our Lord Jesus Christ, your Son,
who lives and reigns with you and the Holy Spirit,
one God, for ever and ever.
Amen.

Pastorial Care of the Sick (Anointing Within Mass)

Reality Check

"The family should live in such a way that its members learn to care and take responsibility for the young, the old, the sick, the handicapped, and the poor."

(*Catechism of the Catholic Church*, 2208)

Celebrate!

One of the ways family members express their love is by asking forgiveness of one another. Celebrate your forgiveness of one another with a special meal.

Take Home

Be ready for this unit's Take Home:

Chapter 15: Fostering forgiveness and reconciliation in the family

Chapter 16: Planning to receive the Sacrament of Penance

Chapter 17: Helping people who are ill

Chapter 18: Learning about the Anointing of the Sick in your parish

Chapter 19: Sharing ways to honor Mary

We Turn to God

✝ We Gather in Prayer

Leader: God calls us to turn to him each day. Let us listen to this call in the Word of God.

Reader: A reading from the Letter of Saint Paul to the Colossians

"Put on then, as God's chosen ones, holy and beloved, heartfelt compassion, kindness, humility, gentleness, and patience, bearing with one another and forgiving one another, . . . as the Lord has forgiven you, so must you also do."
(Colossians 3:12–13)

The word of the Lord.

All: Thanks be to God.

♫ We Belong to God's Family

Refrain:
We belong to God's family.
Brothers and sisters are we,
singing together in unity about
one Lord and one faith, one family.

We all share a forgiveness that
flows from sea to sea,
gentle mercy that breaks all bonds
and sets the prisoner free.
(Refrain)

Jesus calls us to conversion.

WE GATHER

✝ *Lord, help us to believe in you.*

When people talk about growing, they often mean more than changing physically. What are some other ways people change? Have you changed in any of these ways over the past year?

WE BELIEVE

During his ministry, Jesus Christ preached a message that the people had heard before. The prophets, including John the Baptist, had told the people to repent. Like those before him, Jesus wanted the people to change, to turn away from sin and toward God. Jesus told the people, "The kingdom of God is at hand. Repent, and believe in the gospel" (Mark 1:15).

Jesus helped his followers turn to God his Father with all their hearts. By the way he lived and the things he did, Jesus showed them how to follow God's law. He showed them how to pray and the ways to treat others with mercy and justice.

Jesus often taught his followers to show their love for God by loving and forgiving others. Jesus once told them this parable.

📖 Luke 15:11–24

"A man had two sons, and the younger son said to his father, 'Father, give me the share of your estate that should come to me.' So the father divided the property between them. After a few days, the younger son collected all his belongings and set off to a distant country."

The young man wasted all of his money, spending it foolishly. So he had to work on a farm taking care of animals. He was so hungry that he wanted to eat the animals' food, but no one offered him any of it.

The young man began to think about his father's hired workers who had more than enough to eat. Yet here he was suffering from hunger. He decided to go to his father and say, "Father, I have sinned against heaven and against you. I no longer deserve to be called your son; treat me as you would treat one of your hired workers."

The young man started the journey back to his father. He was still a distance from home when his father saw him. Filled with compassion, his father ran to him and hugged and kissed him. The son said, "Father, I have sinned against heaven and against you; I no longer deserve to be called your son." But his father said to the servants, "Quickly bring the finest robe and put it on him. . . . Then let us celebrate with a feast, because this son of mine was dead, and has come to life again; he was lost, and has been found." Then there was a great celebration. (Luke 15:11–13, 18–19, 21, 22–24)

What happened in this story? What does the parable mean to you?

Jesus told this parable to help us understand what it means to be sorry for our actions and to turn back to God. God is like the forgiving father in this story. He welcomes us back when we have gone away from him. He rejoices when we decide to turn back to him.

A turning to God   God constantly calls us to turn back to him. Over and over again he calls us to conversion. Conversion is a turning to God with all one's heart. It happens again and again. If we trust God, he will show us how to change and grow into the people he wants us to be. Conversion leads us to live our lives according to God's great love for us. God the Holy Spirit gives us this desire to change and grow. With the support of the Church, we respond to God's call every day.

No matter how much we have responded to God's love, there is always room to grow. Our love for God can grow stronger by praying, celebrating the sacraments with our parish community, and working as Jesus did for justice and peace.

Jesus invites us to turn to God. He calls us to change and grow. He leads us to God our Father.

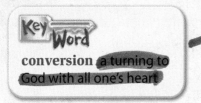

Key Word

conversion a turning to God with all one's heart

Work in a group to come up with a modern-day story about being sorry and turning back to God. Act out the story. Then discuss why this story might help people turn their hearts to God.

Story Script

WE RESPOND

How can you turn to God and grow in his love? Ask the Holy Spirit to strengthen you.

Jesus forgives as only God can do.

WE GATHER

✝ *God, we praise you for your mercy and kindness.*

Why do you think forgiveness is important? What are some examples of ways we forgive and are forgiven?

WE BELIEVE

Unlike the prophets before him, Jesus did more than call people to repentance and conversion. Jesus made this conversion possible. He actually forgave people their sins and reconciled them to his Father.

Some of the leaders were upset when Jesus spent time with sinners and forgave their sins. They knew that only God can forgive people's sins. They did not understand Jesus' ministry of forgiveness and reconciliation.

📖 Mark 2:1–12

After traveling for some time, Jesus returned home. "Many gathered together so that there was no longer room for them, not even around the door, and he preached the word to them."

Four men carrying a paralyzed man came to see Jesus. It was so crowded that they could not even get to Jesus. So through an opening in the roof they let down the mat on which the paralyzed man was lying. When Jesus saw their faith, he said to the paralyzed man, "Child, your sins are forgiven."

Some of the people who were there thought that Jesus should not be speaking this way because only God can forgive sins. Jesus knew what they were thinking. And so that they would know that he had authority to forgive sins Jesus said, "I say to you, rise, pick up your mat, and go home." The man rose, and walked away. They were all amazed because they had never seen anything like it. (Mark 2:2, 5, 11)

174

Jesus' words and actions did not bring all of these religious leaders to believe in him. But many other people believed and had faith, especially those who were healed or forgiven by Jesus. They felt his amazing power and were filled with God's peace.

Given the authority to forgive   After his Death and Resurrection, Christ appeared to his Apostles. He said to them, "'Peace be with you. As the Father has sent me, so I send you.' And when he had said this, he breathed on them and said to them, 'Receive the holy Spirit. Whose sins you forgive are forgiven them, and whose sins you retain are retained'" (John 20:21–23).

Jesus shared his authority to forgive sins with his Apostles. Jesus wanted all people to hear his call to conversion and receive his forgiveness. This forgiveness of sins took place when the Apostles baptized those who believed.

From the beginning of the Church, the forgiveness of sins has first taken place through Baptism. In Baptism we are freed from Original Sin and forgiven any sins we may have committed. Baptism begins our life anew.

Imagine you have been asked to produce a video describing Jesus' ministry of forgiveness and reconciliation. What would your video include? What type of action would take place? Illustrate or design your video here.

What can you do each day to be more accepting and forgiving of others?

Jesus continues to forgive us through the Church.

WE GATHER

✝ *We seek your forgiveness, Lord.*

Think of a time you may have hurt someone you cared about. Did you want to be forgiven? Did you apologize? Did you have to ask for forgiveness?

WE BELIEVE

In Baptism we first receive God's forgiveness. We begin our new life in Christ. Yet we sometimes turn from God and are in need of his forgiveness. The Church celebrates God's forgiveness in the Sacrament of Penance and Reconciliation. This sacrament is a Sacrament of Healing.

Sometimes the choices we make weaken God's life in us. When we think or do things that lead us away from God, we sin. Sin is a thought, word, deed or omission against God's law. Every sin weakens our friendship with God and others.

Sometimes people turn completely away from God's love. They commit very serious sin that breaks their friendship with God. This sin is called *mortal sin*. Those who commit mortal sin must freely choose to do something that they know is seriously wrong. However, God never stops loving people who sin seriously. The Holy Spirit calls them to conversion.

Less serious sin that weakens our friendship with God is called *venial sin*. Even though venial sins do not turn us completely away from God, they still hurt others, ourselves, and the Church. If we keep repeating them, they can lead us further away from God and the Church. However, God offers us forgiveness when we think or do things that harm our friendship with him or with others.

176

The importance of the sacrament Just as he did over two thousand years ago, Jesus forgives those who are truly sorry. Jesus does this through the Church. In the Sacrament of Penance and Reconciliation, which we can call the Sacrament of Penance, our relationship with God and the Church is strengthened or restored and our sins are forgiven.

Every sacrament is a sign of God's love for his people. This is especially true in the Sacrament of Penance. In this sacrament several things happen.

- We receive God's forgiveness. Our sins are forgiven by a priest in the name of Christ and the Church and through the power of the Holy Spirit.

- We are reconciled with God. The life of grace in us is strengthened or made new. Our friendship with God becomes stronger.

- We are reconciled with the Church. Our relationship with the Body of Christ is made stronger and we grow as a forgiving community.

- We are strengthened to live by the Ten Commandments and Jesus' teaching to love one another as he has loved us.

In the Sacrament of Penance, we proclaim our faith in God's mercy. We give thanks for the gift of forgiveness. Together we try to live more faithfully as Christ's disciples.

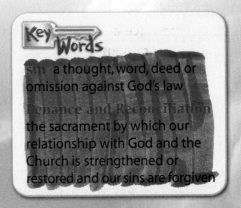

Key Words

sin a thought, word, deed or omission against God's law

Penance and Reconciliation the sacrament by which our relationship with God and the Church is strengthened or restored and our sins are forgiven

---

WE RESPOND

Write a poem or a song about the meaning of being reconciled and the importance of celebrating the Sacrament of Penance.

_____

_____

_____

_____

_____

_____

_____

How can you live as a person of forgiveness?

We are reconciled with God and the Church.

WE GATHER

✝ *We are one body, the Church.*

You are part of your family, your class, your neighborhood, and maybe a team, club, or other group. Think of a time when your actions affected others in one of these groups. How did you know that others were affected?

WE BELIEVE

As members of the Church, we are united by our Baptism. We all share in the life of Christ. We are the Body of Christ. Each time we participate in the celebration of the Eucharist, we are joined more closely with Christ and one another.

As one body, the good works of our members strengthen us as the People of God. The whole Church benefits from our just, loving, and faithful actions. The whole Church also suffers when one person turns from God. So the reconciliation of one member of the Church with God strengthens all of us.

In the Sacrament of Penance we are reconciled with God and one another. We are forgiven. We are also called to forgive others.

Sometimes it is difficult to forgive others. Even the Apostle Peter found it difficult to forgive people all of the time. He asked Jesus, "Lord, if my brother sins against me, how often must I forgive him? As many as seven times?" Jesus told him "I say to you, not seven times but seventy-seven times" (Matthew 18:21, 22). Jesus was telling Peter that he should always be forgiving.

When we forgive others we grow as a loving and reconciling community. Reconciliation with God and the Church contributes to peace and reconciliation in the world. We are better able to stand up for what is right when we are at peace with ourselves, with God, and with the Church. We are able to act with justice.

Justice is based on the belief that all people are equal. Acting with justice respects the rights of others and gives them what is rightfully theirs. All people are created in God's image and share the same human dignity. This makes us one human community. And sin can and does affect that community.

As Catholics...

Part of being reconciled with the Church is admitting that we have not lived as God calls us to live. During Mass the whole assembly confesses that we have sinned. We often pray:

"I confess to almighty God and to you, my brothers and sisters, that I have greatly sinned, in my thoughts and in my words, in what I have done and in what I have failed to do, through my fault, through my fault, through my most grievous fault; therefore I ask blessed Mary ever-Virgin, all the Angels and Saints, and you, my brothers and sisters, to pray for me to the Lord our God."

In this prayer we ask all the members of the Church to pray for us and our forgiveness. Pray that all people will experience God's love and mercy.

Sin can lead to unjust situations and conditions in society. Some results of sin in society are prejudice, poverty, homelessness, crime, and violence. This is social sin. The Church speaks out against social sin. The Church encourages all people to turn to God and live lives of love and respect.

As followers of Jesus we try to do the things he did. We encourage others to respect the needs of all people. We work to stop social sin, the things in society that allow unjust behaviors or conditions to exist.

Work in groups to complete this chart. It lists some of the ways Jesus promoted justice and peace. Brainstorm and list ways the Church can follow Jesus' example. Include things that are already being done in your parish, diocese, or in others parts of the world. Also include new ideas.

Jesus	The Church
• spoke out for freedom even when it threatened public authorities and leaders of the country	
• stood up for those who were treated unjustly because they were ill or poor	
• protected people who could not protect themselves	
• offered the peace and freedom that come from God's love and forgiveness.	

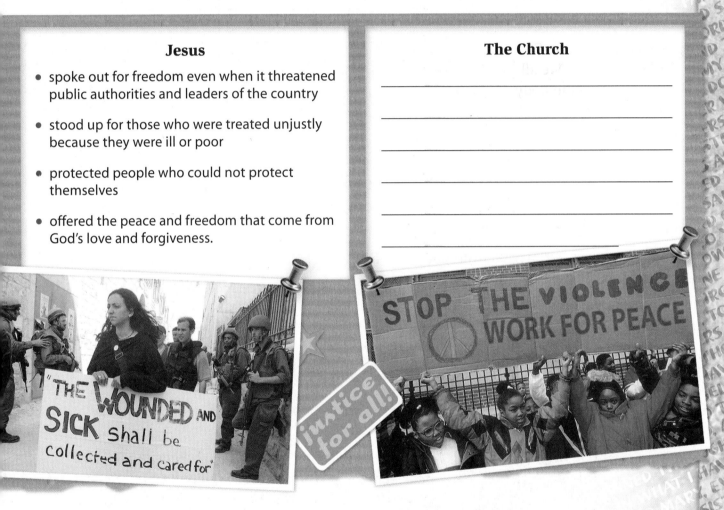

We are the Church. All of us can work for justice and peace. This work can bring about reconciliation in communities all over the world.

WE RESPOND

Discuss what happens when people are reconciled.
What are some situations that need reconciliation in your school, neighborhood, or nation? What can your class do to help bring about understanding and peace in each of the situations?

PROJECT

Show What *you* Know

Complete the crossword puzzle.

Across

3. Sin is a thought, word, deed

or _____ against God's law.

5. In the Sacrament of _____ and Reconciliation our relationship with God and the Church is strengthened or restored and our sins are forgiven.

6. _____ is based on the belief that all people are equal.

Down

1. a turning to God with all one's heart

2. _____ sin is very serious sin that breaks our friendship with God.

4. _____ sin is less serious sin that weakens our friendship with God.

What's *the* Word?

Saint Paul wrote about ways to live in community with others.

"Put on then, as God's chosen ones, holy and beloved, heartfelt compassion, kindness, humility, gentleness, and patience, bearing with one another and forgiving one another, if one has a grievance against another; as the Lord has forgiven you, so must you also do."
(Colossians 3:12–13)

↳ **DISCIPLE CHALLENGE**

• Circle the qualities that are important in order to live in community with others.

• Underline the phrase that tells why we should forgive others.

DISCIPLE

Pray
Learn
Celebrate
Share
Choose
Live

What Would *you* do?

You and your best friend had an argument yesterday. You both left with hurt feelings. After school, you see your best friend walking home alone. You decide to . . .

_____

_____

Saint Stories

Born in Spain in 1170, Saint Dominic spent many years studying before becoming a priest. At first he led a quiet life of prayer, but then he began preaching a message of faith and conversion. He lived by Christ's example. He called many people to God and helped Christians return to the teachings of Christ and the Church. Saint Dominic began the Order of Preachers, a religious community devoted to preaching, also known as the Dominicans. Today there are Dominicans in all parts of the world, preaching the Good News and calling people to conversion. Saint Dominic's feast day is August 8.

SAINT DOMINIC

↳ **DISCIPLE CHALLENGE**
- Circle the name of the religious community founded by Saint Dominic.
- What is another name for this community?

  _____

- When is Saint Dominic's feast day?

  _____

Make *it* Happen

What will you do this week to work for justice and peace?

_____

Take Home

Talk with your family about ways to make your home a more loving and reconciling place for all. Write your ideas here.

_____

_____

_____

Try to put them into action this week.

CHAPTER TEST

Write True or False for the following sentences.
Then change the false sentences to make them true.

1. _____ The sacrament by which our relationship with God is strengthened or restored and our sins are forgiven is called Confirmation.

   _____

2. _____ Jesus shared his authority to forgive sins with his Apostles.

   _____

3. _____ Reconciliation with God and the Church contributes to peace in the world.

   _____

4. _____ Penance and Reconciliation is a Sacrament of Christian Initiation.

   _____

Circle the letter of the correct answer.

5. _____ is a turning to God with all one's heart.

   a. Repentance   **b.** Sin   **c.** Conversion

6. _____ is a thought, word, deed, or omission against God's law.

   a. Conversion   **b.** Sin   **c.** Reconciliation

7. Jesus continues to forgive us through _____.

   a. parables   **b.** the Church   **c.** sin

8. The unjust actions of one person affect _____ of the Church.

   a. all   **b.** some   **c.** none

Write a sentence to answer each question.

9. What did Jesus teach his disciples about forgiving others?

   _____

10. What is one important thing that happens when we celebrate the Sacrament of Penance?

   _____

The Celebration of Penance and Reconciliation

16

✝ We Gather in Prayer

Leader: Let us be still a moment and think about the need for God's forgiveness in our lives.

Reader: A reading from the holy Gospel according to Luke

Reader 1: Once tax collectors and sinners were listening to Jesus teach. "But the Pharisees and scribes began to complain, saying, 'This man welcomes sinners and eats with them.' So to them he addressed this parable."

Reader 2: "What man among you having a hundred sheep and losing one of them would not leave the ninety-nine in the desert and go after the lost one until he finds it? And when he does find it, he sets it on his shoulders with great joy and, upon his arrival home, he calls together his friends and neighbors and says to them, 'Rejoice with me because I have found my lost sheep.'"

Reader 3: "I tell you, in just the same way there will be more joy in heaven over one sinner who repents than over ninety-nine righteous people who have no need of repentance." (Luke 15:2–7)

The Gospel of the Lord.

All: Praise to you, Lord Jesus Christ.

♫ With Open Hands/ Abierto Está Mi Corazón

Refrain:
With open hands and open hearts
we come before you, O God above.
Your loving kindness fills all the earth;
eternal is your love.

Abierto está mi corazón
para encontrarte mi Dios de amor.
Y en todas partes tu cariño está;
eterno es tu amor.

Have mercy on me, O God of goodness,
according to your abundant love.
Wash me clean from all my sins;
restore to me your joy! (Refrain)

The Sacrament of Penance strengthens our relationship with God and others.

WE GATHER

✝ *Lord, help us to become more faithful followers of Jesus Christ.*

When do you look back on the things you have done at school or at home? Is there a time that you do this each day?

WE BELIEVE

As with all the sacraments, we prepare for the celebration of the Sacrament of Penance. One important way we do this is by an examination of conscience. Our **conscience** is our ability to know the difference between good and evil, right and wrong. This gift from God helps us to make decisions and to judge our decisions and actions.

When we examine our conscience, we determine whether the choices we have made showed love for God, ourselves, and others. We think about the ways we are living as disciples of Jesus. We ask ourselves whether we have sinned, either by doing something that we know is against God's law, or by not doing something that God's law calls us to do. We ask the Holy Spirit to help us judge the goodness of our thoughts, words, and actions.

conscience our ability to know the difference between good and evil, right and wrong

Quietly sit and examine your conscience. Use these questions to help you reflect on your relationship with God and others.

Do I make anyone or anything more important to me than God? Have I read from the Bible and prayed?

Do I respect God's name and the name of Jesus?

Do I participate in Mass and keep Sunday holy by what I say and do?

Do I show obedience to God by my obedience to parents, guardians, and teachers?

Have I hurt others by my words and actions? Have I helped those in need?

Do I respect myself? Do I take good care of my body and show respect to others? Do I respect the dignity of everyone I meet?

Have I been selfish or taken the belongings of others without their permission? Have I shared my belongings?

Have I been honest? Have I lied or cheated?

Do I speak, act, and dress in ways that show respect for myself and others?

Have I been happy for others when they have the things they want or need?

Examining our conscience is something we should do daily. Reflecting on the choices we have made helps us to make future choices that bring us closer to God and his people. It helps us to grow as the Body of Christ.

The meaning of the sacrament   The Church calls the Sacrament of Penance by different names. For instance, it has been called the sacrament of conversion, of Reconciliation, of confession, and of forgiveness. Each of these names tell us something about the meaning of the sacrament.

No matter how we name it, this sacrament includes four major parts:

- We express our heartfelt sorrow (contrition).

- We name our sins (confession).

- We show that we are sorry and that we will try not to sin again (penance).

- We experience God's forgiveness and are reconciled with him and the Church (absolution).

Contrition: This is one of our most important actions in the sacrament. Contrition is heartfelt sorrow for our sins. It includes the desire to sin no more. Being truly sorry for our sins, leads us to conversion, to turn back to God the Father. We pray an Act of Contrition as a sign of our sorrow and intention to sin no more.

Confession: We confess, or tell, our sins to the priest. It is important to name the ways we have harmed our relationship with God and others. Naming those ways helps us to take responsibility for our actions and to ask God for forgiveness.

An examination of conscience helps us to know what we need to confess. Serious sins must be confessed because they completely break friendship with God. These sins must be forgiven in order to share in God's grace again. The forgiveness of less serious sins strengthens our weakened friendship with God. It helps us to continue loving God and others.

Penance: A penance is an action that shows we are sorry for our sins. It is sometimes a prayer, the completion of a work of mercy, or an act of service. A penance is a way of making right the harm that we may have caused. Accepting this penance is a sign that we are turning back to God and are willing to change our lives.

Absolution: Our sins are absolved, or forgiven. In the name of Christ and the Church and through the power of the Holy Spirit, a priest grants the forgiveness of sins. This forgiveness brings reconciliation with God and the Church.

In the Sacrament of Penance, we are strengthened to live in God's love. We continue to live as faithful followers of Christ.

WE RESPOND

In the boxes above, design a symbol to describe each of the four parts of the Sacrament of Penance. Your symbols can include pictures, actions, or words. Share your symbols with the class.

Think about your day so far. How have you shown love for God and others? What else can you do today to respond to God's love?

In the Sacrament of Penance, the Church celebrates God's forgiveness.

WE GATHER

✝ *We seek your forgiveness today and always.*

Think about the times you have celebrated the Sacrament of Penance. Were the celebrations always the same? What were they like?

WE BELIEVE

The Church has two usual ways to celebrate the Sacrament of Penance. One way, or rite, is used when an individual meets with a priest for the celebration. The other rite is used when a group gathers to celebrate the sacrament with one or more priests.

Rite for Reconciliation of Several Penitents

Introductory Rites

We gather as an assembly and sing an opening hymn. The priest greets us and prays an Opening Prayer.

Celebration of the Word of God

The assembly listens to the proclamation of the Word of God. This is followed by a homily. Through his Word, God calls his people to repentance and leads them back to him. The readings help us to reflect on the reconciliation that Jesus' life and Death have made possible. They remind us of God's mercy and prepare us to judge the goodness of our thoughts and actions. Then we examine our conscience.

Rite of Reconciliation

The assembly prays together an Act of Contrition to show their sorrow for sinning. We may say another prayer or sing a song, and then pray the Our Father. We ask God to forgive us as we forgive others.

I meet individually with the priest and confess my sins. The priest talks to me about loving God and others. He gives me a penance.

The priest extends his hand and gives me absolution.

After everyone has met with the priest, we join together to conclude the celebration. The assembly praises God for his mercy. The priest offers a concluding prayer of thanksgiving.

Concluding Rite

The priest blesses us, and dismisses the assembly saying "The Lord has freed you from your sins. Go in peace." We respond "Thanks be to God."

Gathering with a group to celebrate the sacrament clearly shows that the sacrament is a celebration of the whole Church. Yet whether we celebrate Penance individually or in a group, we are joined to the whole Church.

Most parishes have a regular schedule for celebrations of the Sacrament of Penance. Normally the sacrament is celebrated in church. There is a special place where a penitent, someone seeking God's forgiveness, can meet with the priest for individual confession and absolution. The penitent can either sit with the priest and speak to him directly, or kneel and speak with him from behind a screen.

We are called to participate in the Sacrament of Penance often. Doing this gives us the peace and comfort that comes from being reconciled with God and the Church. The Church requires us to celebrate the sacrament at least once a year if we have committed serious sin.

Rite for Reconciliation of Individual Penitents

I examine my conscience before meeting with the priest.

Welcoming

The priest greets me and I make the Sign of the Cross. The priest asks me to trust in God's mercy.

Reading of the Word of God

The priest or I may read something from the Bible.

Confession and Penance

I confess my sins. The priest talks to me about loving God and others. He gives me a penance.

Prayer of Penitent and Absolution

I pray an Act of Contrition. The priest extends his hand and gives me absolution.

Proclamation of Praise and Dismissal

The priest says, "Give thanks to the Lord, for he is good." I respond, "His mercy endures for ever." The priest sends me out saying "The Lord has freed you from your sins. Go in peace."

WE RESPOND

🎵 **Psalm 25: To You, O Lord**

Refrain:
> To you, O LORD, I lift up my soul,
> I lift up my soul to you.

> Good and upright is the LORD,
> thus he shows sinners the way.
> He guides the humble to justice
> and teaches the humble his way.

(Refrain)

What do the words of this song tell you about God's love for us?

In the Sacrament of Penance we trust in God's mercy.

WE GATHER

✝ *Loving Father, your mercy endures forever.*

Who are some people that you trust? Why do you put your confidence in them? How do you show them your trust?

WE BELIEVE

In the celebration of the Sacrament of Penance, we trust in God's mercy. We express our thanks for his love and forgiveness. During the celebration, the words of the penitent and of the priest show our trust and thankfulness.

An **Act of Contrition** is a prayer that allows us to express our sorrow. In this prayer we promise to try not to sin again. We can say we are sorry in many ways. The Church gives us several prayers to use as Acts of Contrition. Here is one prayer you may know.

Act of Contrition
My God,
I am sorry for my sins with all my heart.
In choosing to do wrong
and failing to do good,
I have sinned against you
whom I should love above all things.
I firmly intend, with your help,
to do penance,
to sin no more,
and to avoid whatever leads me to sin.
Our Savior Jesus Christ
suffered and died for us.
In his name, my God, have mercy.

As an Act of Contrition we might also pray these words "Lord Jesus, Son of God, have mercy on me, a sinner," or our own words of sorrow.

🧍 Write an Act of Contrition in your own words. You may want to write your prayer in the form of a poem or song.

_____
_____
_____
_____
_____
_____
_____
_____
_____
_____
_____
_____

Key Word

Act of Contrition a prayer that allows us to express our sorrow and promise to try not to sin again

Absolution During the absolution, the priest extends his hand and prays,

"God, the Father of mercies,
through the death and resurrection of
  his Son
has reconciled the world to himself
and sent the Holy Spirit among us
for the forgiveness of sins;
through the ministry of the Church
may God give you pardon and peace,
and I absolve you from your sins
in the name of the Father, and of the Son,
and of the Holy Spirit."

The penitent answers: "Amen."

The words of absolution remind us that our reconciliation comes about by the mercy of the Father, the saving action of Jesus Christ, and the presence of the Holy Spirit. Reconciliation with God is found in and through the Church. The priest acts with the authority of Christ and in the name of the Church.

Celebrating the Sacrament of Penance helps us to focus our lives on God and his loving and just ways. The sacrament helps us to reconcile with others in our daily lives. It directs us to think and act with fairness, to stand up for what is right, and to work for justice and peace in the world.

WE RESPOND

Think of some people who act with fairness and stand up for what is right.

With a group, role-play some ways that you can follow the example of these people.

The priest welcomes us to be reconciled. He is a sign of God's love. He has received the Sacrament of Holy Orders and acts in the name of Christ and the Church and through the power of the Holy Spirit. So it is important to know that only a priest can hear our confession and forgive our sins.

The priest can never, for any reason whatsoever, tell anyone what we have confessed. He is bound to the secrecy of the sacrament. This secrecy is called the *seal of confession*.

Together we turn our hearts and minds to God.

WE GATHER

✝ *Holy Spirit, help us to turn to you.*

Have you ever been left a message in which you have been asked to call someone back? Have you always responded? Why or why not?

WE BELIEVE

God constantly calls us to him. By God's gift of grace, we can turn to God and open our hearts to him. To do this we need to think about the ways we are living as members of the Church. We need to think about what we can change or strengthen in our lives. Examining our conscience is a helpful way to direct our lives to God. It helps us to strengthen our relationship with him.

The community of faith also helps us to turn our lives to God. We are not alone as we try to grow as his children. We are part of the Church. Together we can turn our minds and hearts to God by:

- following Jesus' example and sharing his Good News

- trusting in God when we may be struggling in school or with family or friends

- caring for the physical or spiritual needs of others

- praying daily.

We are the Church. When we act with mercy, others may seek God's mercy. When we respect the dignity of all people and speak out against injustice, others may begin to do the same. If we help people in the community to understand one another and to work to settle differences peacefully, they may experience reconciliation with one another.

Each of us can lead others to turn to God, to rely on him, and to live as he calls us to live.

WE RESPOND

God continually calls us to be a community of faith focused on him and his love. How will you respond this week?

As Catholics...

At every Mass, we have the opportunity to ask forgiveness of our sins as a community. When we pray, "Lord, have mercy. Christ, have mercy. Lord, have mercy" we are seeking forgiveness. This asking of forgiveness together prepares us to celebrate the Eucharist as the one Body of Christ.

PROJECT

Pray
Learn
Celebrate
Share
Choose
Live

Show What *you* Know

Write slogans that tell about the Sacrament of Penance and Reconciliation.

Question Corner

When are good times to examine your conscience?

❏ Every night before going to sleep

❏ Every week before Mass

❏ Before receiving the Sacrament of Penance

❏ Other _____

_____

Pray Today

Jesus,
I know that I am supposed to consider you in every decision I make.
But I sometimes decide on what I think is best for me, without considering its effect on others.

Help me to remember your example when I have a decision to make.
Help me to decide to do the right thing and to remember you as I make my choice.
Guide my actions so they may have a positive effect on others.
Amen.

DISCIPLE

Pray
Learn
Celebrate
Share
Choose
Live

Make it Happen

Make a list of specific ways you can turn your mind and heart to God.

_____

_____

_____

More to Explore

The word *retreat* comes from military language. When an army retreats, it does not run away. It leaves the battle to plan better and new ways of fighting. This is what we do when we join friends and parish members on a retreat. We leave our ordinary way of life for a short time so that we can pray and think about our lives as Christians. We learn and plan ways to follow Christ. Some retreats last for one day. Sometimes retreats last a week or even a month. The Sacrament of Penance is an important part of a retreat. We have the time we need to ask Jesus for help and guidance. We receive God's forgiveness and are strengthened to follow Christ in our daily lives.

DISCIPLE CHALLENGE

• Underline the sentences that say what we do on a retreat.

• Why is the Sacrament of Penance an important part of a retreat?

_____

_____

• Find out what retreats are offered by your parish.

Take Home

Discuss with your family what you learned about the Sacrament of Penance and Reconciliation. Make a plan together for family members to receive the sacrament.

193

CHAPTER TEST

Write the letter that best describes each part of the Sacrament of Penance and Reconciliation.

1. _____ contrition

2. _____ confession

3. _____ penance

4. _____ absolution

a. true sorrow for the sins we have committed and the intention to sin no more

b. our sins are forgiven in the name of Christ and the Church and through the power of the Holy Spirit

c. an action that helps us to show sorrow for our sins

d. telling our sins to the priest

Short Answers

5. The Church calls the Sacrament of Penance by different names. List three of the names.

   _____

6. What ability does our conscience give us?

   _____

7. What are the two usual ways the Church celebrates the Sacrament of Penance?

   _____

8. What is one way we can turn our minds and hearts to God?

   _____

Write a sentence to answer each question.

9. What do we do when we examine our conscience?

   _____

10. What is an Act of Contrition?

   _____

Jesus, the Healer

✝ We Gather in Prayer

Leader: Let us bless the Lord, who went about doing good and healing the sick. Blessed be God now and for ever.

All: Blessed be God for ever.

🎵 **Psalm 23: The Lord Is My Shepherd**

Refrain:
The Lord is my shepherd;
there is nothing I shall want.

Reader: Let us listen to the words of the holy Gospel according to Matthew.

"Jesus went around to all the towns and villages, teaching in their synagogues, proclaiming the gospel of the kingdom, and curing every disease and illness. At the sight of the crowds, his heart was moved with pity for them because they were troubled and abandoned, like sheep without a shepherd." (Matthew 9:35–36)

The Gospel of the Lord.

All: Praise to you, Lord Jesus Christ.

Refrain:
The Lord is my shepherd;
there is nothing I shall want.

Leader: May the almighty and merciful God bless and protect us,
The Father, and the Son, and the Holy Spirit.

All: Amen.

Jesus heals those who are sick.

WE GATHER

✝ *Jesus, your touch heals.*

Think of a time when someone you know or heard about needed some help. If you could have helped this person, what would you have done?

WE BELIEVE

Jesus cared about the needs of all people. However, he had a special concern for those who were sick and suffering. He did not ignore people who had diseases or disabilities. He listened to them and treated them with respect. He also felt love for the family members of those who were ill. Jesus felt great love for those who were suffering, and he healed many of them.

Jesus' amazing love and power healed people. Those who were sick would present themselves to Jesus and beg to be cured. Sometimes their families or friends would bring them to Jesus so that he might heal them.

📖 John 4:46–53

Narrator: "Now there was a royal official whose son was ill in Capernaum. When he heard that Jesus had arrived in Galilee from Judea, he went to him and asked him to come down and heal his son, who was near death. Jesus said to him,

Jesus: 'Unless you people see signs and wonders, you will not believe.'

Narrator: The royal official said to him,

Royal Official: 'Sir, come down before my child dies.'

Narrator: Jesus said to him,

Jesus: 'You may go; your son will live.'

Narrator: The man believed what Jesus said to him and left. While he was on his way back, his slaves met him and told him that his boy would live. He asked them when he began to recover. They told him,

Servants: 'The fever left him yesterday, about one in the afternoon.'

Narrator: The father realized that just at that time Jesus had said to him, 'Your son will live,' and he and his whole household came to believe."

Healing was an important part of Jesus' ministry from the very beginning. And many people grew to believe in Jesus because of his healing.

Jesus desired to heal people from sin, too. Often when he cured the sick, he also forgave their sins. Jesus forgave the sins of people because he knew that sin kept them from loving God.

The healing and forgiving actions of Jesus showed others that he was the Son of God. Jesus' actions showed that God has power over sickness and sin. Jesus' healing of the sick and forgiving of sins were signs of his power to save us and bring us God's life.

By his Death, Resurrection, and Ascension, Jesus has victory over death. Because of Jesus, suffering and death no longer have power over us. He is our Savior.

Design a magazine cover for an issue entitled "Jesus the Healer." Use symbols, pictures, and words. What articles would be featured in the issue? What current happenings or stories might be included?

WE RESPOND

The Church shares Jesus' special concern for those who are sick or suffering. What are some things you can do in your family and neighborhood to care for those in need?

As Catholics...

Jesus calmed the stormy seas, made the blind to see, walked on water, changed water into wine, and even raised the dead to life. These amazing signs were beyond human power. They are called miracles.

Jesus' miracles were a sign to all people that he was the Son of God and that the Father had sent him to save his people. The miracles were special signs that strengthened people's trust and belief in God. These miracles showed people that God's Kingdom had begun.

This week read through the Gospels with your family to find two stories of Jesus' miracles.

VOLUME 2

JESUS
the Healer

U.S.A. $5.99
CANADA/FOREIGN $6.99

Jesus' Apostles preach and heal in his name.

✝ *Jesus, we praise you for your mercy and kindness.*

Think of a book you have read or a movie you have seen that was encouraging or exciting. What was the message and why did it affect you?

WE BELIEVE

Jesus' healing was a sign of God's presence and action in the lives of the people. It encouraged them and strengthened their faith in the one true God. His healing was a sign that God's Kingdom had begun in Jesus himself.

Sometimes it was difficult for Jesus to take care of everyone. He needed rest like all of us do. Once Jesus "withdrew in a boat to a deserted place by himself. The crowds heard of this and followed him on foot from their towns. When he disembarked and saw the vast crowd, his heart was moved with pity for them, and he cured their sick"
(Matthew 14:13–14).

Jesus wanted all people to feel God's power and presence, so he shared his ministry with the Apostles. Sometimes the Apostles were with Jesus as he preached and healed. Other times Jesus sent them to different towns and villages to share the message of the Kingdom of God. He sent them out to preach repentance and to cure the sick.

The Apostles traveled, teaching and healing in Jesus' name. "They anointed with oil many who were sick and cured them."
(Mark 6:13)

This healing ministry of the Apostles took on even greater meaning after Jesus' Death and Resurrection. After his Resurrection Jesus told them to preach the Gospel to the whole world. He told them that they would "lay hands on the sick, and they will recover"
(Mark 16:18).

After the Holy Spirit came upon them at Pentecost, the Apostles went out preaching and baptizing. Strengthened by the Gift of the Holy Spirit, the Apostles healed many people and brought them to believe in the risen Christ.

The Acts of the Apostles records the ministry of the Apostles. Here is one story from it.

On their way to the Temple to pray, Peter and John saw a man who had been paralyzed from birth. Every day he was carried to the Beautiful Gate of the Temple to ask for food and money from people. When he saw Peter and John the man asked them for help. Peter and John looked at the man and asked him to pay attention to them. He did so thinking he would get some food or money.

Peter said, "I have neither silver nor gold, but what I do have I give you: in the name of Jesus Christ the Nazorean, [rise and] walk." Peter then helped the man up. " . . . immediately his feet and ankles grew strong. He leaped up, stood, and walked around, and went into the temple with them, walking and jumping and praising God." (Acts of the Apostles 3:6, 7, 8)

All the people knew he was the one who sat at the Beautiful Gate begging. They were surprised to see him walking and praising God.

Peter told the people that the man had been healed by the power of Christ. Peter called them to believe in Christ and be baptized.

The Apostles continued to preach the Gospel and heal in Christ's name. Many more were baptized and the Church continued to grow.

In groups role-play the story of the event at the Beautiful Gate as if it were happening today. What does the healed man do? How do the people respond?

WE RESPOND

What can you say and do to bring others to believe in Christ?

The Church continues Jesus' healing ministry.

WE GATHER

✝ *May God care for us and give us strength when we are sick.*

When family members or friends are ill, what can we do to help them? When you are ill, what do people do to help you?

WE BELIEVE

From the time of the Apostles, the faithful have turned to the Church for healing and comfort. We see in this account from the letter of Saint James, the beginning of the Sacrament of the Anointing of the Sick.

📖 James 5:13–15

James wrote to one of the early Christian communities about the need for healing. He said that anyone who is suffering should pray. Anyone who is in good spirits should sing praise. Anyone who was sick should call on the priests of the Church, "and they should pray over him and anoint [him] with oil in the name of the Lord, and the prayer of faith will save the sick person, and the Lord will raise him up" (James 5:14–15).

All the sacraments bring us closer to God and one another. However, as a Sacrament of Healing, the Anointing of the Sick celebrates in a special way Jesus' work of healing.

The importance of the sacrament Jesus' healing comes to us through the Church. In the Sacrament of the **Anointing of the Sick**, God's grace and comfort are given to those who are seriously ill or suffering because of their old age. Members of the Church who should definitely receive this sacrament are those who are near death.

Those who celebrate this sacrament receive strength, peace, and courage to face the difficulties that come from serious illness. The grace of this sacrament:

- renews their trust and faith in God

- unites them to Christ and to his suffering

- prepares them, when necessary, for death and the hope of life forever with God.

The grace of this sacrament may also restore them to health.

In the Anointing of the Sick, we proclaim our faith in God's mercy. We support those who are sick and encourage them to fight against illness. In this sacrament we recall that by his own suffering, Death, and Resurrection, Jesus saves us. We ask God to save those who are suffering.

In the Anointing of the Sick, the priest and those gathered represent the whole community in offering comfort and support to the sick. This message of hope and support is also for people who care for those who are sick, especially their families and friends.

Key Word

Anointing of the Sick the sacrament by which God's grace and comfort are given to those who are seriously ill or suffering because of their old age

The priest brings these items to celebrate the Sacrament of the Anointing of the Sick in a home, hospital, or emergency situation.

The stole is a vestment the priest wears.

A small container holds the oil of the sick that the priest uses for anointing.

The priest may have a small *aspergillum*, or container, for sprinkling holy water.

A book which has the prayers and Scripture readings for the sacrament.

WE RESPOND

Think of someone in your school or parish who needs comfort and support. What can your class do to help him or her? Make a plan to do this.

We are all called to care for those who are sick.

✝ *Jesus, your touch heals.*

How have you helped others who have been sick or hurt?

WE BELIEVE

When we care for members of the Church who are sick, we are caring for the Body of Christ. We serve Christ himself.

When comparing the Body of Christ to the human body, Saint Paul wrote that God made the body "so that there may be no division in the body, but that the parts may have the same concern for one another. If [one] part suffers, all the parts suffer with it; if one part is honored, all the parts share its joy" (1 Corinthians 12:25–26).

All who are baptized are joined together in the Body of Christ. What happens to one member affects us all. When a member of the Church is suffering or in pain, he or she is not alone. The whole Church suffers with the person. This is why being kind and considerate to those who are ill is so important. Out of love for Christ and his Body, we work to help others to feel better. We try to provide them with the things they need. We join them in the celebration of the sacraments. These actions are a way to share in Jesus' healing work.

Family and friends are called to support their loved ones by comforting them with words of faith and by praying for them. The sick should be encouraged to receive the Anointing of the Sick when it is necessary.

The Church cares for all those who are sick, not only those who are seriously ill. We support those who are sick in our families and parishes. Those who are sick have different needs. Sick children may want us to read to them or play with them. Parents who are ill may need us to perform chores around the house. An elderly person may enjoy a short visit and the chance to talk to someone. Our concern for them is a way to support them on their road to recovery.

All of us can visit those who are sick and pray with them. Our families, classes, or youth groups can spend time getting to know people in our community who need hope and encouragement. Priests, deacons, and other representatives of the parish visit the sick. They read with them from the Bible, pray with them, bless them, and offer them Holy Communion.

The whole Church remembers in prayer those who are sick, especially when we gather at Sunday Mass. In the Prayer of the Faithful of the Mass we pray for the strength and healing of those who are sick. This is also a good time to remember their family members and those who care for them. On Sunday it is also good to spend time visiting with sick family members and friends.

WE RESPOND

Work with a partner to role-play ways people can reach out to those who are sick or elderly. Then as a class plan your own social outreach to those who are sick or elderly.

PROJECT

Show What *you* Know

Design an advertisement for your parish's weekly bulletin that tells about the Sacrament of the Anointing of the Sick.

What Would *you* do?

An elderly neighbor who lives near you has been hospitalized. She has a pet cat. Most of her family lives out of town. As a disciple of Jesus, you

_____

_____

_____

_____.

Make *it* Happen

Make a list of specific ways fifth-graders can care for the needs of others.

DISCIPLE

Pray
Learn
Celebrate
Share
Choose
Live

More to Explore

Hospice care provides support for those who are dying. It gives loving care to those who are terminally ill. The Sisters of Charity began St. James Hospice in London as a shelter for the dying in 1905. The first hospice in North America opened in 1974 in New Haven, Connecticut. Some hospices offer home care for patients and their families. Other hospices provide residential care for the terminally ill and support for their loved ones.

↳ **DISCIPLE CHALLENGE** Find out more about hospice care. What are some ways your class can support the work of hospice care?

_____

_____

_____

_____

Pray Today

In good times and in bad
in sickness and in health,
we belong to each other
as we belong to you, God ever faithful.
By morning and by night
may your name be on our lips,
a blessing to all our days:
so may kindness and patience be ever
   among us,
a hunger for justice,
and songs of thankfulness in all we do.

We ask this through Christ our Lord. Amen.

Take Home

Think about relatives or family friends who are sick. Write down their names.

_____

_____

_____

_____

_____

With your family, choose one person on the list to do something special for this week. If they are out of town, send them a card, call, or e-mail/message them. If they are in town, visit them. Make a plan to pray for relatives or family friends who are sick.

CHAPTER TEST

Write True or False for the following sentences.
Then change the false sentences to make them true.

1. _____ Jesus' healing and forgiving actions showed people that he was Mary's son.

   _____

2. _____ Anointing of the Sick is a Sacrament of Christian Initiation.

   _____

3. _____ In the Sacrament of Penance God's grace is given to those who are seriously ill or suffering because of their old age.

   _____

4. _____ Jesus healed people by his love and power.

   _____

Short Answers

5. What are two things Jesus' healing of the sick was a sign of?

   _____

6. How did Jesus' healing ministry continue after his Death and Resurrection?

   _____

7. What do those who celebrate the Sacrament of the Anointing of the Sick receive?

   _____

8. Whom do the priest and those gathered for the Anointing of the Sick represent?

   _____

Write a sentence to answer each question.

9. What are two ways that the Church can care for the sick?

   _____

10. What are two things that grace of the Sacrament of the Anointing of the Sick does?

   _____

The Celebration of the Anointing of the Sick

18

✝ We Gather in Prayer

Leader: Blessed be the God of mercy and love.

All: Blessed be God for ever.

Reader: A reading from the holy Gospel according to Mark

"And people were bringing children to him that he might touch them, but the disciples rebuked them. When Jesus saw this he became indignant and said to them, 'Let the children come to me; do not prevent them, for the kingdom of God belongs to such as these' . . . Then he embraced them and blessed them, placing his hands on them." (Mark 10:13–14, 16)

The Gospel of the Lord.

All: Praise to you, Lord Jesus Christ.

Leader: Jesus, come to me.

All: Jesus, come to me.

Leader: Jesus, bless me.

All: Jesus, bless me.

Leader: Let us pray for all children who are sick.

God of love,
ever caring,
ever strong,
stand by us in our time of need.

Watch over your children who are sick,
look after them in every danger,
and grant them your healing and peace.

We ask this in the name of Jesus the Lord.

All: Amen.

Jesus is with us when we are suffering.

WE GATHER

✝ *Jesus, you are with us always.*

Have you ever been so sick that you missed school? Who helped you to get better?

WE BELIEVE

At one time or another in our lives, we will probably get sick. We will catch a cold or come down with the flu. We may be injured while playing sports. Sometimes we may even need surgery.

During these times of sickness, we may become lonely or worried. We may even become discouraged and wonder if God remembers us. Yet God always remembers those who are sick and suffering. They are very special to God. As Christians, we believe that when we are suffering Jesus is with us sharing in our pain. He understands our pain and suffering because he suffered and died on the cross.

Part of human life is realizing that one day we, too, will die. But knowing that Jesus' Death brought us new life with God gives us hope. This hope helps us to live as Jesus did with complete trust that nothing will ever separate us from him.

Our care for those who are suffering around the world helps us to grow closer to Jesus. Jesus taught us that when we care for those who are ill, we care for him.

He said, "Whatever you did for one of these least brothers of mine, you did for me" (Matthew 25:40).

Trust in God, prayer, and hope can help all of us through the difficult times. We learn to rely on God and our faith community. Our family, our friends, and our parish community can help us to realize that Jesus' friendship always strengthens us. We can learn from Jesus that we can care for one another.

WE RESPOND

Work in groups. Brainstorm different ways you can support those who are sick. Share your ideas with the class and choose one thing to do in the next few weeks.

Italian School (17th Century)
Christ Healing the Blind Man of Jericho

The Anointing of the Sick continues Jesus' saving work of healing.

WE GATHER

✝ *We praise you for your mercy and kindness.*

Think of the first time you participated in an event or attended a special celebration. Did you know what to expect? How did you participate?

WE BELIEVE

When people are very sick, they may become anxious and discouraged. They need the special help of God's grace to stay strong and keep their faith alive. In the Sacrament of the Anointing of the Sick, Christ comforts them and suffers with them.

All of us in the Church have a responsibility to those who are seriously weakened by sickness or old age. We need to pray for and with them.

We need to encourage those in need to celebrate the Sacrament of the Anointing of the Sick. In this sacrament the Church community does two very important things. We support those who fight against sickness, and we continue Jesus' saving work of healing.

The sacrament is meant for all the faithful who need it. Children, adults, and the elderly are all invited to be strengthened by God's grace in times of serious sickness. The sacrament is meant to help people in their daily living of the faith. So the Church encourages its members to welcome the grace of this sacrament.

210

The sacrament can be celebrated more than once. For instance, if someone who has been anointed grows more ill, the sacrament can be celebrated again. Or, if a person recovers after being anointed but becomes seriously ill at another time, he or she can receive the sacrament again. When someone is preparing to have serious surgery, he or she can celebrate the sacrament with family, friends, and parish. Those of the faithful who are elderly and growing weaker may also want to be anointed.

Priests have a responsibility to make sure that the Sacraments of Penance and the Eucharist are available to those who are sick. Deacons and extraordinary ministers of Holy Communion can visit the sick to pray with them and bring them Holy Communion. These visits are a sign of the support and concern of the whole community.

As Catholics...

The oil used for the Sacrament of the Anointing of the Sick is called the oil of the sick. It is generally olive oil that has been blessed by the bishop at the Chrism Mass. This is a very special Mass during which the bishop prepares with special blessings the Sacred Chrism used for the anointings in Baptism and Confirmation. He also blesses the oil of the sick and the oil of catechumens, which is used during the time before the person's Baptism.

Do you know when the Chrism Mass is celebrated? Ask someone in your parish who might know.

WE RESPOND

In groups discuss what a motto is and why people use mottoes. Name some different mottoes you know. Then develop a motto for the Anointing of the Sick that will encourage sick people to receive the sacrament.

The Church celebrates the Anointing of the Sick.

WE GATHER

✝ *Jesus, comfort us and all those who need you.*

When are some times you need support and comfort? How do you ask for it? Who offers it to you?

WE BELIEVE

Like all sacraments the Anointing of the Sick is a celebration of the whole community of the faithful. Those present from the parish offer comfort and support to those who are sick. It is wonderful to celebrate the sacrament during Sunday Mass, but most times the sacrament is celebrated outside of the Mass. It is celebrated in hospitals, in homes, at the site of an accident, or wherever someone is in need of it. Whenever possible, friends and family members should be present for the celebration.

The main parts of the Anointing of the Sick are the prayer of faith, the laying on of hands, and the anointing with oil.

Prayer of faith   Jesus often healed people because of their belief and faith in him. The prayer of faith has been an important part of the Church's celebration of the sacrament from the beginning of the Church.

The whole Church is represented by the priest, family, friends, and other parish members gathered to pray. Trusting in God's mercy, they ask for help for those who are sick. Several intentions are offered. After each one those present answer, "Lord, have mercy."

Laying on of hands   In silence, the priest lays his hands on the person who is sick. The laying on of hands is a gesture of healing used by Jesus and the early Church. Many times Jesus healed the sick by the laying on of his hands or by simply touching them. The priest's laying on of hands is a sign of blessing and a calling of the Holy Spirit upon the person.

Anointing with oil   Because the oil has been blessed, the anointing with oil is a sign of the power and presence of the Holy Spirit. It is also a sign of healing and strengthening. Oil has been used for centuries to restore those who are weak and tired. It is known to soothe and comfort those who are sick.

The anointing takes place while the priest prays the following prayer.

The priest anoints the forehead first saying "Through this holy anointing may the Lord in his love and mercy help you with the grace of the Holy Spirit." All respond "Amen."

Then he anoints the hands saying "May the Lord who frees you from sin save you and raise you up." All respond "Amen."

Since the Anointing of the Sick often takes place outside of the celebration of the Mass, the sacrament usually begins with a Liturgy of the Word and is followed by Holy Communion. In this way those being anointed are further strengthened and nourished by the Word of God and by the Body and Blood of Christ. Holy Communion also joins them to their parish community with whom they are unable to celebrate the Eucharist.

"OI" is the abbreviation for *oleum infirmorum,* Latin for "oil of the sick." This holy oil is used in the Sacrament of the Anointing of the Sick.

WE RESPOND

Write a prayer for those who are ill. Pray that they may find God's peace and hope.

_____

_____

_____

_____

_____

_____

_____

_____

_____

Now pray your prayer quietly.

Jesus is with those who hope for eternal life.

WE GATHER

✝ *Jesus, you are with us always.*

What do you think lasts forever? Why do you think this?

WE BELIEVE

The whole Church rejoices in the life that comes to us in the sacraments. We pray in thanks to God for giving us the gift of his Son and the life we share together.

We are blessed with a community that helps us to live out God's love in our lives. They support us when we are sick and in need in any way. As a parish community we pray for all of those who are ill or suffering.

Jesus identifies with those who are ill. He suffers with them. We find Jesus in those who are sick and suffering. It is not surprising, then, that the Church reaches out in a loving way to the sick.

People receive the Sacrament of the Anointing of the Sick at the beginning of a serious illness. It is often called the sacrament of the sick. But Jesus came to give us life. We believe in him and receive his life in the sacraments. He helps us to understand that suffering and death are part of the journey to eternal life. We know that when we die with Christ, we will also rise with him. To help us in this journey through death to eternal life, Jesus Christ gives us himself in the Eucharist.

As a person's life on earth is about to end, he or she receives the Eucharist as viaticum. Viaticum is called the sacrament of the dying. In Latin *viaticum* means "food for the journey." It strengthens the person as he or she prepares for death and the hope of eternal life. The person receives the Body of Christ trusting that Jesus will welcome him or her home.

Jesus told his followers: "Whoever eats my flesh and drinks my blood has eternal life, and I will raise him on the last day" (John 6:54). Jesus acts through his Church to make this promise come true. As a person approaches the hour of death, Jesus gives himself in the Eucharist as viaticum. The Sacraments of Penance, Anointing of the Sick, and the Eucharist as viaticum are sometimes celebrated together and are called the "last sacraments."

WE RESPOND

🎵 I Am the Bread of Life

I am the Bread of life.
You who come to me shall not hunger;
and who believe in me shall not thirst.
No one can come to me unless the
Father beckons.

Refrain:

And I will raise you up,
and I will raise you up,
and I will raise you up on the last day.

PROJECT

Show What *you* Know

Find and circle the words in the box. They can be found up, down, across, and diagonally. Write the remaining letters that were not circled, from left to right, in order on the lines below to reveal the hidden message. Do not use the last two remaining letters.

Anointing
Pain
Strengthen
Viaticum
Comfort
Eternal
Hope
Prayer
Suffering
Care
Encourage
Grace

S	C	M	J	E	P	S	P	A	N
U	O	U	U	A	S	R	N	E	I
F	M	S	I	C	A	O	H	W	L
F	F	N	I	Y	I	T	T	A	G
E	O	H	E	N	G	T	N	R	E
R	R	R	T	N	H	R	A	R	U
I	T	I	E	O	E	C	A	I	S
N	N	R	P	T	E	C	A	L	V
G	T	E	E	W	A	Y	S	Z	W
S	E	N	C	O	U	R	A	G	E

___ ___ ___ ___ ___ ___   ___ ___ ___   ___ ___ ___ ___

___ ___   ___ ___ ___ ___ ___ ___ ___ .

What's *the* Word?

"Is anyone among you sick? He should summon the presbyters of the church, and they should pray over him and anoint [him] with oil in the name of the Lord, and the prayer of faith will save the sick person, and the Lord will raise him up. If he has committed any sins, he will be forgiven." (James 5:14–15)

In this passage, James describes the Sacrament of the Anointing of the Sick. *Presbyters* are those who have authority in the Church. Today, that refers to priests.

- Circle the phrase that means the same thing as laying on of hands.
- Underline the phrase that is a sign of the presence of the Holy Spirit.
- What does the sacrament offer to the sick?

_____

_____

DISCIPLE

Pray Learn Celebrate Share Choose Live

More *to* Explore

The Alexian Brothers is a religious community of brothers that began to care for the sick of Europe in the twelfth century. At that time, the sick and dying were not cared for in hospitals. Their families sometimes were unable to take care of them due to fear of contagious diseases. In the fourteenth century, disease spread through Europe, and the brothers risked their lives to care for many who became sick. The brothers continued to devote themselves to the poor and sick. They chose Saint Alexius, who had worked among the poor, as their patron and became known as the Alexian Brothers.

Today, Alexian Brothers continue to care for the poor and the sick. They serve in hospitals and clinics all over the world.

DISCIPLE CHALLENGE Visit the Alexian Brothers Website (www.alexianbrothers.org) to find out more about Saint Alexius and the Alexian Brothers.

Fast Facts

The *pyx* is a small box in which the priest carries the Eucharist to the sick or dying. Pyxes are often almost flat like a pocket watch. Sometimes they rest on a little stand. Pyxes are made of gold, silver, or brass.

Take Home

Does your parish have a healing Mass? There is a Mass when sick or elderly people celebrate the Sacrament of the Anointing of the Sick. As a family, find out when and where a healing Mass is being celebrated. Plan to attend.

CHAPTER TEST

Choose a word(s) from the box to complete each sentence.

1. The _____ is a sign of healing, strengthening, and the power and presence of the Holy Spirit.

2. Jesus healed the sick by the _____ or by simply touching them.

3. The prayer of _____ is a way for the Church to show its hope and trust in God.

4. The Eucharist as _____ strengthens those who are dying.

> laying on of hands
>
> viaticum
>
> faith
>
> anointing with oil

Underline the correct answer.

5. As Christians, we believe that Jesus is **(with/against)** us when we are suffering.

6. The Sacrament of Anointing of the Sick can be celebrated **(once/more than once)**.

7. Penance, Anointing of the Sick, and the Eucharist as viaticum are sometimes celebrated together and are called the **(first/last)** sacraments.

8. There are **(three/four)** main parts to celebrating the Anointing of the Sick.

Write a sentence to answer each question.

9. Who should receive the Sacrament of the Anointing of the Sick?

_____

10. What should we remember about Jesus in times of sickness?

_____

Mary, Model of Discipleship

19

✝ We Gather in Prayer

Leader: We know Mary as the mother of Jesus and our mother, too. Mary cares about us. She will bring all our needs to Jesus, her son. Think quietly about anything you might be worried about. Is there anything important that you might need? Let us bring our needs to our mother, Mary. Let us ask her to bring them to her son.

All: Mary, bring them to Jesus.
(Response to all petitions.)

Reader 1: For those who are in need in the world . . .

Reader 2: For those who are in need in our country . . .

Reader 3: For those who are in need in our parish . . .

Reader 4: For those who are in need in our families . . .

Leader: Anyone who wishes may name a need. (Response as above.)

Leader: Pray for us, Mother Mary, in the name of your Son, Jesus.

All: Amen.

Mary is Jesus' first disciple.

WE GATHER

✝ *Jesus, bless all of your disciples.*

Who are some people in your parish or local community whom you admire? What is it about these people that makes you want to follow their example?

WE BELIEVE

Throughout the centuries holy men and women in the Church have answered Jesus' call to be disciples. They responded to God's great love for them. They lived lives of love, faith, and service. From them we learn the ways to be a community of faith. However, among all of Jesus' disciples, Mary is the perfect example of discipleship. Mary, the mother of Jesus, is also his first and most faithful disciple. Mary believed in Jesus from the moment that God asked her to be the Mother of his Son.

Mary's "yes" to God What we know about Mary comes from the Gospels. We first learn about her at the Annunciation. The **Annunciation** is the name given to the angel's visit to Mary at which the announcement was made that she would be the Mother of the Son of God.

Annunciation the name given to the angel's visit to Mary at which the announcement was made that she would be the Mother of the Son of God

The Annunciation, (gift from the Philippines), The Basilica of the Annunciation, Nazareth, Israel

Luke 1:26–38

God sent the angel Gabriel to the town of Nazareth in Galilee to a young Jewish woman. Her name was Mary, and she was promised in marriage to a man named Joseph. Joseph was a descendant of David, the great king of Israel. The angel had great news for Mary.

The angel came to Mary and said, "Hail, favored one! The Lord is with you" (Luke 1:28). Mary did not understand what the angel meant, so the angel said to her, "Do not be afraid, Mary, for you have found favor with God. Behold, you will conceive in your womb and bear a son, and you shall name him Jesus" (Luke 1:30–31).

Mary questioned how this could be possible. She was not even married. The angel told Mary that she would conceive her child by the power of the Holy Spirit. "Therefore the child to be born will be called holy, the Son of God." (Luke 1:35)

And Mary said, "Behold, I am the handmaid of the Lord. May it be done to me according to your word"(Luke 1:38).

Mary was chosen by God from among all the women of history to be the Mother of his Son.

We learn from this Gospel account that Mary trusted God completely, and her faith was unshakeable. She did not know what to expect or how Joseph would react to her news about a baby. Yet Mary's love for God brought her to accept his invitation and to believe in his Son completely.

Like Mary we need to be open to the ways God may be calling us. Mary teaches us to trust in God's will for us. Trusting God is not always easy, but it is very important. When we trust God, we show him that we believe in his love for us. Mary helps us to live as faithful disciples. We learn from her to say "yes" to God and to care for others.

Mary loved and cared for Jesus as mothers do. She was with him as he grew and learned. Sometimes she did not understand him. Yet she kept her heart open, trusting, and faithful.

Mary supported Jesus throughout his ministry. She even stood with him as he died on the cross. Her faith in her son did not weaken in times of suffering or loss. She waited in prayer and with hope for the coming of the Holy Spirit. In all of these ways Mary was the first disciple of Jesus and she is a model for all of us.

WE RESPOND

Mary said "yes" to God throughout her life. How can you follow Mary's example and say "yes" to God today? Illustrate one way here.

221

Mary is most blessed among women.

WE GATHER

✝ *Mary, most blessed are you.*

Sometimes we hear people say "I'm blessed." What does this mean? What are some blessings in your life?

WE BELIEVE

When the angel Gabriel visited Mary, he told her something amazing about her cousin Elizabeth. Elizabeth, who had not been able to have children, had become pregnant with a son, even in her old age: "for nothing will be impossible for God" (Luke 1:37).

Mary went to visit her cousin Elizabeth and Elizabeth's husband Zechariah. "When Elizabeth heard Mary's greeting, the infant leaped in her womb, and Elizabeth, filled with the holy Spirit, cried out in a loud voice and said, 'Most blessed are you among women, and blessed is the fruit of your womb. And how does this happen to me, that the mother of my Lord should come to me?'" (Luke 1:41–43).

Elizabeth then told Mary, "Blessed are you who believed that what was spoken to you by the Lord would be fulfilled" (Luke 1:45).

Mary's response to Elizabeth is still sung today. It is known as *The Magnificat*. This prayer can be found on page 327. A version of the prayer is also found as a song called "The Canticle of Mary."

🎵 **The Canticle of Mary**

My soul proclaims the greatness
   of the Lord.
My spirit sings to God, my
   saving God,
Who on this day above all
   others favored me
And raised me up, a light for
   all to see.
Through me great deeds will
   God make manifest,
And all the earth will come to
   call me blest.
Unbounded love and mercy sure
   will I proclaim
For all who know and praise
   God's holy name.
God's mighty arm, protector of
   the just,
Will guard the weak and raise
   them from the dust.
But mighty kings will swiftly
   fall from thrones corrupt.
The strong brought low, the
   lowly lifted up.

Mary was part of God's plan for us. Mary has an important role in our salvation. Mary's visit to her cousin Elizabeth can help us to understand Mary's place in the Church.

As Catholics, what we believe about Mary is based on what we believe about her son, Jesus Christ. Mary was blessed by God and chosen to be the Mother of his Son. For this reason, she was free from Original Sin from the moment she was conceived. This belief is called the **Immaculate Conception**.

Throughout her life Mary loved and obeyed God. She lived a life of holiness. Because Mary did not sin, she had a pure heart. God blessed Mary in another way. We believe that when Mary's work on earth was done, God brought her body and soul to live forever with the risen Christ. This belief is called the **Assumption**.

Immaculate Conception the belief that Mary was free from Original Sin from the moment she was conceived

Assumption the belief that when Mary's work on earth was done, God brought her body and soul to live forever with the risen Christ

WE RESPOND

In the Hail Mary we also hear the words of Elizabeth and the angel Gabriel. Together pray this great prayer honoring Mary.

Hail Mary, full of grace,
The Lord is with you!
Blessed are you among women,
and blessed is the fruit of your womb,
    Jesus.
Holy Mary, mother of God,
pray for us sinners,
now and at the hour of our death.
Amen.

Mary is the greatest of all the saints.

WE GATHER

✠ *Mary, Mother of God, pray for us now and always.*

What makes a person "great"? What do we mean when we say someone is the "greatest"?

WE BELIEVE

Because of Mary's closeness to Jesus, the Church honors her as the greatest of all the saints. Saints are followers of Christ who lived lives of holiness on earth and now share in eternal life with God in Heaven.

Mary shares in God's holiness in a unique way because God chose her to be the Mother of his Son. As the first disciple, Mary is a special example for all of us. The Church has many titles for Mary. These titles help us to understand Mary's role in our lives and in the life of the Church.

Blessed Virgin   We learn from the Annunciation account that Mary was not yet married when the angel visited her. She was a virgin. Her son was conceived by the power of the Holy Spirit. Mary was truly blessed by God with the gift of his Son. We also believe that Mary remained a virgin throughout her married life with Joseph. Sometimes we call Mary the Blessed Virgin, the Blessed Virgin Mary, and the Blessed Mother.

Mother of God   As the mother of Jesus, Mary went through the joys of being pregnant and having a baby. She cared for her son and loved him. She prayed with him, and was an example to him of love and obedience to God. However, Jesus was truly human and truly divine. He is the Son of God, the Second Person of the Blessed Trinity who became man. So Mary is the Mother of God.

Mother of the Church Mary is Jesus' mother. As Jesus was dying on the cross he saw his mother and his disciple John at his feet. Jesus said to Mary, "Woman, behold, your son." He said to John, "Behold, your mother" (John 19:26, 27). Mary is the mother of all those who believe in and follow Jesus Christ. Thus, Mary is the Mother of the Church and our mother, too.

There are many more titles for Mary. We hear some of these titles when we pray a litany of Mary. The word *litany* comes from the Greek word for *prayer*. Litanies are like the Prayer of the Faithful prayed during Mass. They are made up of a list of Mary's titles followed by a short request for her help. Litanies of Mary give praise to God for making a humble young woman the Mother of his Son and the Church.

As Catholics...

We honor Saint Joseph for his love and care of Mary and Jesus. We do not know many things about him. However, we know that he was a just man who listened to the angel sent by God. The angel spoke to Joseph in a dream and told him, "Joseph, son of David, do not be afraid to take Mary your wife into your home. For it is through the holy Spirit that this child has been conceived in her. She will bear a son and you are to name him Jesus, because he will save his people from their sins" (Matthew 1:20–21).

Joseph loved and cared for Mary and Jesus. We call them the Holy Family. As Jesus' foster father, Joseph took care of him. Joseph and Mary prayed with Jesus and taught him the Jewish faith.

Saint Joseph's feast days are March 19 and May 1. Find out some ways the Church honors him.

Read these titles for Mary that come from the Litany of the Blessed Virgin Mary. Choose one of these titles of Mary and design an image for it. Discuss your image with the class. Share ways we can follow Mary's example.

Model of motherhood
Mirror of justice
Health of the sick
Comfort of the troubled
Help of Christians
Queen of all saints
Queen of peace

WE RESPOND

What are some ways you call on Mary? Which of her titles have special meaning to you?

The Church remembers and honors Mary.

WE GATHER

✞ *Mary, you are blessed by God. We honor you.*

What are ways we remember special events that have happened? What are ways we honor special people who have lived before us?

WE BELIEVE

Catholics all over the world honor Mary through prayer. It is important to realize that we do not worship or adore Mary. Our worship and adoration belong to God the Father, God the Son, and God the Holy Spirit. We are devoted to Mary and the saints because of the ways they have responded to God's great love. We ask Mary to pray for us and to speak to her son on our behalf.

In its prayer and liturgy the Church remembers the ways God blessed Mary. We celebrate the special times in her life as the Mother of the Son of God. The Church has many feast days in Mary's honor. On these days and others the Church gathers to celebrate the Eucharist.

There are also popular devotions to Mary. Like litanies and novenas, praying the Rosary is one of these devotions to Mary. We can pray the Rosary alone or with others. We can pray the Rosary at any time of the day.

The Rosary is usually prayed using a set of beads with a crucifix attached. We pray the Rosary by praying the Our Father, Hail Mary, and Glory Be to the Father over and over again. This creates a peaceful rhythm of prayer during which we can reflect on special times in the lives of Jesus and Mary. The mysteries of the Rosary recall these special times. We remember a different mystery at the beginning of each set of prayers, or decade, of the Rosary.

Joyful Mysteries
The Annunciation
The Visitation
The Birth of Jesus
The Presentation of Jesus in the Temple
The Finding of the Child Jesus in the Temple

Sorrowful Mysteries
The Agony in the Garden
The Scourging at the Pillar
The Crowning with Thorns
The Carrying of the Cross
The Crucifixion and Death of Jesus

Glorious Mysteries
The Resurrection
The Ascension
The Descent of the Holy Spirit upon the Apostles
The Assumption of Mary into Heaven
The Coronation of Mary as Queen of Heaven

The Mysteries of Light
Jesus' Baptism in the Jordan
The Miracle at the Wedding at Cana
Jesus Announces the Kingdom of God
The Transfiguration
The Institution of the Eucharist

The Grotto of the Annunciation, Nazareth, Israel

WE RESPOND

Write your own prayer honoring Mary. Then share it with your class.

_____

_____

_____

_____

_____

End

6 Pray the Hail, Holy Queen to end the Rosary.

5 Pray a Glory Be to the Father after each set of small beads.

4 Pray a Hail Mary at every small bead.

3 Pray an Our Father at every large bead.

2 Then pray the Apostles' Creed.

Start

1 Start with the Sign of the Cross.

Here are some of the feast days of Mary:

January 1—Solemnity of Mary, Mother of God

February 11—Our Lady of Lourdes

March 25—The Annunciation

May 25—The Visitation

July 16—Our Lady of Mt. Carmel

August 15—The Assumption

August 22—The Queenship of Mary

September 8—The Birth of Mary

September 15—Our Lady of Sorrows

December 8—Immaculate Conception of Mary

December 12—Our Lady of Guadalupe

227

PROJECT

Show What *you* Know

Your class has been asked to update your school's Web site.
Write and design an on-line profile of Mary. Be sure to include the
Key Words in your profile.

Question Corner

What devotions to Mary
do you plan to practice
more often?

❏ Praying the Rosary

❏ Praying the "Hail Mary"

❏ Praying a litany to Mary

❏ Other _____

_____

➤ **DISCIPLE CHALLENGE** Choose one of the
above and teach it to someone
younger than you.

Fast Facts

The parents of Mary
were Joachim and
Anne. They cared for
Mary, brought her up,
and gave her an example
of good parenting.
The Church honors
them as saints. To find
more saints, visit *Lives
of the Saints* on
www.webelieveweb.com.

DISCIPLE

Pray
Learn
Celebrate
Share
Choose
Live

More to Explore

In 1847, Pope Pius IX proclaimed Mary as "patroness of the United States" under her title of the Immaculate Conception. Later, the bishops of the United States built a national shrine in Washington, D.C. to honor Mary. It is called the Basilica of the National Shrine of the Immaculate Conception, and is the largest Roman Catholic church in North America. People come from all over to pray at the shrine. Within the Basilica, there are seventy-two in total beautifully decorated chapel areas. Many are dedicated to Our Lady in the names by which she is known in countries around the world.

DISCIPLE CHALLENGE

• Who declared Mary to be the patroness of the United States?

_____

• What did the bishops of the United States build to honor Mary?

_____

• Visit the Web site for the National Shrine and take the virtual tour of the Great Upper Church. Which chapel is your favorite?

_____

Why? _____

Mary's "yes" to God teaches us to be open to the ways that God may be calling us. How can fifth-graders be more open to God?

_____

_____

_____

_____

Take Home

What are some ways your family remembers and honors Mary?

_____

_____

_____

_____

_____

CHAPTER TEST

Short Answers

1. Mary has many titles. List three. _____

2. How does the Church remember the ways God blessed Mary? _____

   _____

3. What is *The Magnificat,* the Canticle of Mary? _____

4. What is the Rosary? _____

Write the letter that best defines each term.

5. _____ Annunciation

6. _____ saints

7. _____ Assumption

8. _____ Immaculate Conception

a. followers of Christ who lived lives of holiness on earth and now share in eternal life with God in Heaven

b. the belief that Mary was free from Original Sin from the moment she was conceived

c. the name given to the angel's visit to Mary and the announcement that she would be the Mother of the Son of God

d. the belief that when Mary's work on earth was done, God brought her body and soul to live forever with the risen Christ

e. recalling special times in the lives of Jesus and Mary

Write a sentence to answer each question.

9. Why is Mary the Mother of the Church?

   _____

10. How is Mary a model of holiness?

    _____

> "Yet even now, says the LORD,
> return to me with your whole heart."
>
> Joel 2:12

SEASONAL
CHAPTER 20

This chapter offers preparation for
the season of Lent.

LENT

Lent is a season of preparation for the great celebration of Easter.

WE GATHER

✝ *Holy Spirit, help us to follow Christ.*

What are some ways to become a better student, team player, or class member? Why is it important to try to improve?

WE BELIEVE

During Lent the whole Church prepares for the great celebration of Christ's Paschal Mystery in the Easter Triduum. This season is the final time of preparation for those who will celebrate the Sacraments of Christian Initiation at Easter. It is also a time for all who are already baptized in the Church to prepare to renew their Baptism at Easter. The whole Church thinks and prays about the new life Christ shares with us in Baptism.

The season of Lent begins on Ash Wednesday and lasts forty days. On Ash Wednesday we are marked on our foreheads with blessed ashes. These ashes are a sign of sorrow for our sins and of hope of having life forever with God. During Lent we use deep shades of purple and violet in our churches and during our worship. This is a sign of our need for reconciliation with God. The color also helps us to remember that joy and happiness will come from Christ's Death and Resurrection.

Lent is a season of simple living. We make a special effort to pray, to do penance, and to do good works. We are called to do these things all year long. During Lent, however, they take on added meaning as we prepare to renew our Baptism.

Penance Lent is a time of conversion, of turning to God with all our hearts. God constantly calls us to be with him and to respond to his love. Lent is a special time to think about the ways we follow God's law. It is a time to change our lives so that we can be better disciples of Christ.

Penance is an important part of this conversion. Doing penance helps us to turn back to God and to focus on the things that are important in our lives as Christians. Doing penance is a way to show that we are sorry for our sins. Our penance restores or strengthens our friendship with God and the Church.

We may do penance by giving up things we enjoy, like a favorite food or activity. We can also do without, or fast, from these things. Catholics of certain ages do penance by fasting from food on Ash Wednesday and not eating meat on the Fridays during Lent.

Prayer During Lent we try to give more time to God, and prayer helps us to do this. In Lent we may devote extra time to daily prayers and worship. We can spend more time reading and reflecting on Scripture. We can pray especially for those who are preparing to receive the Sacraments of Christian Initiation. We can gather with our parishes for the Stations of the Cross (found on page 327) and for the celebration of the Sacrament of Penance.

Good works During Lent we also show special concern for those in need. A way to do penance is to practice a work of mercy or to give of our time in a special way. We follow Jesus' example of providing for the hungry and caring for the sick. We try to help other people get the things they need and to make sure that people have what is rightfully theirs. Many parishes have food and clothing drives during this time of year. Families may volunteer at soup kitchens, visit those who are sick, and practice other works of mercy. We remember that good works should happen all year long.

👤 In what ways can you grow closer to Christ and others this Lent?

I will pray by _____

_____

I will turn to God by _____

_____

I will care for the needs of others by

_____

Passion (Palm) Sunday After five weeks of preparing through prayer, penance, and doing good works, Lent is nearly over. The Sunday before the Easter Triduum is known as Passion Sunday. This Sunday is also called Palm Sunday. We recall Jesus' Passion: the judgment to put him to Death, his carrying of the cross, and his suffering and dying on the cross. We also celebrate his joyous entrance into Jerusalem just days before he was to die.

📖 Matthew 21:1–11

Jesus and his disciples were traveling to Jerusalem for the great feast of Passover. As they neared the city, Jesus sent two disciples ahead to find a mule on which he could ride. They did as Jesus ordered. When they returned they placed their cloaks upon the animal, and Jesus sat upon it.

"The very large crowd spread their cloaks on the road, while others cut branches from the trees and strewed them on the road. The crowds preceding him and those following kept crying out and saying:

'Hosanna to the Son of David;
   blessed is he who comes in the
      name of the Lord;
hosanna in the highest.'

And when he entered Jerusalem the whole city was shaken and asked, 'Who is this?' And the crowds replied, 'This is Jesus the prophet, from Nazareth of Galilee.'" (Matthew 21:8–11)

LENT

233

The original Hebrew meaning of the word *hosanna* is "O Lord, grant salvation." But it had come to be an acclamation of joy and welcome. The crowds were overjoyed to see Jesus.

On Passion Sunday, a joyful procession takes place to celebrate Jesus' entrance into Jerusalem. We may gather away from the church building, and palm branches are blessed with holy water. We listen to the story of Jesus' entrance into Jerusalem, and a short homily may be given. The procession then begins to the church. We all sing hosanna and wave our branches to praise and welcome Jesus as the crowds of Jerusalem once did.

When we arrive at the church, Mass begins. During the Liturgy of the Word the Gospel reading is the Passion of our Lord Jesus Christ. This is one of the longest Gospel readings we hear all year long. It helps to prepare us for the celebration of the Easter Triduum that will begin four days later on Holy Thursday evening.

The palm branches that are blessed on Passion Sunday remind us that Lent is a time of renewal and hope. After Mass many people place these branches near the cross or crucifix in their home. The palm branches often remain there until the celebration of Passion Sunday the following year. These branches are also burned before Lent of the next year to make ashes for the Ash Wednesday celebration.

WE RESPOND

In your family or parish are there any other traditions or practices regarding the palm branches?

What are some other signs of new life and hope that help people to follow Christ?

Passion Sunday

234

✠ We Respond in Prayer

Leader: The Lord calls us to days of penance and mercy. Blessed be the name of the Lord.

All: Now and for ever.

Reader: A reading from the Book of Joel
"Yet even now, says the LORD,
return to me with your whole heart,
with fasting, and weeping, and mourning;
Rend your hearts, not your garments,
and return to the LORD, your God.
For gracious and merciful is he,
slow to anger, rich in kindness." (Joel 2:12–13)
The Word of the Lord.

All: Thanks be to God.

🎵 Sign Us with Ashes

Refrain
Sign us with ashes, the sign of your cross.
Give us the grace to know your mercy, Lord.
Renew our spirits and open our hearts.
Help us remember the love you gave us.

Help us pray so we might be closer
to you and to God's family. (Refrain)

Help us fast so we might know the want
of those within God's family. (Refrain)

Help us give so we might share of what
we have to serve God's family. (Refrain)

PROJECT DISCIPLE

Pray
Learn
Celebrate
Share
Choose
Live

Show What *you* Know

Write a paragraph about Lent.

What's *the* Word?

"Then the devil took him [Jesus] up to a very high mountain, and showed him all the kingdoms of the world in their magnificence, and he said to him, 'All these I shall give to you, if you will prostrate yourself and worship me.' At this, Jesus said to him, 'Get away, Satan! It is written, 'The Lord your God, shall you worship and him alone shall you serve.'" (Matthew 4:8–10)

↳ **DISCIPLE CHALLENGE** Read the rest of the story (Matthew 4:1–11). Why do you think the Gospel story of the temptation of Jesus is sometimes read at Mass on the first Sunday of Lent?

_____

_____

Take Home

Lent is a season of simple living. With your family, make a list of ways that you can live more simply during this season. Where can you all add extra time to pray, do penance, and to do good works as a family?

_____

_____

_____

Fast Facts

"Remember . . . you are dust and to dust you will return." The priest may speak these words as he marks the foreheads of the Christian faithful with ashes on Ash Wednesday.

"Jesus knew that his hour had come
to pass from this world to the Father.
He loved his own in the world and
he loved them to the end."

John 13:1

SEASONAL

CHAPTER 21

**This chapter includes the three days from Holy
Thursday evening until Easter Sunday.**

The Easter Triduum is our greatest celebration of the Paschal Mystery.

WE GATHER

✝ *Jesus, remember us when you come into your Kingdom.*

Think of someone in your family whom you care about and love very much. How do you show him or her your love?

WE BELIEVE

All during his life Jesus showed his love for his disciples. Jesus' greatest act of love for us was his dying for our sins. However, Jesus' Death was not the end of his love for us. Three days after his Death, Jesus rose to new life. His Death and Resurrection restores our relationship with God. They make it possible for us to have life forever with God. We celebrate Christ's Paschal Mystery of dying and rising to new life during the Easter Triduum. These three days are the holiest days of the year.

It is a Jewish tradition to mark the day as beginning at sundown and ending at sundown of the next day. Since Jesus followed this tradition, the Church also counts Sundays and solemnities from one evening to the next. So the Triduum begins on Holy Thursday evening and ends on the evening of Easter Sunday.

Holy Thursday The Evening Mass of the Lord's Supper on Holy Thursday begins the Easter Triduum. This celebration is not simply a remembering of the events of the Last Supper. It is a celebration of the life that Jesus gives us in the Eucharist. We are thankful for the unity that we have because of the Eucharist. We celebrate the love and service Christ calls us to everyday.

At the Last Supper Jesus washed his disciples' feet as a sign of his love for them. Jesus calls each of us to love and serve others, too. During the Mass on Holy Thursday, we have a special ceremony of the washing of the feet. This commits us to follow the example of Jesus' love and service. During this Mass we also take a special collection for those who are in need.

We do not actually end this liturgy. After everyone has received Holy Communion, the Blessed Sacrament is carried through the church in procession. It is reserved in another chapel. Back in the main church the altar is stripped, and the church is silent. This reminds us of the connection between Holy Thursday and Good Friday.

Good Friday On Good Friday we have the Celebration of the Lord's Passion. This often takes place in the afternoon. The cross is the central image of this day's liturgy. The cross is a sign of Christ's suffering and Death. It is also a sign of his victory over death and the salvation he brings to the whole world.

We enter the church quietly, and the priest and deacon wear the color red as a sign of Christ's Death. The Liturgy of the Word includes the reading of the Passion from the Gospel of John. There are ten General Intercessions that include prayers for the whole world. They are sometimes sung to show their special importance in this liturgy.

We also honor the cross with a special procession. We hear the words: "This is the wood of the cross, on which hung the Savior of the world. Come, let us worship." Then all gathered are invited to give reverence to the cross.

Though the Mass is not celebrated, the liturgy continues with the distribution of Holy Communion. Then all depart in silence.

TRIDUUM

Word. We hear again all the wonderful things God has done for his people. We have not sung the Alleluia since Lent began, but we sing it now with great joy. Jesus has indeed risen from the dead! One high point of this vigil is the celebration of the Sacraments of Christian Initiation. We welcome new members into the Church and praise God for the new life we have all received in Christ. We renew our own baptismal promises and rejoice in the newness of our own lives. We continue to share in Christ's life in the celebration of the Eucharist that follows.

The third day of the Triduum begins Saturday evening and continues until the evening of Sunday. Parishes gather on Easter Sunday for the celebration of the Mass. We sing with joy that the Lord is risen!

Holy Saturday   During the day we spend time thinking and praying. We remember that Jesus died to save all people, and we thank God for this gift. In the evening we gather with our parish for the celebration of the Easter Vigil.

We begin in darkness, waiting for the light of Christ. When we see the light of the large Paschal candle, we sing with joy. At this vigil there are many readings in the Liturgy of the

WE RESPOND

Illustrate the Easter Triduum. Show that it is one celebration that spans three days from evening to evening.

✞ We Respond in Prayer

Leader: The grace of our Lord Jesus Christ be with us all, now and forever.

All: Amen.

Reader: A reading from the first Letter of John
"Beloved, let us love one another, because love is of God. . . In this way the love of God was revealed to us: God sent his only Son into the world so that we might have life through him. . .Beloved, if God so loved us, we also must love one another." (1 John 4:7, 9, 11)

The Word of the Lord.

All: Thanks be to God.

Leader: The Lord Jesus, when he had eaten with his disciples, poured water into a basin and began to wash their feet saying: This example I leave you.

All: Lord, help us to follow your example of love and service.

Leader: If I, your Lord and Teacher, have washed your feet, then surely you must wash one another's feet.

All: They will know we are his disciples if there is love among us.

♫ This Is My Commandment

This is my commandment,
that you love one another
that your joy may be full.

PROJECT DISCIPLE

Pray Learn Celebrate Share Choose Live

Celebrate!

Complete the chart by describing what we celebrate and what happens on each day of the Easter Triduum.

Day	What We Celebrate	What Happens
Holy Thursday		
Good Friday		
Holy Saturday		

Fast Facts

Two Greek letters A (alpha) and Ω (omega) are carved into the Easter, or Paschal candle. The letters are referred to in Scripture. "'I am the Alpha and the Omega,' says the Lord God, 'the one who is and who was and who is to come, the almighty.'" (Revelation 1:8)

The Paschal candle is lit at the Easter Vigil as a symbol of Jesus' Resurrection.

Take Home

With your family plan to take a walk or drive during the Triduum. What signs of new life did you see? Write down some of these.

_____

_____

_____

_____

Choose a word or phrase from the box to complete each sentence.

1. When we examine our _____, we determine whether the choices we have made showed love for God, ourselves, and others.

2. God constantly calls us to turn back to him. A turning to God with all one's heart is called _____.

3. _____ is the sacrament by which God's grace and comfort are given to those who are seriously ill or suffering because of their old age.

4. The mysteries of the _____ recall special times in the lives of Jesus and Mary.

5. An Act of _____ is a prayer that allows us to express our sorrow and promise to try not to sin again.

6. A thought, word, deed, or omission against God's law is a _____.

Assumption
Immaculate Conception
conscience
Contrition
Anointing of the Sick
Penance
Rosary
conversion
sin

7. In the Sacrament of _____ our relationship with God and the Church is strengthened or restored and our sins are forgiven.

8. The belief that Mary was free from Original Sin from the moment she was conceived is called the _____.

Fill in the circle beside the correct answer.

9. A prayer, a work of mercy, or an act of service that shows we are sorry for our sins is called _____.

   ○ a confession   ○ absolution   ○ a penance

10. Penance, the Anointing of the Sick, and the Eucharist as _____ are often celebrated together by those who are sick.

   ○ litany   ○ viaticum   ○ initiation

continued on next page   243

11. Unjust situations and conditions in society such as prejudice, poverty, and violence are examples of _____.

    ○ absolution   ○ contrition   ○ social sin

12. Because of _____, the priest cannot tell anyone what we have confessed in the Sacrament of Penance.

    ○ absolution   ○ the seal of   ○ the Act of Contrition
                            confession

13. The _____ is also known as the Canticle of Mary.

    ○ *Magnificat*   ○ Annunciation   ○ Assumption

14. In Anointing of the Sick we proclaim our faith in God's _____.

    ○ justice   ○ mercy   ○ litany

15. The main parts of the Anointing of the Sick are the prayer of faith, the _____, and the anointing with oil.

    ○ laying on of hands ○ absolution   ○ examination of conscience

16. Mary is Jesus' _____ disciple.

    ○ last   ○ first   ○ oldest

Answer the questions.

17–18. What are two effects of celebrating the Sacrament of Penance?

19–20. What are some ways that the Sacrament of the Anointing of the Sick offers God's grace and comfort to those who are ill, and to those who love and care for them?

Human Dignity

Part 1 **I Open My Heart**

The Catholic Church teaches that honoring the dignity of every person is a basis of morality. Human dignity is the value and worth that come from being created in God's image and likeness.

Look at the picture below.

What does it say to you about human dignity? Draw your own image of human dignity.

Human Dignity

Part 2 We Come Together for Prayer

Leader: Let us begin by thinking of this message from our Holy Father, Pope Francis: "We are all jars of clay, fragile and poor, yet we carry within us an immense treasure." (Pope Francis, Twitter, August 9, 2013)

Let us pray. God, you created all human beings in your image, and our human dignity is an immense treasure.

Reader 1: "It is [God] who gives to everyone life and breath and everything. He made from one the whole human race to dwell on the entire surface of the earth." (Acts of the Apostles 17:25–26)

Reader 2: "In his hand is the soul of every living thing." (Job 12:10)

Reader 3: "For God so loved the world that he gave his only Son, so that everyone who believes in him might not perish but might have eternal life." (John 3:16) (*Pause for reflection.*)

Leader: God, you call us to recognize one another's dignity and to share the love of your Son with all people. Often, however, human dignity is cast aside and people are left in need. As followers of your Son, we try to work to end these social injustices. We pray for an end to all social sin, including:

All: (*Take turns naming examples of social sin aloud, such as prejudice, poverty, homelessness, crime, violence, or even bullying, gossip, or excluding others.*)

Leader: The Church speaks out against social sin. Imagine you are using social media to speak out against one of the social sins we named. What would your message say? (*All silently write their messages.*)

Let us conclude by praying the Our Father. (*All pray the Our Father.*)
Amen.

Human Dignity

Part 3 I Cherish God's Word

"God created man in his image;
   in the divine image he created him;
   male and female he created them."

(Genesis 1:27)

Detail from *The Creation of Adam,*
by Michelangelo, on the Sistine
Chapel ceiling, painted circa 1511–12

READ the quotation from Scripture. Read slowly. Pay close attention to what you are reading.

REFLECT on what you read. Think about:

- How does being aware that everyone is created in God's image change the way I feel about myself? about others? about my life?

- What are the wonderful things about being created in God's image? What are the challenges?

- How would the world be different if everyone truly lived as God's image?

SHARE your thoughts and feelings with God in prayer. Let your thoughts and feelings come naturally. Speak to God as a friend.

CONTEMPLATE, or sit quietly and allow your attention to remain focused on God's Word in the Scripture passage from Genesis above.

Human Dignity

Part 4   I Value My Catholic Faith

Imagine you are on a "Human Dignity Quest," finding words about upholding human dignity. Write the words here.

_____

_____

_____

_____

_____

In the space below, make a signpost for the "Human Dignity Labyrinth" with one of the words you found.

As you walk the labyrinth, look at all the signs you pass. Think about examples of living each of these out.

HUMAN DIGNITY

Catholic Identity Retreat

Human Dignity

Part 5 I Celebrate Catholic Identity

Work with your group to complete the contract to promote justice and respect human dignity. After it has been completed and signed by all, copy the words of the contract here.

Contract to Promote Justice and Respect Human Dignity

Signed:

Share this with your family at home. Ask them to commit to and sign it, too.

_____

_____

Catholic Identity Retreat

Human Dignity

Part 6   I Honor My Catholic Identity

Leader: Holy Spirit, help us to honor the teaching that everyone is made in the image of God. Guide us to be aware of this teaching and let it direct the way we treat everyone, including ourselves. We pray that everyone will promote justice and respect human dignity.

We go forth now to honor the dignity of every person. Let us close with the prayer of Saint Francis of Assisi. As you pray, think about a special gift or strength you have that helps you to be an instrument of God's peace.

Saint Francis of Assisi

All: Lord, make me an instrument of
    your peace:
  where there is hatred, let me
      sow love;
  where there is injury, pardon;
  where there is doubt, faith;
  where there is despair, hope;
  where there is darkness, light;
  where there is sadness, joy.

O divine Master, grant that I may
    not so much seek
to be consoled as to console,
to be understood as to
    understand,
to be loved as to love.
For it is in giving that we receive,
it is in pardoning that we are
    pardoned,
it is in dying that we are born
    to eternal life. Amen.

Catholic Identity Retreat

Bringing the Retreat Home

Human Dignity

Retreat Recap

Review the pages of your child's *Celebrating Catholic Identity: Morality* retreat. Ask your child to tell you about the retreat. Talk about what human dignity means:

- God created us in his image.
- Human dignity is the value and worth that come from being created in God's image.
- Honoring the presence of God in every human being is a basis for living a moral life.

Human Dignity Contract

Review your child's "Contract to Promote Justice and Respect Human Dignity" from Part 5 of the retreat. Make your own family contract that names specific ways your family can promote justice and respect human dignity. Examples might include any local charitable runs/walks, bowl-a-thons, dance-a-thons, or sporting events.

Family Contract to Promote Justice and Respect Human Dignity

Take a Moment

Part of your child's retreat was a labyrinth, a maze-like path that is walked through in a meditative state. Arrange for the family to take a peaceful, meditative walk or bike ride together. Choose surroundings where you might quietly observe nature.

Family Prayer

Pray this at mealtime or when your family is together. Finish the last line of the prayer together.

Almighty God,
you created us in your image.
We have dignity.
We are valuable and wondrous creations of God.
May we always treat one another
with the respect we deserve.
May we always remain aware
of the dignity of all human beings
and share with them the love of Christ.
Give us the strength to help and protect
all those whose human dignity is not honored
in our world, including:

_____

_____

For more resources, see the *Catholic Identity Home Companion* at the end of this book.

Why We Believe
As a Catholic Family

What if someone asks us:

- Why should we protect human life in all its stages?
- What does the Church say about war and violence?
- Why should Catholics work to end poverty?

The following resources can help us to respond:

As Catholics, we believe that all human life is sacred.

🌿 What does Scripture say?

"The Lord God formed man out of the clay of the ground and blew into his nostrils the breath of life, and so man became a living being." (Genesis 2:7)

"Then God said: 'Let us make man in our image, after our likeness. Let them have dominion over the fish of the sea, the birds of the air, and the cattle, and over all the wild animals and all the creatures that crawl on the ground.'" (Genesis 1:26)

"Do you not know that your body is a temple of the holy Spirit within you, whom you have from God, and that you are not your own?"

(1 Corinthians 6:19)

God created us to reflect who he is. We have God's "breath of life." We each have a soul, a conscience, and a free will. As the *Catechism of the Catholic Church* says, this is part of the "outstanding manifestation of the divine image" (CCC, 1705).

The Son of God, Jesus Christ, the Second Divine Person of the Trinity, took on a human nature. And the fact that he took on our human life is the greatest testimony we have to the dignity and sacredness of human life. God gives us the responsibility of loving, caring for, and protecting his gift of life.

God gave us the Fifth Commandment: "You shall not kill" (Exodus 20:13). This commandment is based on the truth that all life is sacred, created by God. It demands that we respect and protect human life in many different ways.

🌿 What does the Church say?

Right to life "Human life must be respected and protected absolutely from the moment of conception." (CCC, 2270)

War and violence "The Church insistently urges everyone to prayer and to action so that the divine Goodness may free us from the ancient bondage of war." (CCC, 2307; see Gaudium et spes 81 § 4.)

Poverty "Not to enable the poor to share in our goods is to steal from them and deprive them of life. The goods we possess are not ours but theirs." (Saint John Chrysostom, one of the Church Fathers, A.D. 347–407, from Hom. in Lazaro 2, 5, as quoted in CCC, 2446)

Notes:

We Love and Serve As Jesus Did

UNIT 4

Seasonal Chapter

DEAR FAMILY

In Unit 4 your child will grow as a disciple of Jesus by:

- choosing to practice the virtues of faith, hope and love and living the Beatitudes that Jesus taught
- learning the ways disciples of Jesus can follow him as laypeople, ordained men, or religious
- appreciating that the Sacrament of Matrimony is celebrated as a life-long covenant
- understanding that in the Sacrament of Holy Orders men are ordained to serve as deacons, priests, and bishops
- recognizing the four special marks or characteristics of the Church: one, holy, catholic, and apostolic.

Fast Facts

The Christian symbol used for the virtue of hope is an anchor. The anchor is also seen as a representation of Christ's Cross, through which we are saved and so have hope. How does hope anchor your family today?

Picture This

Look at the photos on pages 252–253 that show people acting in loving ways toward others. Talk about the ways your family can show love to your neighbors, your parish family, your community. Plan on doing a loving act together for someone in need.

Reality Check

"The Christian home is the place where children receive the first proclamation of the faith."

(*Catechism of the Catholic Church*, 1666)

Show That You Care

The Church is enriched by generous people who follow their vocations with faithfulness and love. Who are the married couples, single people, priests, deacons, brothers and sisters your family knows? Do something to celebrate their vocations and to thank them for their Christian examples—send an e-mail or a card, call them, or invite them for dinner.

Take Home

Be ready for this unit's Take Home:

Chapter 22: Discussing ways to live out the Beatitudes

Chapter 23: Choosing to be active in your parish

Chapter 24: Deciding to be the "domestic Church"

Chapter 25: Working together on family tasks

Chapter 26: Participating in a local service project

Faith, Hope, and Love

✝ We Gather in Prayer

Leader: Loving God, fill our hearts with peace and share your love with us. Blessed be the name of the Lord.

All: Now and for ever.

Reader: A reading from the first Letter of Saint Paul to the Corinthians

". . . If I have all faith so as to move mountains, but do not have love, I am nothing. If I give away everything I own . . . but do not have love, I gain nothing.

Love is patient, love is kind . . . faith, hope, love remain, these three; but the greatest of these is love."

(1 Corinthians 13:2–4, 13)

The Word of the Lord.

All: Thanks be to God.

Leader: May God bless us with his love, strengthen us in faith, and bring us hope.

All: Amen.

♫ God's Greatest Gift

Love, love, Jesus is love.
God's greatest gift is the
   gift of love.
All creation sings together,
   praising God for love.

We believe in God and all that the Church teaches.

WE GATHER

✝ *God, we are your children, people of faith.*

What are some choices you have had to make recently? Were your decisions easy or difficult to make? How did your decisions affect you and others?

WE BELIEVE

Every day Christ calls us to follow him and to live by his teachings. We answer Jesus' call to discipleship by believing in him and by loving God and others as he did. The grace God shares with us in the sacraments helps us to live by the commandments and by Jesus' teachings. The Holy Spirit guides us to live as Jesus' disciples and to follow Jesus' example of loving God and one another.

Every day we have the opportunity to act as Jesus' disciples. The choices that we make show whether or not we follow Jesus' example. Sometimes we do not even realize that we are making a choice. We show love and respect because we are in the habit of doing it. A **virtue** is a good habit that helps us to act according to God's love for us.

The *theological virtues* of faith, hope, and love bring us closer to God and increase our desire to be with God forever. They are called theological because *theo* means "God," and these virtues are gifts from God. They make it possible for us to have a relationship with God—the Father, the Son, and the Holy Spirit.

As Catholics...

The theological virtues are the foundation of the human virtues. The human virtues are habits that come about by our own efforts. They lead us to live a good life. They result from our making the decision, over and over again, to live by God's law. These human virtues guide the way we think, feel, and behave. Four of these are called "Cardinal" Virtues: prudence, justice, fortitude, and temperance.

Prudence helps us to make sound judgments and direct our actions toward what is good. Justice, also called righteousness, leads us to respect the rights of others, give them what is rightfully theirs, and work for change so people can live better lives. Fortitude enables us to act bravely in the face of troubles and fears. Temperance helps us to keep our desires under control and to balance our use of material goods.

Each day try to practice these virtues and make choices that lead you to follow Jesus.

The virtue of **faith** enables us to believe in God and all that the Church teaches us. Faith helps us to believe all that God has told us about himself and all that he has done. The gift of faith helps us to believe that God is with us and is acting in our lives.

God makes faith possible, but faith is still a choice we make. Jesus once said, "Blessed are those who have not seen and have believed" (John 20:29). We choose to respond to God's gift of faith. We choose to believe. Faith leads us to want to understand more about God and his plan for us, so that our belief in him can grow stronger.

Our faith is the faith of the Church. It is through the community of the Church that we come to believe. Through this community of faith we learn what it means to believe. Our faith is guided and strengthened by the Church.

Jesus' followers once asked him to "increase our faith" (Luke 17:5). They understood that faith could grow by the power of God. To grow in faith, we need to read the Bible,

pray to God to make our faith stronger, and give witness to our faith by the way we live. We give witness to Christ when we speak and act based upon the Good News. As Christ's disciples we are called to show others our belief in God and to help them believe.

WE RESPOND

Find a word, starting with each of the letters below, that describes faith.

F _____
A _____
I _____
T _____
H _____

How can you grow in faith this week?

Pray together this Act of Faith.

O God, we believe in all that Jesus has taught us about you.
We place all our trust in you because of your great love for us.

Key Words

virtue a good habit that helps us to act according to God's love for us

faith the virtue that enables us to believe in God and all that the Church teaches us; it helps us to believe all that God has told us about himself and all that he has done

We trust in God and are confident in his love and care for us.

WE GATHER

✝ *Lord, we place our hope in you.*

Think about the things that you hope for. What are you hoping for today?

WE BELIEVE

From the beginning of his ministry, Jesus gave people a reason to hope in God's mercy. God had not forgotten his people. He had sent his only Son to be with them and to share his life and love with them. Jesus brought all people God's forgiveness and healing. He gave all of us the hope of peace and life with God.

The Beatitudes are a very important teaching of Jesus. Each beatitude begins with the word *blessed* which means "happy." In the Beatitudes, Jesus describes the happiness that comes to those who follow his example of living and trusting in God's care.

📖 Matthew 5:3–10 ✦ ✦ ✦ ✦ ✦ ✦ ✦ ✦ ✦ ✦

The Beatitudes	Living the Beatitudes
"Blessed are the poor in spirit, for theirs is the kingdom of heaven.	We are "poor in spirit" when we depend on God and make God more important than anyone or anything else in our lives.
Blessed are they who mourn, for they will be comforted.	We "mourn" when we are sad because of the selfish ways people treat one another.
Blessed are the meek, for they will inherit the land.	We are "meek" when we are patient, kind, and respectful to all people, even those who do not respect us.
Blessed are they who hunger and thirst for righteousness, for they will be satisfied.	We "hunger and thirst for righteousness" when we search for justice and treat everyone fairly.
Blessed are the merciful, for they will be shown mercy.	We are "merciful" when we forgive others and do not take revenge on those who hurt us.
Blessed are the clean of heart, for they will see God.	We are "clean of heart" when we are faithful to God's teachings and try to see God in all people and in all situations.
Blessed are the peacemakers, for they will be called children of God.	We are "peacemakers" when we treat others with love and respect and when we help others to stop fighting and make peace.
Blessed are they who are persecuted for the sake of righteousness, for theirs is the kingdom of heaven."	We are "persecuted for the sake of righteousness" when others disrespect us for living as disciples of Jesus and following his example.

250

Jesus teaching the Beatitudes from the motion picture *Jesus of Nazareth.*

The Beatitudes describe the ways Christ's disciples should think and act. They are a promise of God's blessings. They give us reason to hope in the Kingdom of God, also called the Kingdom of Heaven.

The virtue of **hope** enables us to trust in God's promise to share his life with us forever. Hope makes us confident in God's love and care for us. Hope keeps us from becoming discouraged or giving up when times are difficult. Hope helps us to trust in Christ and to rely on the strength of the Holy Spirit.

Hope is a gift that helps us to respond to the happiness that God offers us now and in the future. Hope helps us work to spread the Kingdom of God here on earth, and to look forward to the Kingdom in Heaven.

Key Word

hope the virtue that enables us to trust in God's promise to share his life with us forever; it makes us confident in God's love and care for us

WE RESPOND

Work in groups and discuss how the Beatitudes can help us to live as Christians. Then pick two beatitudes and describe ways that people can live them.

_____

_____

_____

_____

Role-play some of these ways.

What can you do in your family, school, and community to live by the Beatitudes?

Pray together this Act of Hope.

O God, we never give up on your love. We have hope and will work for your kingdom to come and for a life that lasts forever with you in heaven.

We are able to love God and one another.

WE GATHER

✝ *God, help us to know and love others.*

Think about what you are like at home, in school, and around your neighborhood. What are some ways you show care for others? for yourself?

WE BELIEVE

All love comes from God. Out of his great love, God first created humans. Then because of his love God sent his Son to save all people. God sent his Son so that all people everywhere could share in God's life and love more fully.

The carnation, an ancient symbol of love.

During his ministry Jesus taught the people about many things. He explained God's law and the way to live it. He talked about the meaning of the Ten Commandments. He offered the Beatitudes as a model for living and working toward future happiness. By doing these things, Jesus showed the people that God's law is a law of love.

Once Jesus was asked what commandment of God's law was the greatest. Jesus responded by saying "You shall love the Lord, your God, with all your heart, with all your soul, and with all your mind. This is the greatest and the first commandment. The second is like it: You shall love your neighbor as yourself" (Matthew 22:37–39).

Love is possible because God loves us first. God's love for us never ends. He is always there for us, especially through the Church community. The virtue of **love** enables us to love God and to love our neighbor. Love is the greatest of all virtues. All the other virtues come from it and lead back to it. Love is the goal of our lives as Christians.

Jesus showed us how to love like no one else could. Before he died Jesus told his disciples, "I give you a new commandment: love one another. As I have loved you, so you also should love one another. This is how all will know that you are my disciples, if you have love for one another" (John 13:34–35).

Key Word

love the greatest of all virtues that enables us to love God and to love our neighbor

Jesus showed us how to love. He kept his promises, lived by the virtues, took care of his family and friends, and treated all people with respect. He listened to people and cared for their needs, even when he was tired. He stood up for the rights of others and helped them to find peace and comfort. He continued to love his disciples even when they were too afraid to return that love.

Jesus is our example of unconditional love. When we practice the virtues of love, or charity, we love as Jesus did. Unconditional love does not depend upon our own actions. It is a love that continues no matter what we do or fail to do. It is a love that is shown even when it is not returned.

WE RESPOND

 How can you recognize Jesus' disciples? Work in groups and act out some ways.

Pray together this Act of Love.
O God, we love you above all things.
Help us to love ourselves and one another as Jesus taught us to do.

The saints are models for living the life of virtue.

WE GATHER

✝ *Holy women and men, pray for us.*

Discuss these questions together. Have you ever known that someone was a Christian even before he or she told you so? How could you tell that this person was a follower of Jesus?

WE BELIEVE

Ever since Jesus first preached his message of love, people have followed him. From the very beginning of the Church, Christ's disciples have given witness to their faith in him. Some of them were inspired by the Holy Spirit to record their stories in the New Testament. These stories tell us of many other disciples who believed. These disciples spread the Good News of Jesus Christ, followed the teaching of the Apostles, and lived as a community of believers.

Many of these early disciples were martyrs, people who died rather than give up their belief in Christ. The word *martyr* comes from the Greek word for "witness." We remember and honor these martyrs, and the many others throughout history who have given their lives for their faith.

The Martyrs of Vietnam   In the sixteenth century, Christian missionaries first brought the faith to Vietnam. During the next three centuries, Christians in Vietnam suffered for their beliefs. Many were martyred, especially during the years of 1820 to 1840. In 1988, Pope John Paul II proclaimed a group of one hundred seventeen of these martyrs as saints.

The majority of those honored were lay-people. There were also many priests, some bishops, and religious sisters and brothers. Many of them were missionaries. Andrew Dung-Lac was a Vietnamese priest who was martyred, along with Father Peter Thi.

Andrew Trong Van Tram was a soldier and later an officer in the army, so he had to

Saint Andrew Trong Van Tram

keep his faith a secret. In 1834 the authorities discovered that Andrew, who was Catholic, was helping the missionaries. His position as an officer was taken away from him, and he was put in prison because of his faith. He was given the chance to be freed if he would stop practicing his faith. He refused to do so, and in 1835 he died for his belief.

Anthony Dich Nguyen was a wealthy farmer who contributed to the Church.

Saint Anthony Dich Nguyen

He helped the missionaries of the Paris Foreign Mission Society who served in Vietnam. He hid priests who were trying to escape government persecution. Anthony was arrested and beaten because of his faith and because he sheltered these Catholic priests.

These holy people made it possible for future generations of Vietnamese to know Christ and learn the faith.

The feast day of the martyrs of Vietnam is November 24. We also remember and honor some of these martyrs with their own feast days: Andrew Dung-Lac and Peter Thi on December 21 and Andrew Trong Van Tram on November 28.

Saint Josephine Bakhita   There are many other holy women and men who have given witness to Christ and are examples of faith, hope, and love. One example of such a life of virtue is Saint Josephine Bakhita.

Saint Josephine Bakhita

This holy woman was born in Sudan in 1869. She was kidnapped at an early age, and the frightening experience made her forget her name. Her kidnappers gave her the name Bakhita, which means "fortunate." Although she was sold into slavery and suffered greatly, she eventually was taken in by a family who treated her in a loving and kind way.

This family was Italian and took Bakhita to live with them in Italy. When their daughter, Mimmina, was born Bakhita became her nanny and friend. Mimmina and Bakhita were once left in the care of the Canossian Sisters in Italy. It was there that Bakhita came to know about God. After several months, Bakhita, who was now in her twenties, received the Sacraments of Christian Initiation and was given the new name, Josephine. It was January 9, 1890.

Bakhita became more aware of God, and her love for him grew. She believed that God had led her to him, almost as if he had been guiding her by the hand. So Bakhita asked to stay with the Canossian Sisters. She wanted to serve God. And in 1896 she became a Canossian Sister, a Daughter of Charity. She lived in the community in Italy, and she cooked, sewed, did embroidery, and answered the door.

For fifty years, she was a true witness of the love of God. Her voice was pleasing to the children, comforting to the poor and suffering, and encouraging for those who knocked at the door.

As she grew older she became painfully sick, but Mother Bakhita, as she was now known, continued to witness to faith and goodness. She did not complain about her illness but put her hope in Christ. She died in 1947 at the Canossian convent in Italy. A crowd gathered at the convent and asked for her protection from Heaven. The fame of her holiness has spread all around the world, and many ask for her intercession.

We look to the saints as examples for living the virtues of faith, hope, and love. There are many people around us who live by these virtues, too. We thank God for all these people in our lives.

WE RESPOND
Discuss some other saints that you know about. In what ways did these saints show that they were Christ's followers? How can we follow their example?

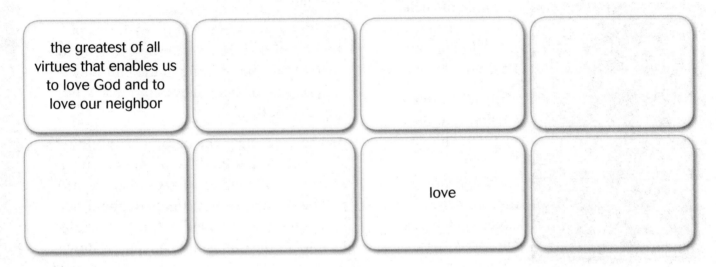

PROJECT

Show What *you* Know

Make a memory game using the Key Words. Write the remaining Key Words and definitions in different squares. Then, cover each square with a sticky note or scrap paper. Play the game by asking a partner to choose squares to find matching pairs of Key Words and definitions.

the greatest of all virtues that enables us to love God and to love our neighbor			
		love	

Make *it* Happen

What are some ways that you can show faith, hope, and love? Make a list here:

_____

_____

_____

_____

_____

↳ **DISCIPLE CHALLENGE** Look over your ideas. Circle one that you will live out this week at school, at home, and in the community.

Pray Today

Dear God,
I know you created me out of love.
You love me no matter what—just the way I am.
God, you see my hidden talents and know what I can do.
Sometimes I am not happy being me.
Help me to see myself as you see me.
Amen.

DISCIPLE

Pray
Learn
Celebrate
Share
Choose
Live

What Would you do?

Your mother has recently started a part-time job. You notice that she doesn't have the time to do all the things that she used to do. You

_____

_____.

Remember, every day we have the opportunity to act as Jesus' disciples.

Now, pass it on!

More to Explore

The Lives of the Saints

The Church has a special process to honor people who have lived very holy lives and have witnessed to Jesus Christ. This process, is called *canonization*. During this process Church leaders examine the life of a person whose name has been submitted for sainthood. They gather proof that the person has lived a life of faith and holiness. When someone is canonized, his or her name is officially entered into the worldwide list of saints recognized by the Catholic Church. Each saint is remembered on a special day during the Church year. What is the Church's special process of becoming a saint called? For a person to be named a saint, what kind of life would they have lived?

↳ **DISCIPLE CHALLENGE** Visit www.vatican.va to find the answers to these questions about canonization.

- What are two titles that the Church gives to people of virtue who are not yet saints?

  _____

- What evidence is used to prove a person worthy of sainthood?

  _____

Take Home

Gather your family together. Look over the chart on page 250 which describes some ways to live the Beatitudes. Choose a beatitude that your family will live out this week.

_____

_____

_____

CHAPTER TEST

Write the letter of the definition that matches each term.

1. _____ faith

2. _____ love

3. _____ hope

4. _____ martyrs

a. enables us to trust in God's promise to share his life with us

b. disciples who died rather than give up their belief in Christ

c. enables us to believe in God and all that the Church teaches us

d. the greatest of all virtues that enables us to love God and our neighbor

e. a habit that comes about by our own efforts

Write True or False for the following sentences.
Then change the false sentences to make them true.

5. _____ The new commandment teaches us to love only ourselves.

_____

6. _____ The theological virtues are gifts from God that make it possible for us to have a relationship with God.

_____

7. _____ A virtue is a good habit that helps us to act according to our wants.

_____

8. _____ Love is the greatest of all virtues.

_____

Write a sentence to answer each question.

9. What does Jesus teach us in the Beatitudes?

_____

10. Choose one of the saints you learned about in this chapter. How did this person live out the theological virtues?

_____

Called to Live As Jesus' Disciples

23

✞ We Gather in Prayer

Leader: Lord, may we follow your call to do good in whatever work we do.

Reader: A reading from the holy Gospel according to John

"Whoever believes in me will do the works that I do, and will do greater ones than these, because I am going to the Father. And whatever you ask in my name, I will do, so that the Father may be glorified in the Son." (John 14:12–13)

The Gospel of the Lord.

All: Praise to you, Lord Jesus Christ.

Leader: Lord you ask us to continue your work. Be with us as we share your love and peace with others.

All: Lord, make me an instrument of your peace:
where there is hatred, let me sow love;
where there is injury, pardon;
where there is doubt, faith;
where there is despair, hope;
where there is darkness, light;
where there is sadness, joy.

O divine Master, grant that I may not
    so much seek
to be consoled as to console,
to be understood as to understand,
to be loved as to love.
For it is in giving that we receive,
it is in pardoning that we are pardoned,
it is in dying that we are born
    to eternal life.

Amen.

Jesus calls the baptized to serve him in the priesthood of the faithful.

WE GATHER

✝ *We are here to do your will, Lord.*

Think of a time when a group that you were part of was given a job to do. What was the job? How did the group get it done? Did different people do different things? Why or why not?

WE BELIEVE

When Jesus was baptized at the Jordan, the Spirit of the Lord came upon him. This anointing by the Holy Spirit marked Jesus as priest, prophet, and king. Our anointing at Baptism makes us sharers in Christ's role as priest, prophet, and king.

Jesus offered the greatest sacrifice. No one else could offer the sacrifice that Jesus did. He gave himself to save us from sin and to bring us God's own life. Jesus Christ is the one true priest.

All those who are baptized share in Christ's priestly mission. This is known as the **priesthood of the faithful**. In the priesthood of the faithful, each and every one of us is called to:

- worship God

- spread the Good News of Jesus Christ

- serve one another and the Church.

In the Sacrament of Holy Orders, priests and bishops become members of the ordained priesthood. They participate in Christ's priestly mission in a unique way. They receive the grace to act in the name of and in the person of Christ.

Being part of the priesthood of the faithful is not the same thing as being an ordained priest. However, members of the priesthood of the faithful work with ordained priests to lead and care for God's people.

priesthood of the faithful
Christ's priestly mission in which all those who are baptized share

These women and men help us to participate in Christ's priestly mission. They help us to learn the faith, to worship, and to care for the needs of others.

Living out the priesthood of the faithful

Each of us can live out the priesthood of the faithful in many ways. We can gather with our parish for the celebration of the Mass and other sacraments. When we worship God the Father, God the Son, and God the Holy Spirit we are strengthened to be more like Christ. We can also open our hearts to God by praying. We can pray for all those who lead and serve in the Church and we can ask God to help us grow together in faith. With God's grace and the help of our community, we can focus on loving God and others.

As members of the priesthood of the faithful, we are called to spread the Good News of Christ. We can tell others who Jesus is and what he means to us. We can show others who Jesus is by following his example. Our love for one another is a sign of Jesus' love

for us. So we continue to learn about Jesus' teachings and the teachings of the Church. We try to live by them to the best of our ability.

As members of the priesthood of the faithful, we are called to treat people fairly and equally. All people share the same human dignity. All people are created by God, and we should love and care for them as Jesus did. We are called to protect the rights of children and those in need. We are called to care for people who are without a home or for those who are new to our country.

All the things that we do and say can help others to believe in and follow Christ.

WE RESPOND

How can you share in Jesus' work? What is one thing you and your family can do this week to show others that you are doing the work of Jesus?

 Illustrate ways people of all ages can show they are part of the priesthood of the faithful.

The laity share in the mission to bring the Good News of Christ to the world.

WE GATHER

✝ *Christ, help us respond to your love in our lives.*

One way that God shares his love with us is through other people. How can we show God's love and care to the people in our lives?

WE BELIEVE

Because all Christians share in the priesthood of the faithful, we all share a common vocation, too. Our common vocation is to grow in holiness and spread the message of Jesus' life and saving work. An important part of our common vocation is responding to God's love throughout our lives.

We respond to God's love when we pray and participate in the sacraments. We also respond to God's love when we follow the Ten Commandments, live by the Beatitudes, and love God and others as Jesus did. When we respond to God's love, others can see Christ in us. We are witnesses to the Good News of Christ and we spread the Kingdom of God.

God calls each of us to love and serve him and the Church. He calls each of us to live out our common vocation in a particular way. We do this as laypeople, religious, or ordained ministers.

Laypeople are all the baptized members of the Church who share in the mission to bring the Good News of Christ to the world. Laypeople are also known as the Christian faithful or the laity. All Catholics begin their lives as laypeople. Most Catholics remain members of the laity for their entire lives. They follow God's call either in the single life or in marriage.

Single people and married people serve God and the Church in many ways. They share God's love in their families and parishes. A husband and wife share God's love in a special way with each other and form a new Christian family. Much of their time and energy is focused on loving and caring for their families.

Single people often devote themselves to sharing their gifts and talents with others through their work. Sometimes they care for their brothers or sisters or take on extra responsibility in caring for their parents. They may also dedicate more of their time to their parishes and local communities. In these ways they work to make the world a better, safer, and more holy place.

laypeople all the baptized members of the Church who share in the mission to bring the Good News of Christ to the world

The role of the laity Laypeople, single or married, live their faith as citizens, voters, and workers. They have a responsibility to bring the Good News of Christ to their work places and local communities. They do this when they treat others equally, fairly, and justly. Laywomen and men are called to be involved in city, state, and national governments. They also serve the Church. In these situations they often take on leadership positions and make many decisions. They have a responsibility to act and make decisions based on the teachings of Jesus and on their faith.

The Christian faithful are called to be active in their parishes. They take part in the parish community in many ways. They:

- participate in the celebration of the sacraments and parish programs

- serve as lay ecclessial ministers, on the pastoral council, as school principals or as directors of religious education, or in music, liturgy, and youth ministry

- assist during the Mass as ushers and greeters, or as altar servers, musicians, readers, and extraordinary ministers of Holy Communion.

The laity serve in their dioceses, too. They may work in or lead offices for education, worship, youth and social ministries, and other ministries.

Right now you are a member of the Christian faithful. You are called to share the Good News at home, in school, and in your neighborhood. You can take part in your parish celebrations and activities. Every day you can live as Jesus taught. You can be an example of Christian living for others.

Together with your family and your parish, you can care for the needs of others. You can help others to see Christ's love for them and his presence in the world. You can stand up for what is right and just at home, in school, around your neighborhood, and in the world. You are called by Christ to live as one of his followers.

WE RESPOND

Think of one thing you really enjoy doing as a layperson in the Church. Make up a song or poem to encourage others your age to take an active part in the Church.

_____

_____

_____

_____

_____

Now imagine yourself ten years from now. In what ways do you see yourself taking part in the work of the Church?

Women and men in religious life serve Christ, their communities, and the whole Church.

WE GATHER

✝ *Thank you Lord, for communities of religious women and men.*

Think about some promises that you have made. Why did you make them?

Who helps you to keep your promises?

WE BELIEVE

God calls some women and men to the religious life. **Religious** refers to the women and men who belong to communities of service to God and the Church. They are known as religious sisters, brothers, and priests. They devote themselves to Christ's work through the work of their communities. Religious make vows, or promises, to God. By taking these vows religious try to follow Jesus' example of living each day for God.

The vows that religious sisters, brothers, and priests often make are:

Chastity. They choose to live a life of loving service to the Church and their community. They do not marry. Instead they promise to devote themselves to the work of God and to the Church as members of their communities.

Poverty. They promise to live simply as Jesus did. They agree to share their belongings and to own no personal property. This helps them focus their hearts and minds on God without being distracted by material things.

Obedience. They promise to listen carefully to God's direction in their lives by obeying the leaders of the Church and of their communities. They serve wherever their community and the Church need them. Religious try to live the way Christ did and follow God's will.

religious women and men who belong to communities of service to God and the Church

Community life   Many religious live as a family in one community. They pray together, share their meals, and work with the other members of their community. Other religious may live away from their community and work where they are needed. Yet even when they are away, they are still part of that community.

There are different types of communities and different ways to serve as religious sisters, brothers, and priests. Some communities are set apart from the rest of society. These religious usually live in places called monasteries. They devote their lives to praying for the world. They provide for their needs through their prayer and work.

Whether they farm, prepare food to sell, or work on computers, their work is a way of prayer.

Other communities combine prayer with a life of service outside their communities. These religious sisters, brothers, and priests may serve in many different parish ministries. They may also be teachers, missionaries, doctors, nurses, or social workers. In these ways they can directly help those who are poor, elderly, suffering, or in any type of need.

Together the laity, religious, and ordained ministers make up the Church. No one group is more important or special than another. The Church needs all members to be able to continue Jesus' work. We all have a role in spreading the Good News and sharing God's great love with others.

WE RESPOND

In groups share any questions you may have about religious life. Talk about the ways religious sisters, brothers, and priests may serve in your community. Then thank God for their example of faith and service.

🎵 **Prayer of St. Francis/Oracion de San Francisco**

Make me a channel of your peace.
Where there is hatred, let me bring your love.
Where there is injury, your pardon, Lord,
And where there's doubt, true faith in you.

O Master, grant that I may never seek
So much to be consoled, as to console,
To be understood, as to understand,
To be loved, as to love with all my soul.

Hazme un instrumento de tu paz,
donde haya odio lleve yo tu amor,
donde haya injuria, tu perdón, Señor,
donde haya de haya duda fe en ti.

Maestro, ayúda me a nunca buscar
el ser consolado sino consolar,
ser entendido sino entender,
ser amado sino yo amar.

Friendships prepare us for future vocations.

WE GATHER

✝ *Lord, may we always respect ourselves and others.*

What qualities does a good friend have? How can you be a good friend to others?

WE BELIEVE

Every now and then you probably think about your future and the vocation God may be calling you to live. For most of us discovering our vocation is a process that takes many years. We are encouraged to pray and think about the things we enjoy doing. We are encouraged to think about our talents and abilities. The Holy Spirit will guide and help us as we pray about our future. Our families, friends, and parish also support us as we try to find out what God is calling us to do.

You might not realize it, but you are actually preparing for your future vocation. The ways that you are responding to God and other people in your life right now are preparing you to respond to God in the future.

Right now you are discovering the importance of responsibility, faithfulness, and self-respect. These values are essential in all of your relationships. They help make you a loving and trustworthy person. You are also learning about love and service in your families and with your friends.

Friendships are an important part of finding out what it means to be faithful to Christ and one another. Good friends are true to each other. They are honest. They keep their promises. They stand up for each other. However, friends sometimes make mistakes. They may forget something important or hurt each other's feelings. But they learn to forgive each other. They encourage each other to be fair and loving in the future.

Good friends help us to be the people God wants us to be. These friendships help us to live as disciples of Christ at home, in school, and in our neighborhood. They also prepare us to serve God in whatever vocation we accept and follow. This preparation is not only something that takes place when we are young. It happens all through life as we grow and learn more about ourselves and God's call.

WE RESPOND

Silently reflect on the ways God might be calling you to live. Then pray together this Prayer for Vocation.

Dear God,
    You have a great and loving plan for
        our world and for me.
    I wish to share in that plan fully,
        faithfully, and joyfully.
    Help me to understand what it is you
        wish me to do with my life.

    How might you be calling me to live?
    Help me to be attentive to the signs that you
        give me about preparing for the future.

    And once I have heard and understood
        your call, give me the strength and
        the grace to follow it with generosity
        and love.
    Amen.

As Catholics...

All of us are called to share in the mission of the Church. We can do this by our prayers, words, and actions. We are called to share the Good News of Christ and to live lives of holiness. Laypeople, religious, and ordained ministers can also do this as missionaries.

Missionaries serve here in our own country and in places all over the world. Various religious communities and dioceses have missionary programs for which laypeople volunteer. High school and college students, adults, and whole families can devote time to missionary work.

Missionaries may spend weeks, months, or even years doing mission work. They live with the people they serve and share their love with them. Some missionaries learn the customs and traditions of the people they serve. They may even learn a new language so that they can teach about Jesus and the Catholic faith.

Missionaries may work to build better homes, schools, and hospitals. They may teach people to farm. They may help people to provide for their needs in other ways, too. But everything missionaries do involves bringing the Good News of Christ to those who need his love and comfort.

Find out what missionary opportunities your parish and diocese offer.

Pray
Learn
Celebrate
Share
Choose
Live

PROJECT

Show What *you* Know

Using L for laypeople and/or R for religious, identify the groups that correspond to each statement.

1. _____ Through Baptism, share in the priesthood of the faithful.

2. _____ Live their faith as citizens, voters, and workers.

3. _____ Make vows of chastity, poverty, and obedience.

4. _____ May follow God's call in the married life.

5. _____ Devote themselves to Christ through the work of their religious community.

What Would *you* do?

Good friends help us to be the people God wants us to be. What advice could you give to someone about making new friends?

_____

_____

_____

_____

_____

Fast Facts

The monastery of Saint Anthony the Great is the oldest active Christian monastery in the world. Built in 356 A.D. on the burial site of Saint Anthony, the monastery is located in an oasis of the Egyptian desert.

DISCIPLE

Celebrate!

In 1963 Pope Paul VI designated the Fourth Sunday of Easter as the World Day of Prayer for Vocations. On this day, all members of the Church, throughout the world, are called to pray for those who are serving in the vocations to the priesthood and religious life, and for those whom God is calling to those vocations.

More to Explore

When a parish does not have a resident priest to serve the people, the bishop of the diocese appoints a pastoral administrator to serve the parish. Pastoral administrators may be religious sisters and brothers as well as laypeople. A pastoral administrator serves as the leader of parish life. Pastoral administrators make sure parish communities have worship, religious education, and social outreach programs. They often lead their faith communities in prayer services and community outreach. The bishop assigns a priest to celebrate the Mass and other sacraments for the parish, or the community joins with another parish for the celebration of the sacraments.

- Who might lead the parish if a priest is not available?

_____

- Who can be a pastoral administrator?

_____

- Does your parish have a pastoral administrator?

_____

Take Home

What are some ways that your family, as members of the Christian faithful, can be active in your parish?

_____

_____

_____

↳ **DISCIPLE CHALLENGE** With your family, choose one idea from your list to live out this week.

CHAPTER TEST

Circle the letter of the correct answer.

1. _____ are baptized members of the Church who share in the mission to bring the Good News of Christ to the world.

    a. Laypeople   **b.** Vows   **c.** Vocations

2. _____ are men and women who belong to communities in which they dedicate their lives to the service of God and the Church.

    a. Christian faithful   **b.** Laity   **c.** Religious

3. _____ are an important part of finding out what it means to be faithful to Christ and one another.

    a. Vocations   **b.** Laity   **c.** Friendships

4. The _____ is Christ's priestly mission in which all those who are baptized share.

    a. laypeople   **b.** ordained priesthood   **c.** priesthood of the faithful

Short Answers

5. Name three things that help us to live out the priesthood of the faithful.

    _____

6. As Christians, what is our common vocation?

    _____

7. Name three ways that laypeople can be active and serve in their parish community.

    _____

8. What are the three vows, or promises, that religious might make to God?

    _____

Write a sentence to answer each question.

9. What are two ways men and women in religious life serve others?

    _____

10. How do friendships prepare us for future vocations?

    _____

Matrimony: A Promise of Faithfulness and Love

24

✝ We Gather in Prayer

Leader: Let us bless the Lord,
by whose goodness we live
and by whose grace we love one another.
Blessed be God for ever.

All: Blessed be God for ever.

Reader: A reading from the Book of
Deuteronomy

"Hear, O Israel! The LORD is our God, the
LORD alone. Therefore, you shall love the
LORD, your God, with all your heart, and
with all your soul, and with all your
strength. Take to heart these words which
I enjoin on you today. Drill them into your
children. Speak of them at home and
abroad, whether you are busy or at rest."
(Deuteronomy 6:4–7)

The word of the Lord.

All: Thanks be to God.

Leader: May the God of hope fill us with
every joy in believing.
May the peace of Christ abound in
our hearts.
May the Holy Spirit enrich us with his gifts,
now and for ever.

All: Amen.

Marriage was part of God's plan from the very beginning.

✝ *Thank you, God, for your love and care.*

Think about any wedding photos that you may have seen. How are these photos alike? How are they different?

WE BELIEVE

God created humans to love and to be loved. He made us in his image and likeness. Because of this we are able to think, to make choices, and to love. When God created the first humans, he made them male and female. God created them to be different but equal, and he found this very good.

The differences between girls and boys, women and men are good. These differences are part of God's plan. Even though we are different, we are equal. We share the same human dignity that comes from being made in God's image.

God told the first man and woman to "Be fertile and multiply" (Genesis 1:28). In this way God blessed the first man and woman to bring new life into the world. He wanted them to have children and to share in his plan for creating the human family.

Marriage was also part of this plan. "That is why a man leaves his father and mother and clings to his wife, and the two of them become one body." (Genesis 2:24)

The importance of Matrimony We learn in the Old Testament that marriage was part of God's plan from the very beginning. We learn in the New Testament that Jesus showed the importance of marriage by attending a wedding in Cana and helping the couple who had been married. Since that time marriage has been an effective sign of Jesus' love and presence. Jesus' love is made present through the love of a husband and wife. This is what the Church celebrates in the Sacrament of Matrimony.

In the Sacrament of **Matrimony**, a man and woman become husband and wife. They promise to be faithful to each other for the rest of their lives.

In this sacrament a man and woman are united as loving partners. As a married couple they:

- promise to love and be true to each other always

- lovingly accept their children as a gift from God, not preventing conception by unacceptable means

- are strengthened by God's grace to live out their promises to Christ and each other.

With members of the Church community present, their love is blessed and strengthened by the grace of this sacrament. By this grace Christ is with the couple as they love and work. Christ shares his love with them so that they can love and forgive each other. Christ supports and strengthens them to live as loyal and trustworthy partners.

Matrimony the sacrament in which a man and woman become husband and wife and promise to be faithful to each other for the rest of their lives

WE RESPOND

Ask God to help all people live out their promises to him and to one another.

How can you be a loyal and trustworthy family member, friend, and neighbor?

Wedding at Cana,
**Notre Dame de Quebec,
Canada**

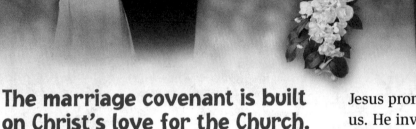

The marriage covenant is built on Christ's love for the Church.

WE GATHER

✝ *Jesus, give us the strength to keep our word.*

Describe an agreement you have made with a family member. What did you agree to do? What did he or she agree to do? How were you true, or faithful, to your agreement?

WE BELIEVE

We read in the Old Testament that God made covenants, or special agreements, with his people. God's covenant with Moses and the Israelites is very special. In this covenant God promised to protect the people and to help them live in freedom. He promised to be their God.

In return the people promised to be God's people. They agreed to live as God wanted them to live. This covenant is about the faithfulness between God and his people. God remains true to his word, and the Jewish People continue to live by the covenant today.

Christians believe there is also a new covenant. This covenant is between Jesus Christ and the Church. It is based on the Son of God's complete love for his Church.

Jesus promises to love us always and be with us. He invites us to trust and believe in him. He calls us to love him with all our hearts. He even sends the Holy Spirit to help us respond to his invitation.

In return, we, the Church, promise to love Jesus and one another. We promise to be faithful to and to follow his teachings and the teachings of the Church. We promise to do our best to live as Jesus calls us to live.

The Church sees marriage as a covenant, too. The **marriage covenant** is the life-long commitment between a man and woman to live as faithful and loving partners. The marriage covenant reminds us of Christ's covenant with the Church. Christ faithfully loves his people and keeps his covenant with them. In marriage a husband and wife try to model their love on Christ's love for his Church, sometimes called the Bride of Christ.

The love between a husband and a wife is a sign of God's love for all his people. It is a sign of Christ's love for his Church. The love between a husband and wife is meant to be generous, faithful, and complete. Their love can bring about a child, the gift of life.

marriage covenant
the life-long commitment
between a man and woman
to live as faithful and
loving partners

Key Word

A married couple promises to share and express this love only with each other. That is why polygamy, having more than one spouse at the same time, is against the marriage covenant.

Forever faithful   Christ will always love us. He will forever keep his promise to share God's life and love with us. So Christ's love for the Church is permanent. In the same way, the marriage covenant is meant to be permanent, too. Divorce breaks the marriage covenant. Catholics who are divorced and remarried are not separated from the Church, but cannot receive the Eucharist.

Once Jesus was teaching about marriage, and he said, "What God has joined together, no human being must separate" (Matthew 19:6). Christ and the Church teach us that the marriage covenant is not to be broken. In the Sacrament of Matrimony, the husband and wife agree to be loyal and true to each other for the rest of their lives.

If a married couple does have difficulty in their relationship, they can turn to their family and parish community for prayer and support. God's grace helps married couples. And they can turn to the Sacraments of Eucharist and Penance to strengthen and heal their relationship.

Often during these kinds of difficulties, children do not understand what is happening to their parents. They may be confused and sad. It is important that they not blame themselves for these difficulties. They are not responsible if their parents get separated or divorced.

Though separation and divorce are very painful, God continues to offer his healing to all who need it. Though things change in our lives, God always loves and cares for all of us.

WE RESPOND

♫ **Love Is Colored Like a Rainbow**

All the world's a family,
may our love resound
'til there's love for ev'ryone,
there will God be found.

Where there's love for ev'ryone,
There will God be found.
Though our minds may not be one,
By love are we all bound.

Refrain:
Love is colored like a rainbow
and it shines through ev'ryday.
There are many colors in a rainbow
for we love in many ways.

275

In the Sacrament of Matrimony, a man and woman promise to always love and be true to each other.

WE GATHER

✝ *Blessed Trinity, guide and inspire us.*

Preparation gets us ready for things that will be happening in the future. What are some things you prepare for? How does it help you to prepare for these things?

WE BELIEVE

A man and woman who want to be married in the Church spend time preparing to celebrate the sacrament. The parish priest or deacon usually explains to the couple the Church's teachings about marriage and makes sure that the couple are free to marry one another. Often married members of the parish community assist in preparing couples for Matrimony.

During their preparation the couples learn about the holiness and duties of Christian marriage. They grow to appreciate Jesus' place in their married life. They prepare their marriage ceremony with great detail. They also may participate in a program or retreat with other couples who are also preparing for marriage. And Catholics can celebrate the Sacrament of Penance in preparation for the Sacrament of Matrimony.

In all the other sacraments, Jesus acts through his ordained ministers to offer the grace of the sacrament. But in the Sacrament of Matrimony, the bride and groom are the celebrants. A priest or deacon does not "marry" the couple.

The bride and groom marry each other. Jesus acts through the couple and through their promise to always love and be true to each other. The priest or deacon is the official witness of the sacrament, and he blesses the union that God has joined together.

Key Word

fidelity faithfulness to a person and to duties, obligations, and promises; in marriage, the loyalty and the willingness to be true to each other always

The Rite of Marriage The celebration of the Sacrament of Matrimony often takes place within the Mass. When it does, the Liturgy of the Word includes readings selected by the couple themselves. The Rite of Marriage takes place after the Gospel is proclaimed.

The Rite of Marriage usually begins with the deacon or priest asking the couple three important questions. Are they free to give themselves in marriage? Will they love and honor each other as husband and wife for the rest of their lives? Will they lovingly accept children from God and raise them in the faith?

After answering these questions, the bride and groom then pledge their love for each other by exchanging their vows. They may say words such as these: "I take you to be my husband (or wife). I promise to be true to you in good times and in bad, in sickness and in health. I will love you and honor you all the days of my life."

The deacon or priest receives the couple's promises and asks God to strengthen their love and faithfulness and to fill them with many blessings. The rings are then blessed and the couple exchanges them as a sign of their love and fidelity. **Fidelity** is faithfulness to a person and to duties, obligations, or promises. In marriage, fidelity is loyalty and the willingness to be true to each other always.

The whole assembly prays the Prayer of the Faithful, and the Mass continues with the Liturgy of the Eucharist. After the Lord's Prayer, the priest faces the couple and prays a special prayer asking for God's favor on this new marriage. This is called the *nuptial blessing*. *Nuptial* is another word for the marriage or wedding ceremony.
Here is part of the nuptial blessing:

"Keep them faithful in marriage
   and let them be living examples of
      Christian life.

Give them the strength that comes from
   the gospel
so that they may be witnesses of Christ
   to others."

The bride and groom, if they are Catholic, receive Holy Communion. Their Communion is a sign of their union with Jesus who is the source of their love.

WE RESPOND

In the Rite of Marriage the priest prays "Let them be living examples of Christian life." Write down some ways that you can show others what it means to be an example of Christian life.

_____

_____

_____

Let us pray:
Jesus, help us all to be living examples of Christian life.

Families are very important communities.

WE GATHER

✝ *Loving God, bless and protect our families.*

What makes a group of people a family? What are some qualities that you think are necessary for a family to have?

WE BELIEVE

The Sacrament of Matrimony is a Sacrament at the Service of Communion. Those who celebrate this sacrament are strengthened to serve God and the Church.

With God's grace a husband and wife remain loyal to their marriage promises and to each other. As Christian faithful, married couples are called to share the Good News of Christ and give witness to their faith. They do this at home, at work, and in their local community. They are called to live out their fidelity to God and each other in their home, in their jobs, and in their neighborhoods.

By creating a loving family, married couples express their love. When they share the goodness of their love with others, their own love for each other and for Christ grows.

Families are communities, and they are very important to our society. Some families are small, and some are large. Some families include members who live far away. Others are made up of relatives who all live in the same area. In some families a grandparent, aunt, uncle, cousin, or even a brother or sister is the guardian who provides a home for all the children of the family.

Family responsibilities Being part of a family means having duties and responsibilities. Parents and guardians try to provide a safe, loving home for the children. They protect and care for their children, and they teach them about the world that they live in. Parents and guardians have a responsibility to show the children how to respect the rights of others, how to help people who may be in need, and how to take proper care of the gifts of God's creation.

Children learn what it means to be a disciple of Christ and member of the Church by the example of their parents, guardians, and family members. Parents and guardians are the first teachers of their children. They are called to live by their faith and to share their belief with their children. They make sure that their children are taught about Jesus Christ. Parents and guardians need to spend time praying with their children. They try to help them to learn the difference between good and evil. And they offer support and encouragement as their children make decisions about their future vocations.

Children have many duties and responsibilities, too. They are called to honor their parents and guardians by loving and obeying them. They are to do the just and good things that are asked of them, and to cooperate with their parents and guardians. They try to help out around the house by doing chores and showing their appreciation for whatever their family members do for them.

As children grow older, the ways they show their love and appreciation often change. But the love between children and their parents and guardians is meant to stay strong and to continue to grow.

WE RESPOND

In groups come up with a slogan that encourages families to be loving, faithful communities. Then design a billboard to show others what wonderful things can happen in families where there is love for God and one another.

As Catholics...

Christian families are called to be communities of faith, hope, and love. Every family is called to be a domestic Church, or a "Church in the home." It is in the family that we can first feel love and acceptance. We can experience Jesus' love when our family members love and care for us. We can learn to forgive and be forgiven, to grow in faith as we pray and worship together. In our families we can learn to be disciples of Jesus and to help and comfort those in need. We can learn to stand up for what we believe and to reach out to other families in our own area and around the world.

Talk with your family about the ways that you can be a domestic Church.

Pray Learn Celebrate Share Choose Live

PROJECT

Show What *you* Know

Use your hands to communicate. Can you sign the **Key Words**: Matrimony, marriage covenant, and fidelity?

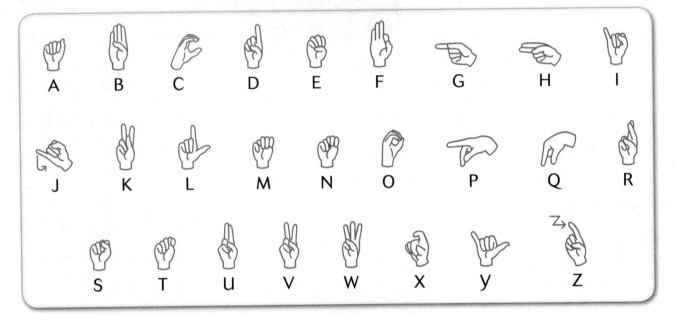

Then, write a sentence for each Key Word on the lines below.

_____

_____

_____

What's *the* Word?

Brides and grooms often select the following as a reading for the Rite of Marriage.

"Love is patient, love is kind. It is not jealous, [love] is not pompous, it is not inflated, it is not rude, it does not seek its own interests, it is not quick-tempered, it does not brood over injury, it does not rejoice over wrongdoing but rejoices with the truth. It bears all things, believes all things, hopes all things, endures all things. Love never fails." (1 Corinthians 13:4–8)

↳ **DISCIPLE CHALLENGE** Why is the above passage appropriate for the Sacrament of Matrimony?

_____

DISCIPLE

Pray
Learn
Celebrate
Share
Choose
Live

Saint Stories

Margaret was an English princess born in 1045. When she was older, she and her mother moved to Scotland where Margaret married King Malcolm. As Queen of Scotland, Margaret worked to make Scotland a better place. She gave her husband wise advice and helped him to live a life of virtue. They prayed together and fed the poor. Margaret and Malcolm had eight children. She was devoted to her family, her faith, and the people of Scotland. She wanted the Scots to learn and practice their faith, so she made great efforts to get good teachers and had churches built. Margaret is a great example to wives and mothers.

↳ DISCIPLE CHALLENGE

- Underline the phrase that describes how Margaret helped the Scots learn and practice their faith.

Visit the *Lives of the Saints* on www.webelieveweb.com to answer the questions about Saint Margaret.

- When is the feast day of Saint Margaret?

  _____

- What was the name of her son who became a saint?

  _____

Fast Facts

The *Catechism of the Catholic Church* states, "Marriage is based on the consent of the contracting parties, that is, on their will to give themselves, each to the other, mutually and definitively, in order to live a covenant of faithful and fruitful love" (*CCC*, 1662).

Take Home

Talk with your family about some ways that a family can be a domestic Church, or "a Church in the home."

Make a list here:

_____

_____

_____

_____

Put a check next to each way your family shows it is a domestic Church.

281

Short Answers

1. How do children first learn what it means to be a disciple of Christ and a member of the Church?

_____

2. What is the role of the priest or deacon in the Sacrament of Matrimony?

_____

3. What are the three questions the couple is asked by a priest or deacon at the beginning of the Rite of Marriage?

_____

4. How does the marriage covenant remind us of Christ's love for the Church?

_____

Write True or False for the following sentences.
Then change the false sentences to make them true.

5. _____ Marriage is an effective sign of Jesus' love and presence.

_____

6. _____ Fidelity is the sacrament in which a man and woman become husband and wife, and promise to be faithful to each other for the rest of their lives.

_____

7. _____ The Sacrament of Matrimony is a Sacrament of Christian Initiation.

_____

8. _____ Being part of a family means having duties and responsibilities.

_____

Write a sentence to answer each question.

9. How can a man and woman prepare to celebrate the Sacrament of Matrimony?

_____

10. In the Rite of Marriage, what do the bride and groom promise each other?

_____

Holy Orders: A Promise of Service for the People of God

25

✝ We Gather in Prayer

Leader: Christ, you call us to follow you every day of our lives. Give us the courage to trust in you as your first disciples did.

Reader 1: A reading from the holy Gospel according to Matthew

"As he was walking by the Sea of Galilee, he saw two brothers, Simon who is called Peter, and his brother Andrew, casting a net into the sea; they were fishermen. He said to them, 'Come after me, and I will make you fishers of men.' At once they left their nets and followed him."

(Matthew 4:18–20)

Reader 2: "As Jesus passed on from there, he saw a man named Matthew sitting at the customs post. He said to him, 'Follow me.' And he got up and followed him."

(Matthew 9:9)

The Gospel of the Lord.

All: Praise to you, Lord Jesus Christ.

♫ Come, Follow Me

Refrain:
Come, follow me, come, follow me.
I am the way, the truth, and the life.
Come, follow me, come, follow me.
I am the light of the world, follow me.

You call us to serve with a generous heart;
in building your kingdom each one has a part.
Each person is special in your kingdom of love.
Yes, we will follow you, Jesus!

(Refrain)

Jesus shares his ministry in a special way with the Apostles.

WE GATHER

✝ *Jesus, help us to serve one another.*

Have you ever worked together with friends or classmates to complete a task? Who gave the directions? How did you know what to do?

WE BELIEVE

From the beginning of his ministry, Jesus Christ invited people to be his disciples. Jesus called all types of people to follow him. He called people who were young and old, wealthy and in need. Fishermen and tax collectors followed him. Women and men, fathers and mothers, brothers and sisters, and friends and strangers believed in Jesus and became his disciples.

One day Jesus went to a mountain where he spent all night praying to his Father. "When day came, he called his disciples to himself, and from them he chose Twelve, whom he also named apostles." (Luke 6:13) Jesus chose the Apostles to share in his ministry in a special way.

Jesus spoke to the Apostles about God his Father. He taught them about the Kingdom of God. He showed them ways to bring God's love to people, especially those who were poor or who were ignored by the rest of society. He then sent the Apostles out to share his message. He sent them to preach and to cure people in his name. He told them, "Whoever receives the one I send receives me" (John 13:20).

Jesus did not ask the Apostles to do his work alone. He called the twelve of them to work together. "He summoned the Twelve and began to send them out two by two." (Mark 6:7) They shared the same work, and this work united them wherever they were.

Once the Apostles argued among themselves about who was the greatest. Jesus told them that whoever wanted to be great must be a servant to the others. He told them, "I am among you as the one who serves" (Luke 22:27). Jesus wanted his Apostles to follow his example and to lead others by serving them.

In groups talk about the ways family members serve one another and the ways members of a neighborhood serve their community. Then write down some ways that you serve your family and your classmates.

_____

_____

_____

_____

_____

_____

_____

Christ Appearing to His Disciples at the Mount of Galilee
Duccio di Buoninsegna (1278–1319)

The mission of the Apostles Before he returned to his Father, Jesus promised his Apostles that they would receive the Gift of the Holy Spirit. The Holy Spirit would help them to remember all that Jesus had said and done. The Holy Spirit would help them to continue Christ's saving mission.

After his Death and Resurrection, the risen Jesus gave the Apostles the authority to continue his work. He commissioned them, or sent them out, saying, "'Peace be with you. As the Father has sent me, so I send you.' And when he said this, he breathed on them and said to them, 'Receive the holy Spirit'" (John 20:21–22).

With these words Jesus trusted the Apostles with his own work, and they received their mission. Jesus sent them out to all parts of the world to lead his community and to bring people to share in his Kingdom. They were to teach and to baptize people. The Holy Spirit strengthened the Apostles to carry out their mission.

WE RESPOND

Pray that the whole Church, strengthened by the Holy Spirit, may continue to follow Jesus and spread the Good News to all the world.

Holy Orders is the sacrament through which the Church continues the Apostles' mission.

WE GATHER

✝ *Lord, bless us to continue your work.*

Who are some people who help you to grow in faith? How do they help you to believe in and follow Christ?

WE BELIEVE

Strengthened and guided by the Holy Spirit, the Apostles went out to preach the Good News and baptize. They helped others to believe in and follow Jesus Christ. Everywhere they went the Apostles gathered believers into local Church communities. With the help of each local Church, they chose leaders and ministers for the community. The Apostles laid hands on those chosen and commissioned them. In this way the Apostles passed on what Christ had given them: the Gift of the Holy Spirit and the authority to carry out the mission of Jesus Christ.

These local leaders served their communities in various ways. Some were responsible for the worship within the community. Some assisted in caring for those who were sick or in need. Others led the community by preaching the Good News of Jesus Christ and sharing the teachings of the Apostles. All of these leaders continued the Apostles' work in their local communities and acted on behalf of the Apostles. They continued the Apostles' ministry and were the successors of the Apostles. They eventually became known as bishops.

Other local leaders who worked with the bishops became known as priests. And those who assisted in the worship and service of the community were called deacons.

As the Church continued to grow, the bishops, the successors of the Apostles, commissioned others to continue the ministry of the Apostles. In this way, the leadership of the Church throughout history can be traced back to the Apostles.

Early Christian Communities

From one generation to the next, the Holy Spirit guided Church leaders to share Jesus' authority with others. They did this by the laying on of hands and by a special prayer to the Holy Spirit. The Church still does this today in the Sacrament of Holy Orders.

The importance of Holy Orders Holy Orders is the sacrament in which baptized men are ordained to serve the Church as deacons, priests, and bishops. It is a Sacrament at the Service of Communion. While there are many ministries in the Church, deacons, priests, and bishops are the only ordained ministers. Those who receive Holy Orders take on a special mission in leading and serving the People of God.

In the Sacrament of Holy Orders:

- Men are ordained by the bishop's laying on of hands and prayer of consecration.

- Those ordained receive the grace necessary to carry out their ministry to the faithful.

- Men are imprinted with an indelible sacramental character, a permanent spiritual seal on their souls.

As Catholics...

The pope is the Bishop of Rome because he is the successor of the Apostle Peter, who was the first leader of the Church of Rome. As the Bishop of Rome, the pope has a special responsibility to care for and lead the Church. The bishops are called to work with the pope to lead and guide the whole Church. The bishops, with the pope as their head, are called to watch over all those under their care, especially those who are in need in any way.

- The Church, through its ordained ministers, continues the mission that Jesus Christ first gave to his Apostles.

Some baptized men, single or married, are ordained permanent deacons. They share in Christ's mission and remain deacons for life. They may work to support themselves and their families. Other baptized men are ordained deacons as a step in their preparation for the priesthood. These men remain unmarried and continue their study to become ordained priests.

Just as all priests are first ordained deacons, all bishops are first ordained priests. The pope, with the help of other bishops and Church members, chooses some priests to be ordained bishops.

Holy Orders the sacrament in which baptized men are ordained to serve the Church as deacons, priests, and bishops

WE RESPOND

In what ways do the members of your parish work with the priests and deacons who serve you?

Design a thank-you card to show your appreciation for the priests and deacons who serve your parish.

Bishops, priests, and deacons serve the Church in different ways.

WE GATHER

✝ *Holy Spirit, bless our ordained ministers.*

In your school there are many leaders. They are of different ages and have different responsibilities. Name some of these people and talk about the different ways they show that they are leaders.

WE BELIEVE

Bishops, priests, and deacons have different roles and responsibilities in the Church. Through the Sacrament of Holy Orders, they are given the grace to serve God's people. Preaching the Good News of Jesus Christ and leading the Church is part of each of their ministries. However, bishops are fully and completely responsible for the care of the whole Church.

Bishops are the successors of the Apostles. They are called to continue the Apostles' mission of leadership and service in the Church. A bishop usually leads and cares for a diocese. A diocese is a local community of Christian faithful. A diocese is made up of parish communities, schools and colleges, and even hospitals.

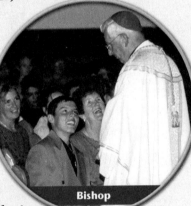

Bishop

The bishops are the chief teachers of the Church. They are called to make sure that the faithful receive the teachings of Jesus and the beliefs of our faith. The bishops help us to understand and live out these teachings.

The bishops are the chief leaders and pastors of the Church. They have authority in their dioceses, and together with the pope they are the pastors of the whole Church. The bishops lead their people and oversee the work of their dioceses. In the United States, the bishops meet twice a year to make decisions that affect the Church in our country.

The bishops are the chief priests in their dioceses. They make sure that the Christian faithful in the diocese have the opportunity to participate in the celebration of the sacraments, most especially the Eucharist. By providing for the liturgy of the diocese, the bishop helps all the faithful to live Christian lives and to grow in holiness.

The bishop does not care for his diocese by himself. He appoints priests to represent him and carry out his ministry in the parishes. The bishop also appoints deacons, religious, and lay women and men to work with the priests in caring for the people of his diocese.

Priests are ordained by their bishops and are called to serve the Christian faithful by leading, teaching, and most especially celebrating the Eucharist and other sacraments. Priests are co-workers with their bishops. There are two kinds of priests: diocesan priests and religious priests. Religious priests are those who belong to religious communities.

Diocesan priests are ordained to serve in a diocese. They usually serve in parishes. But diocesan priests may also serve in hospitals, schools, the military, prisons, or other institutions.

Priest

Bishops usually appoint one priest to serve as the pastor of a parish. The pastor is responsible to see that the life of the parish grows stronger. He is especially responsible for the celebration of the liturgy, prayer, education, care for those in need, and upkeep of parish buildings. He leads the parish community in spreading the Good News of Jesus Christ and working for justice and peace in the community. The pastor is not alone in doing his work. There may be other priests and many women and men of the parish who work with him.

Religious priests serve wherever their communities send them. They usually take the vows of chastity, poverty, and obedience. They might be pastors of parishes, or they might be missionaries, teachers, doctors, writers, or work in any field where their service is needed. They might spend their time in prayer and work within their community. All priests are called to make prayer, most especially the Mass, the heart of their ministry. This strengthens them to help the Church grow in faith through prayer and worship.

Missionary Priest

Deacons are baptized men who are not priests but are ordained by their bishops to the work of service for the Church. They are ordained by their bishops for an important role in worship, leadership, and social ministries.

Deacons are called to serve the community in worship. They may preach the Word of God and baptize new members of the Church. They may witness marriages and preside at Christian burials.

At Mass they proclaim the Gospel, preach, prepare the altar, distribute Holy Communion, and send the gathered community out to serve others.

Deacons help the parish to reach out to people in the community. They have a special responsibility to care for those who are suffering or who are in need. In these ways deacons are called to the ministry of service.

Deacon

bishops the successors of the Apostles who are ordained to continue the Apostles' mission of leadership and service in the Church

priests ordained ministers who serve the Christian faithful by leading, teaching, and most especially celebrating the Eucharist and other sacraments

deacons baptized men who are not priests but are ordained to the work of service for the Church

WE RESPOND

There are many people who minister to and lead the members of your parish community. Name some of them and explain their ministries. Which of them are ordained ministers? What is your role in your Church community?

_____

_____

_____

_____

The laying on of hands and prayer of consecration are the main parts of the Sacrament of Holy Orders.

WE GATHER

✝ *God, we pray for all who hear your call to serve the Church.*

God calls each of us to love and serve him. What are some ways that you can hear God calling you?

WE BELIEVE

A candidate for Holy Orders is a baptized man who has been called by God to serve as deacon or priest and has been accepted into a period of preparation. Candidates spend several years preparing in a special school called a seminary. They pray daily and participate in the liturgy. They study Scripture and learn Church teachings and practices. They develop caring ways to listen to people's needs and to help them with their problems. In these ways they grow into ministers who care for and serve a community. The celebration of the Sacrament of Holy Orders, or ordination, marks the end of the candidates' seminary preparation and the beginning of their ordained ministry.

A priest who is to become a bishop has already been serving the Church as a member of the ordained priesthood. He is not called a candidate but a bishop-elect.

The Sacrament of Holy Orders is a wonderful celebration for the Church. The whole Church community in the diocese gathers together for the celebration. A bishop is always the celebrant of this sacrament. Only a bishop can ordain another bishop, a priest, or a deacon.

The celebration of Holy Orders always takes place during the celebration of the Mass. The ordination of deacons, priests, and bishops is similar. In all three cases, the Liturgy of the Word includes readings about ministry and service. After the Gospel reading, those to be ordained are presented to the bishop celebrant.

The celebrant speaks to the people about the roles these men will have in the Church. He reflects on the ways they are called to lead and serve in Jesus' name. He talks about their responsibilities to teach, to lead, and to worship. The celebrant then speaks directly to those being ordained. He asks them some questions to make sure that they understand their responsibilities and are willing to accept them.

The celebrant invites the whole assembly to pray. They pray that God will bless those to be ordained so that they may serve as Jesus calls them to serve.

Signs of Service

Deacon	He is given a stole as a sign of his ministry as deacon. It is worn across the left shoulder and fastened at the right.
	He is given the *Book of the Gospels* as a sign of the deacon's role in preaching the Good News.
Priest	His stole is rearranged as a sign of his ministry as priest. It is now worn around the neck and down over his chest.
	The palms of his hands are anointed so that he can serve to make the People of God holy through the sacraments.
	He is given the chalice and paten as a sign that he may now celebrate the Eucharist to offer the sacrifice of the Lord.
Bishop	His head is anointed, and he is blessed to perform his duties as bishop.
	He is given a miter, a pointed hat that is a sign of his office as bishop.
	He is given a ring as a sign of his faithfulness to Christ and the Church.
	He is given a pastoral staff as a sign of his role as shepherd. He will care for and watch over the Church, the flock of Christ.

Now the laying on of hands takes place. During the laying on of hands, the bishop celebrant prays in silence. When a priest is ordained, the other priests who are present also lay their hands upon the candidate.

This is a sign of their unity in priesthood and service to the diocese. When a bishop is ordained, other bishops lay their hands upon the bishop-elect as a sign of their unity in service to the Church.

After the laying on of hands, the bishop celebrant prays the prayer of consecration. Through this prayer these men are consecrated or dedicated for a particular service in the Church. The bishop celebrant extends his hands, and by the power of the Holy Spirit consecrates the candidates or the bishop-elect to continue Jesus' ministry. The words of the prayer of consecration are different for deacons, priests, and bishops.

The laying on of hands and the prayer of consecration are the main parts of the Sacrament of Holy Orders. It is through these two actions that the candidates or the bishop-elect are ordained.

They are forever marked by Holy Orders. The newly ordained are presented with signs of their service and ministry in the Church.

WE RESPOND

Design your own sign of service to show others that you are a follower of Christ and member of the Church. It might be an object, logo, or image.

PROJECT

Show What *you* Know

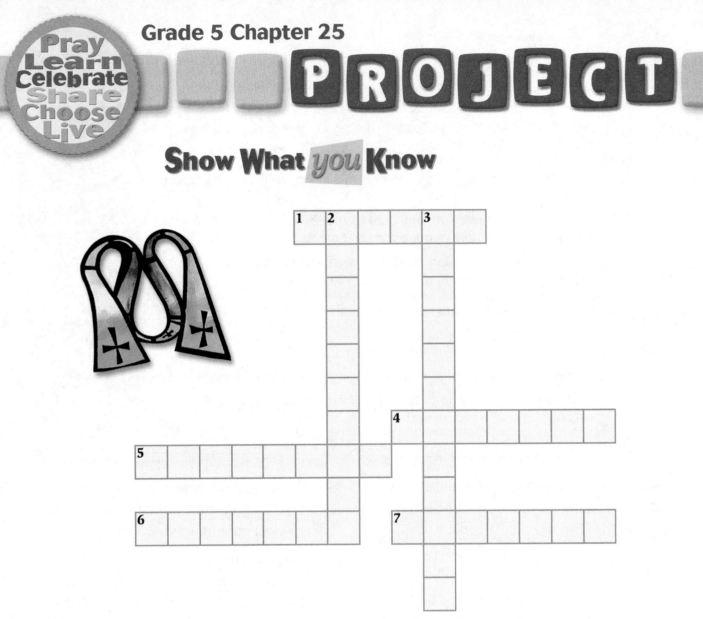

Across

1. Bishops, priests, and deacons serve the _____ in different ways.

4. ordained ministers who serve the Christian faithful by leading, teaching, and most especially celebrating the Eucharist and other sacraments

5. Jesus shared his ministry in a special way with the _____.

6. baptized men who are not priests but are ordained to the work of service for the Church

7. the successors of the Apostles who are ordained to continue the Apostles' mission of leadership

Down

2. the sacrament in which baptized men are ordained to serve the Church as deacons, priests, and bishops (two words)

3. The laying on of hands and prayer of _____ are the main parts of the Sacrament of Holy Orders.

DISCIPLE

Pray
Learn
Celebrate
Share
Choose
Live

Fast Facts

The title of *Monsignor* is given to certain priests who have been honored by the pope for faithful and esteemed service to the Church. The bishop of a diocese usually nominates candidates for this honor and submits them to the Vatican for approval.

Saint Stories

Andrew Kim Taegon was baptized a Catholic in Korea when he was fifteen years old. He later traveled over a thousand miles to China to study for the priesthood. He became Korea's first native priest. He was famous for the faith and witness he gave to Christ. At that time, the Church in Korea was persecuted. Father Andrew helped many Christians escape to China. He also tried to bring some French missionaries to Korea. Because he tried to continue the work of Christ and the Church, he was captured and put to death. He was the first of 103 Korean Catholics to be martyred for their faith. He was only twenty-five years old when he was killed. His feast day is September 20.

↳ DISCIPLE CHALLENGE

- Underline the phrase that describes why Father Andrew was put to death.
- What hardships did Father Andrew go through for his vocation?

_____

_____

Visit *Lives of the Saints* on **www.webelieveweb.com** to learn more about saints and holy people.

Take Home

Jesus called his Apostles to work together. As family members we may have certain daily work we are expected to do. With your family, take time to make a list of family tasks that need to be done on a daily/weekly basis.

_____

_____

_____

293

Choose a word(s) from the box to complete each sentence.

1. _____ is the sacrament in which baptized men are ordained to serve as deacons, priests, and bishops.

2. _____ are ordained ministers who serve the Christian faithful by leading, teaching, and most especially celebrating the Eucharist and other sacraments.

3. _____ are baptized men who are not priests but are ordained to the work of service for the Church.

4. _____ are the successors of the Apostles who are ordained to continue the Apostles' mission of leadership and service in the Church.

Deacons

Bishops

Holy Orders

Priests

Eucharist

Short answers

5. How did the Holy Spirit help the Apostles carry out Jesus' mission?

_____

6. Who is the celebrant of Holy Orders?

_____

7. What was the Apostles' mission?

_____

8. What are the two main parts of the Sacrament of Holy Orders?

_____

Write a sentence to answer each question.

9. What is the importance of the Sacrament of Holy Orders?

_____

10. What are two ways deacons serve the community in worship?

_____

One, Holy, Catholic, and Apostolic

26

✝ We Gather in Prayer

Leader: Blessed be the name of the Lord.

All: Now and for ever.

Reader: A reading from the Letter of Saint Paul to the Ephesians

". . . you are fellow citizens with the holy ones and members of the household of God, built upon the foundation of the apostles and prophets, with Christ Jesus himself as the capstone."
(Ephesians 2:19, 20)

The Word of the Lord.

All: Thanks be to God.

Leader: The Church is one.

All: Make us one, Lord.

Leader: The Church is holy.

All: Share your holiness with us, Lord.

Leader: The Church is catholic.

All: Lord, help us to share your good news with people everywhere.

Leader: The Church is apostolic.

All: Lord, thank you for the faith of the Apostles passed on to us through all generations.

Bless us always. Amen.

The Church is one and holy.

WE GATHER

✝ *Loving Jesus, lead us to unity and holiness.*

What are some qualities or characteristics that describe you?

How can these qualities and characteristics help you to grow closer to your family and community? your family and community to grow closer to you?

WE BELIEVE

In the sacraments we receive God's grace to live as Jesus' followers. We are united by our belief in Christ and celebrate our faith as a community. In the sacraments we profess our faith. In the celebration of the Eucharist, we do this when we pray the Nicene Creed. In the Nicene Creed we state that "we believe in one, holy, catholic and apostolic Church." These four characteristics are the **marks of the Church**. The Church is one, holy, catholic, and apostolic.

The first mark is that the Church is one. We read in the New Testament that there is "one body and one Spirit, . . . one Lord, one faith, one baptism; one God and Father of all" (Ephesians 4:4, 5–6).

The Church is one because all her members believe in the one Lord, Jesus Christ. The Church is one because we all share the same Baptism, and together are the one Body of Christ. The Church is one because we are guided and united by the one Holy Spirit. The Church is one because of the leadership of the pope and bishops, the sacraments we celebrate, and the laws of the Church that help us to live as members of the Church.

Cathedral of Our Lady of the Angels, Los Angeles, California

> **Key Word**
>
> **marks of the Church**
> the four characteristics of the Church: one, holy, catholic, and apostolic

The second mark of the Church is that she is holy. God alone is good and holy. But God shared his holiness with all people by sending his Son to us. Christ shares his holiness with us today through the Church, where we are first made holy in Baptism. Throughout our lives God and the Church call us to holiness. Our holiness comes from the gift of grace that we receive in the sacraments. It comes from the gifts of the Holy Spirit and from the practice of the virtues. Our holiness grows as we respond to God's love in our lives, and from living as Christ asks us to live.

God calls the whole Church to holiness. The Christian faithful, religious sisters and brothers, and ordained ministers live out this call in different ways. These differences make the Church an amazing sign of God's goodness and holiness.

We are not perfect. We do not always live according to Christ's example or God's law for us. Yet we always have the chance to begin again. The sacraments help us to turn to God and his love. When we follow Jesus' example to pray, respect all people, live fairly, and work for justice and peace, we grow in holiness.

WE RESPOND

With a partner describe the different events that show that your parish is one and holy. Then role-play some of these events.

What is one thing you can do this week that can help you grow in holiness?

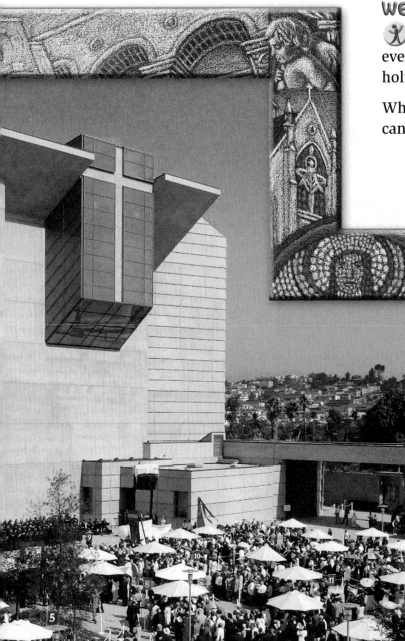

As Catholics...

The laws of the Church are found on page 329. They are also called the precepts of the Church. These laws remind us that we are called to grow in holiness and serve the Church. They help us to see that loving God and others is connected to our life of prayer and worship and to our life of service. They guide our behavior and teach us how we should act as members of the Church.

The laws of the Church help us to know and fulfill our responsibilities as members of the Church and to unite us as followers of Jesus Christ. They make all Church members more aware that the Church is one, holy, catholic, and apostolic.

Read the laws of the Church together and discuss ways you can follow them.

The Church is catholic and apostolic.

WE GATHER

✝ *Holy Spirit, inspire us to spread God's Word.*

🚶 With a partner list some words that can be described by the adjective *universal*. Share your words with the class.

_____

_____

_____

_____

_____

_____

_____

WE BELIEVE

The third mark of the Church is that she is catholic. The word *catholic* means "universal." The Church is worldwide, and it is open to all people everywhere. The Church has been universal since her very beginning. Jesus commissioned his Apostles saying, "Go, therefore, and make disciples of all nations, baptizing them in the name of the Father, and of the Son, and of the holy Spirit" (Matthew 28:19).

Some of the Apostles traveled to different parts of the world. They preached the Gospel message. They baptized believers and established local Church communities. The Church continued to grow, and today there are Catholics all across the world.

The Church is truly catholic, or universal. She is made up of people from all over the world. Often Catholics have different ways of living, dressing, and celebrating. These different customs and traditions are part of the Church's life. They add beauty and wonder to the Church. Yet with all of our differences, we are still one. We are united by our faith in Jesus and by our membership in the Church. We are joined by the celebration of the Seven Sacraments and by our Holy Father, the pope, and all of the bishops. We are the Body of Christ and the People of God.

We experience the Church as worldwide in our parishes, too. Our parish community is a community of faith. Together we grow and celebrate our faith.

298

In this family of faith we learn what it means to be Catholic. We are joined with Catholics who may be very different from us. We may be from different countries. We may speak different languages and have different customs. But we are united by our love for Christ and our common call to holiness. These things strengthen us to love as Jesus loved and to continue his work for justice and peace.

Because the Church is catholic, she is missionary, too. The Church welcomes all people as Jesus Christ did. We are to tell everyone about the saving love of Christ and the Church.

The fourth mark of the Church is that she is apostolic. The word *apostolic* comes from the word *apostle*. The Church is apostolic because she is built on the faith of the Apostles. We read about their ministry and the work of the early Church in the New Testament. The faith we profess and practice is based on some of the earliest creeds, or written statements of belief. The Apostles' Creed tells us about Jesus, his teachings, and the teachings of the Apostles. We still pray the Apostles' Creed today.

The Church is apostolic because the life and leadership of the Church is based on that of the Apostles. Jesus chose the Apostles to care for and lead the community of believers. He gave them the mission of spreading the Good News and baptizing new members of the Church.

The bishops, the successors of the Apostles, are called to continue the ministry of the Apostles. Today the pope and bishops carry out the Apostles' mission, and all baptized Catholics share in this work.

WE RESPOND

In groups, discuss different ways that the Church is catholic and apostolic. Then illustrate some of these ways.

What is one thing you can do this week to welcome others and share your faith with them?

Let us pray the Apostles' Creed together. (See page 325.)

The Church respects all people.

WE GATHER

✞ *God our Father, help us cherish all your children.*

List some things that you have in common with:

your classmates

_____

your neighbors

_____

people in your country

_____

people in our world.

_____

Then as a class discuss how these things can bring people together.

Ecumenical Prayer Service
Toronto, Canada

WE BELIEVE

Christians believe in and follow Jesus Christ. At the Last Supper Jesus prayed, "I pray not only for them, but also for those who will believe in me through their word, so that they may all be one" (John 17:20–21). Yet Christians are not one as Jesus prayed. Among Christians there are Catholics, Orthodox Christians, and Episcopalians. There are Lutherans, Methodists, Presbyterians, Baptists, and many others. There are some very important things that we have in common.

Christians are baptized and believe that Jesus is both divine and human. They believe that he died and rose to save us from sin. Christians also share the belief that the Bible was inspired by the Holy Spirit.

The Catholic Church is the Church founded by Christ himself. We are working with other Christian communities to bring about the unity of the Church. This work to promote the unity of all Christians is called **ecumenism**.

The differences among Christians are serious, but the Church is committed to the work of ecumenism. Each year in January the Church celebrates a week of prayer for Christian Unity. Together Christians try to grow in love and understanding.

Respect for all faiths Christians are people of faith who believe in and follow Jesus Christ. Not everyone in the world believes in Jesus as Christians do, but that does not mean that they are not people of faith. We respect all Christians and acknowledge that elements of sanctification and truth are found in other Christian communities and in other faiths. We respect the right of others to practice and live their faith in different ways.

The Christian faith has a special connection to the Jewish faith. Jesus himself grew up as a Jew.

So the Jewish People are our ancestors in faith. Many Christian beliefs and practices come from the Jewish faith. Today Jewish People everywhere continue to live their faith in the one true God.

People of other religions and faiths include Muslims, Buddhists, Hindus, and native tribes. There are many other people of faith. They, too, follow a set of beliefs and show their faith in different ways. The Church respects the rights of all people to practice their faith. We join with people of all faiths in living and working to make the world a better place.

> Key Word
>
> **ecumenism** the work to promote unity among all Christians

Studying the Torah
in a Jewish synagogue.

Studying the Koran
in a Muslim mosque.

WE RESPOND

Imagine that you are writing an invitation to Jesus asking him to come and give a talk on "Faith in our World." What questions would you ask him to answer? What do you think other faith community leaders would ask him to speak about?

The Church works for justice and peace.

WE GATHER

✝ *Loving God, guide our work for justice and peace.*

What do you think the word *justice* means? How would you describe a just action? a just person? a just law?

WE BELIEVE

Justice is something we often hear about. Justice means respect for the rights of others. When we are just we give people the things that are rightfully theirs. Justice is based on the simple fact that all people have human dignity. All people have the value and worth that come from being created in God's image. We believe that all people have the same human rights. They have the right to practice faith and have a family. They have the right to receive an education and to work. They have the right to equal treatment and to safety. They have the right to housing and to health care. And all people have the most basic human right, the right to life.

Jesus respected the dignity of others and protected their rights. He began his ministry by saying,

"The Spirit of the Lord is upon me,
because he has anointed me
to bring glad tidings to the poor.
He has sent me to proclaim liberty to captives
and recovery of sight to the blind,
to let the oppressed go free,
and to proclaim a year acceptable to the Lord."
(Luke 4:18–19)

Jesus then did all these things. He worked to be sure that people had what they needed. He healed the sick and fed the hungry. He listened to people when they told him about their needs. Jesus stood up for those who were neglected or ignored by society. And he spoke out against leaders who did not take care of people.

Jesus wanted his disciples to care for the needs of others, too. He wanted them to be just and fair. The whole Church continues Jesus' work for justice. The pope and our bishops remind us to respect the rights of all people. They are called to teach us about the need to protect human life, to care for those who are poor, and to work for peace and justice. Our parishes serve those in need and work together to build better communities. In our families, schools, and neighborhoods, we try to live out Jesus' command to love others as Jesus loves us.

Together we can work to change the things in society that allow unjust behaviors and conditions to exist. With other Church members, we can visit those who are sick or elderly. We can volunteer in soup kitchens or homeless shelters. We can help those who have disabilities. We can help those from other countries to find homes and jobs and to learn the language. We can write to the leaders of our state and country asking them for laws that protect children and those in need.

Stewardship God freely created the world to share his love and goodness and to show his glory and power. God's creation is a marvelous gift for which we praise him. We also praise God for giving humans the responsibility to care for his creation. God asks us to protect and take care of creation—people, animals, and the resources of the world. He asks us to be stewards of creation. **Stewards of creation** are those who take care of everything that God has given them.

God intended all people to use the goods of his creation. We use God's gifts each day for our food, our shelter, our work, and even for our relaxation. But it is important to make sure that all people share in the goodness of creation. We need to be mindful that people in many places in the world do not have the water, food, or fuel that they need to survive.

Justice is sharing the resources that come from God's creation with those who do not have them. Justice is using the resources we have in a responsible way. We cannot use so much food, water, and energy that there is not enough for others.

The world is not only God's gift to us. It is also his gift for the generations of people to come. We must work together to protect our environment and the good of all God's creation.

stewards of creation those who take care of everything that God has given them

WE RESPOND

How can you work for justice and peace? Make a plan of action. Include things you can do with your family and with your parish.

JUSTICE AND PEACE JUSTICE AND PEACE JUSTICE AND PEACE JUSTICE AND PEACE JUSTICE AND PEACE JUSTICE AND PEACE JUSTICE AND PEACE JUSTICE AND PEACE

PROJECT

Show What *you* Know

Complete the word webs by writing words or phrases that relate to each Key Word.

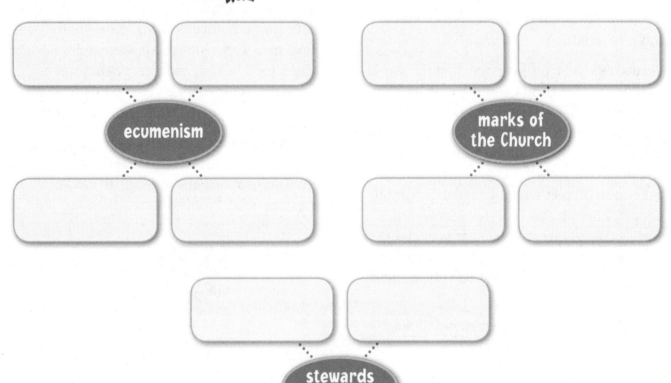

Make *it* Happen

The world is not only God's gift to us. It is also his gift for the generations of people to come. What are some ways that fifth-graders can protect our environment and the good of all God's creation?

_____

_____ **Now, pass it on!**

DISCIPLE

Pray
Learn
Celebrate
Share
Choose
Live

Fast Facts

There are over one billion Catholics in the world, which is about 17 percent of the world population. The percentage of Catholics has remained about the same for more than 35 years. The 2008 *Official Catholic Directory* lists the Catholic population in the United States as 67,117,016. Catholics represent about 22 percent of the total U.S. population.

Reality Check

What do you think "a year acceptable to the Lord" is like? (Hint: see pages 302–303.)

_____

_____

_____

Pray Today

Mary, Queen of Peace,
save us all, who have so much trust in you,
from wars, hatred, and oppression.
Make us all learn to live in peace, and educate
ourselves for peace,
do what is demanded by justice and respect
the rights of every person,
so that peace may be firmly established.
Amen.

(Pope John Paul II)

Take Home

Look over the list you wrote in *Make It Happen*. With your family, find local service projects that will help bring about one of the items on your list.

↳ **DISCIPLE CHALLENGE** Together, plan to help this local service project this week.

_____

_____

CHAPTER TEST

Write the mark of the Church that best completes each sentence.

1. The Church is _____ because God shares his holiness with us in the sacraments, and through the gifts of the Holy Spirit and the virtues.

2. The Church is _____ because all of her members believe in the one Lord, Jesus Christ, are led by the pope and bishops, and participate in the sacraments.

3. The Church is _____ because she is built on the faith of the Apostles. The Church's life and leadership is based on that of the Apostles.

4. The Church is _____ because she is universal and missionary. All people are welcomed to believe in Jesus Christ.

Short Answers

5. How are all Christians alike?

   _____

6. What is a steward of creation?

   _____

7. What is one way the Church works for justice?

   _____

8. How does the Catholic Church practice ecumenism?

   _____

Write a sentence to answer each question.

9. What are some things that unite Catholics?

   _____

10. How can we grow in holiness?

   _____

alleluia

Let us shout out our joy and happiness,
and give glory to God, the Lord of all,
because he is our King, alleluia.

SEASONAL CHAPTER 27

This liturgical chapter celebrates the entire Easter season.

EASTER

The Easter season is a special time to rejoice over the new life we have in Christ.

WE GATHER

✝ *Lord, we praise you with our hearts and voices.*

What are some exciting or joyful school or neighborhood events that you have been a part of? What make these times so happy and full of fun?

WE BELIEVE

On Easter Sunday the celebration of the Mass is very festive. It is a joyous time with bells ringing and flowers filling the church. There are other signs of new life, too. During this Mass we listen to the Gospel reading about Jesus' Resurrection.

Mark 16:1–10

Narrator: "When the sabbath was over, Mary Magdalene, Mary, the mother of James, and Salome bought spices so that they might go and anoint him. Very early when the sun had risen, on the first day of the week, they came to the tomb. They were saying to one another,

Women: 'Who will roll back the stone for us from the entrance of the tomb?'"

Narrator: "When they looked up, they saw that the stone had been rolled back; it was very large. On entering the tomb they saw a young man sitting on the right side, clothed in a white robe, and they were utterly amazed." He said to them,

Young man: "Do not be amazed! You seek Jesus of Nazareth, the crucified. He has been raised; he is not here. Behold, the place where they laid him. But go and tell his disciples and Peter, 'He is going before you to Galilee; there you will see him, as he told you.'" (Mark 16:1–7)

Narrator: The women ran from the tomb not knowing what to think. Later that morning the risen Christ appeared to Mary Magdalene, and she went and told his other disciples. But they did not believe. Christ appeared to two other disciples, and still the others did not believe. But when the risen Christ appeared to the Apostles, the Apostles and disciples finally believed.

In groups talk about why the other disciples might not have believed. Imagine you are among the first disciples to see the empty tomb or to see the risen Jesus. What might you be thinking? What might you be feeling? Who or what helps you to believe in the risen Christ?

We celebrate Christ's Resurrection every Sunday. The risen Christ is among us, and there are signs of new life all around us. However, the Easter season is a special time to remember and rejoice over the new life we have in Christ.

The deep purple used during Lent is changed to a brilliant white and joyous gold. White and gold are the colors of light, life, and Resurrection. Gold is the most precious metal there is, and we often use it as a sign of God and Heaven.

We sing, "Alleluia!" The word *alleluia* means "Praise God!" All during Lent, we did not sing or say alleluia in the liturgy.

Now during the Easter season, we say it and sing it over and over again! Jesus is risen, Alleluia! He has conquered death forever, Alleluia!

In the Easter season the first reading during the Mass is from the Acts of the Apostles, not the Old Testament. The Acts of the Apostles records the life of the Apostles after Jesus' Ascension into Heaven. It tells of the beginning of the Church. During this reading we hear of the wonderful way the first Christians spread the Good News of Christ and formed a community of faith.

The season of Easter lasts fifty days and ends on Pentecost Sunday. As in all the seasons of the year, we remember Mary and the saints for their belief in Christ and witness to his Good News. We enter into the month of May sometime during the Easter season.

Honoring Mary In many areas of the world, May is a special month of devotion to Mary. We honor and celebrate Mary because she is the Mother of the Son of God. Her trust and faith in God teach us how to be disciples, and we ask her to pray with and for us. There are many popular devotions to Mary. For many people the month of May has been a time for the crowning of Our Lady's statue. We call Mary Queen because her Son Jesus is the King of Kings whose Kingdom will never end. In fact, all followers of Christ are promised the "crown of glory" (1 Peter 5:4) and "the crown of life" (James 1:12).

In a May crowning, a statue of Mary may be crowned with a wreath of flowers or a simple crown. The May crowning ceremony is often celebrated in grottos, outdoor shrines, or parish gardens. It does not take place during the liturgy. Many times there is a procession accompanied by singing, Scripture readings, and requests for Mary to pray for us. We rejoice with her that one day we, too, may receive the "crown of glory."

WE RESPOND

How can you follow the examples of Mary and the saints? What will you do this week to give witness to Jesus?

✞ We Respond in Prayer

Leader: We praise you, Lord, in this daughter of Israel,

All: Mary, your faithful one and our mother.

Reader: A reading from the holy Gospel according to Luke

"When Elizabeth heard Mary's greeting, the infant leaped in her womb, and Elizabeth, filled with the holy Spirit, cried out in a loud voice and said, 'Most blessed are you among women, and blessed is the fruit of your womb. And how does this happen to me, that the mother of my Lord should come to me?'" (Luke 1:41–43)

The Gospel of the Lord.

All: Praise to you Lord, Jesus Christ.

Leader: Pray for us, holy Mother of God.

All: That we may become worthy of the promises of Christ.

🎵 Holy Mary

Refrain

Holy Mary, we come to honor you.
We crown you this day,
the queen of our hearts.
Mary, you are filled with the Lord's own grace.
Salve Regina, Holy Mary.

We crown you this day
the mother of our Savior.
You show us the way
to Jesus Christ our Lord. (Refrain)

We crown you this day
the virgin blest and chosen.
The gift of your life
has shown us how to love. (Refrain)

EASTER

PROJECT DISCIPLE

Pray
Learn
Celebrate
Share
Choose
Live

Show What *you* Know

Make a word search using the following terms related to the season of Easter. Exchange your puzzle with a classmate or family member. As each term is found and circled, talk about its significance to the season of Easter.

Resurrection
Good News
white and gold
rejoice
new life
Alleluia
Jesus Christ
fifty days
Sunday
Easter

What's *the* Word?

"Jesus came and stood in their midst and said to them, 'Peace be with you.' When he had said this, he showed them his hands and his side. The disciples rejoiced when they saw the Lord. [Jesus] said to them again, 'Peace be with you. As the Father has sent me, so I send you.'"
(John 20:19–21)

- What are some ways you can bring peace to others this Easter Season?

_____

_____ **Now, pass it on!**

Take Home

Encourage your family to do something "green" this Easter season. Suggestions might include: begin a family garden (indoors or outdoors), turn off lights when leaving a room, repair leaky faucets, etc.

Write another way for your family to go "green."

_____

_____

UNIT TEST

Write True or False for the following sentences.
Then change the false sentences to make them true.

1. _____ There are three marks of the Church. She is one, holy, and catholic.

   _____

2. _____ Deacons are the successors of the Apostles who are ordained to continue the Apostle's mission of leadership and service in the Church.

   _____

3. _____ The saints are models for living a life of virtue.

   _____

4. _____ The love between a husband and wife is a sign of God's love for all his people and of Christ's love for his Church.

   _____

5. _____ Laypeople are all the baptized members of the Church who share in the mission to bring the Good News of Christ to the world.

   _____

6. _____ In the Sacrament of Matrimony the bride and groom are the celebrants. Jesus acts through them and through their promise to always love and be true to each other.

   _____

7. _____ The laying on of hands and prayer of consecration are the main parts of the Sacrament of Matrimony.

   _____

8. _____ Love is the greatest of all virtues; it is the goal of our lives as Christians.

   _____

continued on next page

Write the letter that best defines each term.

9. _____ catholic

10. _____ Holy Orders

11. _____ stewards of creation

12. _____ fidelity

13. _____ priesthood of the faithful

14. _____ religious

15. _____ virtue

16. _____ faith

a. women and men who belong to communities of service to God and the Church

b. Christ's priestly mission in which all those who are baptized share

c. the virtue that enables us to believe in God and all the Church teaches us, it helps us to believe all that God has told us about himself and all that he has done

d. the sacrament in which baptized men are ordained to serve the Church as deacons, priests, and bishops

e. those who take care of everything God has given them

f. a good habit that helps us act according to God's love for us

g. universal, worldwide, open to all people

h. faithfulness to a person and to duties, obligations, and promises; in marriage the loyalty and the willingness to be true to each other always

i. the promises to live simply as Jesus did

Answer the questions.

17–18. Friendships prepare us for future vocations. What would you tell a good friend who asks you to tell him about all the possible vocations?

19–20. As a fifth grader, how can you show that you are a disciple of Jesus?

Forms of Prayer

Part 1   I Open My Heart

Complete these statements about a special person . . . YOU!

I am a blessing because _____.

One thing I need God's help with is _____.

My biggest concern for the world is _____.

I am most thankful for _____.

I praise you, God, because _____.

Share responses with a partner.

Here are the five forms of Catholic prayer.

Blessing: prayer that dedicates someone or something to God or makes something holy in God's name

Petition: prayer in which we ask something of God

Intercession: prayer in which we ask God for something on behalf of another person or a group of people

Thanksgiving: prayer that shows our gratitude to God for all he has given us

Praise: prayer that gives glory to God for being God

Together turn one of your statements above into one of these forms of prayer. Share the prayer with the group. Pray from the heart, without writing down or practicing the prayer. Have others guess the form of prayer.

Catholic
Identity
Retreat

Forms of Prayer

Part 2   We Come Together for Prayer

Leader: "According to Scripture, it is the *heart* that prays." (*CCC*, 2562) In the quiet of your heart, talk with God. Use the form of prayer—blessing, petition, intercession, thanksgiving, or praise—that works best for you now. (*Write prayer below.*)

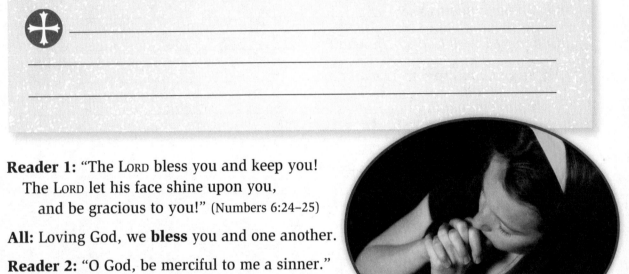

Reader 1: "The Lord bless you and keep you!
The Lord let his face shine upon you,
   and be gracious to you!" (Numbers 6:24–25)

All: Loving God, we **bless** you and one another.

Reader 2: "O God, be merciful to me a sinner."
(Luke 18:13)

All: Merciful God, forgive us. Hear our **petitions**
for forgiveness.

Reader 3: "We always pray for you, that our God may make you worthy of his calling . . . that the name of our Lord Jesus may be glorified in you, and you in him."
(2 Thessalonians 1:11–12)

All: Caring God, we pray for the needs of others. (*Pray specific **intercessions** for the needs of the class, parish, community, and beyond.*)

Reader 4: "Give thanks to the Lord, for he is good, / for his kindness endures forever."
(1 Chronicles 16:34)

All: God of all goodness, we **thank** you for your gifts! Your generosity is beyond measure.

Reader 5: "I will praise your name forever." (Psalm 145:2)

All: Glorious God, we **praise** you!

Leader: Dear Heavenly Father, hear our prayers. We ask this in the name of your Son, our Lord Jesus Christ.

All: Amen.

Forms of Prayer

Part 3   I Cherish God's Word

"[A blind man] shouted, 'Jesus, Son of David, have pity on me!'. . . . When he came near, Jesus asked him, 'What do you want me to do for you?' He replied, 'Lord, please let me see.' Jesus told him, 'Have sight; your faith has saved you.' He immediately received his sight and followed him, giving glory to God. When they saw this, all the people gave praise to God." (Luke 18:38, 40–43)

READ the quotation from Scripture. Read slowly. Pay close attention to what you are reading.

REFLECT on what you read. Think about:

- The blind man was not afraid to come to Jesus with his needs. What holds you back from going to Jesus for help? Do you pray without giving up?

- How do you thank or praise God when he answers your prayer? What if his answer is not what you expect?

SHARE your thoughts and feelings with God in prayer. Let your thoughts and feelings come naturally. Speak to God as a friend.

CONTEMPLATE, or sit quietly and allow your attention to remain focused on God's Word in the Scripture passage from the Gospel of Luke above.

Christ Heals the Blind-Born Man, by Eustache Le Sueur (1617–1655)

Forms of Prayer

Part 4   I Value My Catholic Faith

God gives us the gift of imagination. During the next few minutes, give your imagination to God.

Imagine you are in a peaceful, relaxing setting. You see Jesus there. You go to him.

What would you like to say to Jesus? Is there something you wish to thank him for? Do you have something to ask of him? praise for him? requests to help others? a blessing to ask upon someone or something?

What happens next? Imagine and then write or draw the rest of the story. Underneath, write the type(s) of prayer you experienced in your meeting with Jesus: blessing, petition, intercession, thanksgiving, or praise.

_____

_____

_____

_____

_____

_____

Forms of Prayer

Part 5   I Celebrate Catholic Identity

Jesus said, "Where two or three are gathered together in my name, there am I in the midst of them" (Matthew 18:20).

Recall one of the prayers of blessing, petition, intercession, thanksgiving, or praise you have prayed in this retreat. Write your chosen prayer in the space below. Link your prayers in a chain. Commit to praying for all of these intentions as a group.

Then together decide on something you can *do* to put these prayers into action.

Catholic **I**dentity **R**etreat

Forms of Prayer

Part 6 I Honor My Catholic Identity

Leader: Music can be a powerful way to pray. Let us lift our voices in praise as we sing:

🎵 **With Open Hands/Abierto Está Mi Corazón**

Refrain:
With open hands and open hearts
we come before you, O God above.
Your loving kindness fills all the earth;
Eternal is your love.

Abierto está mi corazón
para encontrarte mi Dios de amor.
Y en todas partes tu cariño está;
eterno es tu amor.

Leader: With our hearts and hands open, we come before God to listen and to ask for continued help in learning how to pray.

Reader: "[Jesus] was praying in a certain place, and when he had finished, one of his disciples said to him, 'Lord, teach us to pray.'" (Luke 11:1)

Saint Ignatius Loyola

All: Jesus Christ, you teach us to pray by words and example. Help us to pray always, in blessing, petition, intercession, thanksgiving, and praise.

Leader: Let us close by praying the *Anima Christi*, a centuries-old Catholic prayer often prayed to Christ by Saint Ignatius Loyola (1491–1556). We ask Jesus Christ to keep us close to him throughout our lives of prayer.

All: Soul of Christ, sanctify me.
Body of Christ, save me . . . .
O good Jesus, hear me . . . .
Do not permit me to be parted from you.
From the evil foe protect me.
At the hour of my death call me.
And bid me come to you,
to praise you with all your saints
for ever and ever. Amen.
(From the *Anima Christi*)

Catholic Identity Retreat

Bringing the Retreat Home

Forms of Prayer

Retreat Recap

Review the pages of your child's *Celebrating Catholic Identity: Prayer* retreat. Ask your child to tell you about the retreat. Talk about the five forms of Catholic prayer (see page R25 for definitions):

- Blessing
- Petition
- Intercession
- Thanksgiving
- Praise

Practicing Prayer

Ask your child for ideas about the kinds of things your family needs to pray about. Together compose your own family prayer of blessing, petition, intercession, thanksgiving, or praise. Pray this together at mealtime or another time your family is gathered. Share with other family members the five forms of prayer, and tell the family which one you and your child used in your prayer. Invite family members to practice each form of prayer.

Take a Moment

Find a favorite traditional prayer. Examples might include the Our Father or the *Anima Christi* from your child's retreat. You may wish to look in *Prayers and Practices* or the *Catholic Identity Home Companion* at the end of your child's book for ideas. Share this traditional prayer with your child, and spend time praying it together.

Family Prayer

Pray this family blessing prayer together. Name the members of the family where prompted.

Lord Jesus, bless our family.
Bless each person individually, including (name each family member):

_____

_____

May each of us develop a stronger relationship with you day by day.

Bless us as a whole family.
May your light and love shine upon all our actions and endeavors.
Bless all we say and do. Amen.

For more resources, see the *Catholic Identity Home Companion* at the end of this book.

Why We Believe
As a Catholic Family

What if someone asks us:

- What if God doesn't answer my prayers?
- Why not consult other means, such as horoscopes or psychics, for help?

The following resources can help us to respond:

Jesus taught us to pray with patience and complete trust in God. When we have a particular need we are praying about, we might worry that God may not hear us. We might say the words of our prayer but keep our hearts and minds in a state of distrust and anxiety.

🌿 What does Scripture say?

"Have no anxiety at all, but in everything, by prayer and petition, with thanksgiving, make your requests known to God. Then the peace of God that surpasses all understanding will guard your hearts and minds in Christ Jesus." (Philippians 4:6–7)

Jesus said, "Your Father knows what you need before you ask him. . . .

Look at the birds in the sky; they do not sow or reap, they gather nothing into barns, yet your heavenly Father feeds them. Are not you more important than they? Can any of you by worrying add a single moment to your life-span?" (Matthew 6:8, 26–27)

"Ask and you will receive; seek and you will find; knock and the door will be opened to you," said Jesus (Luke 11:9).

Jesus said, "And whatever you ask in my name, I will do" (John 14:13).

Jesus clearly asks us to trust in God alone, praying for our needs and being confident that God will hear us. Trust in God is part of following the First Commandment: *I am the LORD your God: you shall not have strange gods before me.* This commandment, found in Exodus 20:2–5, calls us to honor, love, and respect God as the one true God. When we have concerns about our lives, we must not consult horoscopes, seek the advice of psychics, or try to predict the future. These are all offenses against the First Commandment. We are called to instead trust God as our loving Father.

🌿 What does the Church say?

"Believing in God, the only One, and loving him with all our being has enormous consequences for our whole life. . . . It means trusting God in every circumstance, even in adversity." (CCC, 222, 227)

"Let nothing disturb you, nothing cause you fear. All things pass; God is unchanging. Patience obtains all. Whoever has God needs nothing else." (Saint Teresa of Ávila, Doctor of the Church, 1515–1582)

"Pray, hope, and don't worry. Worry is useless. God is merciful and will hear your prayer." (Saint Pio of Pietrelcina, 1887–1968)

Notes:

Across

2. To be _____ is to be blessed with holy oil.

4. The call to holiness that all Christians share is our _____ vocation.

5. _____, Confirmation, and the Eucharist are the Sacraments of Christian Initiation.

8. The mission of the Church is to share the Good _____ of Christ and to spread the Kingdom of God.

9. A sacrament is an effective sign given to us by Jesus through which we share in God's _____.

10. The _____ is all those who believe in Jesus Christ, have been baptized in him, and follow his teachings.

Down

1. In Baptism the bishop, priest, or deacon who celebrates the sacrament for and with the community is the _____.

2. The bishops of the Church are the successors to the _____.

3. Some men are ordained as _____ to assist the bishops in works of service to the Church.

6. _____ is another word for Christ that means "anointed one."

7. Sanctifying _____ is the gift of sharing in God's life that we receive in the sacraments.

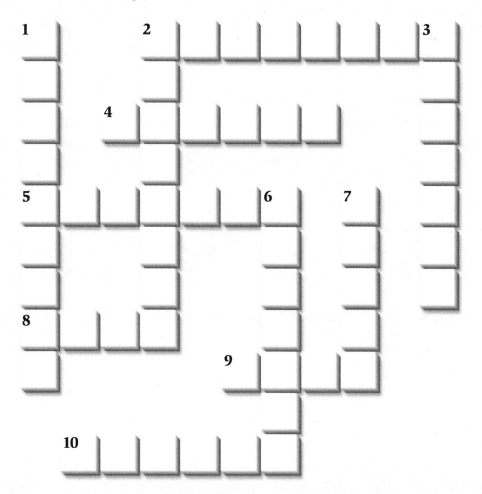

**Grade 5
Unit 2**

Using the clues, unscramble the letters to make words. Then write the words in the spaces and the circles.

1. In this sacrament we receive the Gift of the Holy Spirit in a special way. TIMANOCFIRON

   _ _ _ _ _ _◯_ _ _ _ _

2. In the _____ Jesus becomes truly present under the appearances of bread and wine. SURATEICH

   _ _◯_ _◯_ _ _

3. This feast celebrates the coming of the Holy Spirit. COTTENEPS

   _ _ _ _ _ _ _ _◯

4. At this part of the Eucharistic Prayer the bread and wine become Christ's Body and Blood. NOITANOCCRES

   _ _ _ _ _ _ _◯_ _ _◯

5. Jesus celebrated this Jewish feast with the Apostles on the night before he died. VERASOPS

   _ _ _◯_ _ _

6. At Mass, during the _____ of the Word, we listen and respond to God's Word. GUILTRY

   ◯_ _ _ _ _ _

7. Among the gifts of the Holy Spirit are _____, understanding, fortitude, and piety. DOMSIW

   _ _◯_ _ _

8. _____, kindness, joy, and self-control are some of the fruits of the Holy Spirit. ATENPICE

   _ _ _ _◯_ _ _

9. The Eucharist is a memorial, a meal, and a _____. CRAISICEF

   _◯_ _ _ _ _ _ _

10. In _____ we open our minds and heart to God. YERRAP

    _ _◯_ _ _

Write the circled letters here.

◯◯◯◯◯◯◯◯◯◯

Then unscramble these letters to find the word that completes this sentence.

_ _ _ _ _ _ _ _ _ _ _ _ _ are blessings, actions, and objects that help us respond to God's grace.

316

Use the spaces below to design three prayer cards.

1. The first will be a card to give to someone who is about to celebrate the Sacrament of Penance.

2. The second will be a card to give to someone who is caring for someone who is elderly or sick.

3. The third will be a card dedicated to Mary, honoring her under one of her titles or on one of her feast days.

You may use pictures, symbols, prayers, or any combination of words and images that you think best conveys the message of each card.

(front of card 1) (front of card 2) (front of card 3)

(back of card 1) (back of card 2) (back of card 3)

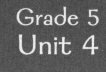

In the spaces below write four brief prayers asking God to bless those called to love and serve him in different vocations.

In each prayer mention one or more specific ways in which someone in that particular vocation is called to love and serve God and the Church.

• Ask God to bless someone called to serve him as a layperson living in the world.

_____

_____

_____

_____

• Ask God to bless someone called to serve him through the Sacrament of Matrimony.

_____

_____

_____

_____

• Ask God to bless someone called to serve him as a member of a religious community.

_____

_____

_____

_____

• Ask God to bless someone called to serve him through the Sacrament of Holy Orders.

_____

_____

_____

_____

**CONGRATULATIONS
ON COMPLETING
YOUR YEAR AS
A GRADE 5 DISCIPLE!**

Fold on this line.

PROJECT DISCIPLE LOG

Pray
Learn
Celebrate
Share
Choose
Live

**A RECORD OF MY JOURNEY
AS A GRADE 5 DISCIPLE**

_____

Name

✂ Cut on this line.

My conscience helps me to choose between right and wrong.

Sometimes when I need help in making a choice, I

- talk to _____

- pray to _____

A loving choice I made this year was

_____

_____

_____

_____

_____

Sacramentals—blessings, actions, and objects—are part of the Church's prayer life.

The sacramentals that help me to pray are

- blessings

- making the Sign of the Cross with holy water

- a crucifix

- a rosary

- _____

  _____

  _____

This year I learned about the Seven Sacraments of the Catholic Church.

One thing I learned about the

- Sacraments of Christian Initiation

  _____

  _____

- Sacraments of Healing

  _____

  _____

- Sacraments at the Service of Communion

  _____

  _____

2

✂ Cut on this line.

As a disciple of Jesus, I share my faith with others.

A friend with whom I can share my faith is

_____

_____

This person is a good friend because

_____

_____

An adult with whom I can share my faith is

_____

_____

I share my faith with family and friends by

_____

_____

6

As a disciple of Jesus, I have lived out my faith this year when I

- forgave someone who _____

  _____

- cared for the environment by _____

  _____

- when I encouraged someone who _____

  _____

- when I took care of myself by _____

  _____

- when I helped someone by _____

  _____

This summer I will live out my faith by

_____

7

As Jesus' disciple, I gather with others to celebrate the liturgical year.

My favorite liturgical season is _____

_____

I celebrate this season with

- my family by _____

  _____

- my friends by _____

  _____

- my parish by _____

  _____

During this season I can help others by

_____

3

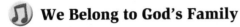
End-of-Year Prayer Service

✝ We Gather in Prayer

🎵 We Belong to God's Family

We belong to God's family.
Brothers and sisters are we,
singing together in unity about
one Lord and one faith,
one family.

We are one in the water,
the fountain of rebirth.
We are God's new creation
and our song will cover the earth

Leader: Let us gather together to give praise to our God.

All: Loving God,
We thank you for the sacraments that draw us together in love.

Leader: Immerse us in your grace,

All: And help us to grow stronger in our faith each day.

Leader: Remind us to seek forgiveness from those we have hurt,

All: And to forgive those who have hurt us.

Leader: Give us compassionate hearts,

All: And generous spirits.

Leader: As we look forward to a safe and happy summer, help us to remember that Jesus is always present in our lives.

All: Amen!

The Lives of the Saints

Saint Dominic Savio

⤳ **Born:** April 2, 1842 ⤳ **Died:** March 9, 1857
⤳ **Feast Day:** March 9

What he said

"I am not capable of doing big things, but I want to do everything, even the smallest things, for the greater glory of God."

What the world was like

During Dominic Savio's short lifetime, Italy was not one country; rather it was made up of many city-states. A city-state was made up of a city and the region surrounding it. Each city-state had its own government. Many of these city-states fought against each other and other countries. While Dominic Savio was alive, the Italians tried to unite their country. Italy became one unified country shortly after Dominic died.

During Dominic Savio's lifetime, the first transatlantic telegraph cable was laid and the first safety elevator was used. The postage stamp was introduced and anesthesia was used for the first time during an operation.

Who he was

Dominic Savio was one of ten children. His father was a blacksmith and his mother was a seamstress. They lived in Italy, near Turin. At the age of four, Dominic could recite all of his prayers and one year later, he became an altar boy. Dominic received his first Holy Communion at the age of seven. On that day, he wrote, "I will go to confession very often and go to communion as often as my confessor gives me permission. I will celebrate Sundays and feast days as holy days. Jesus and Mary will be my friends."

When Dominic was twelve years old, he entered a school that was run by John Bosco. Dominic was always cheerful, studied hard, and helped his friends. He taught them about religion, took care of them when they were sick, and broke up many fights. Dominic was well liked and known for praying frequently, often praising God through song. Dominic obeyed those in charge and he enjoyed playing games.

Shortly before his fifteenth birthday, Dominic became ill. He was sent home to get better, but he died one month before his fifteenth birthday.

What this saint means to us today

Dominic lived his life doing ordinary things with a smile and a cheerful heart. He did everything to the best of his ability. He used Jesus as a role model and tried to imitate him in all situations. As a student, as a friend, as a son, as a brother, and as a teenager, Dominic lived his life focused on God. As students, as friends, as sons or daughters, as brothers or sisters, we can live our lives focused on God in everything we do. Dominic is the patron saint of children's choirs.

The Lives of the Saints

Name _____

Saint Dominic Savio

As a young boy, Dominic did many of the things that children today do. He went to school and studied hard. He had many friends and enjoyed playing games.

Praying was important to Dominic. He would often leave the playground and go into church. He prayed everyday, sometimes praising God through song.

Like Dominic, we can praise God through song. Create your own song to praise God. Write a prayer giving praise to God. Set this prayer to music by using a familiar tune. Share your musical prayer with your family, friends or your class.

_____

_____

_____

_____

_____

_____

_____

_____

_____

_____

_____

For saints, games, study guides and more, visit www.webelieveweb.com.

You are learning and living out ways to be a disciple of Jesus Christ.
Look what awaits you in **WeBelieve** Grade 6: We Are God's People.

You will learn about and live out that

• God formed a covenant.

• God's people built a covenant nation.

• God redefined the covenant people.

• The covenant is fulfilled in Jesus.

Until next year, pay attention each time you read Scripture. Take quiet time to reflect. Listen to God's Word.

Here is one thing that I know about the Old Testament.

_____

_____

_____

_____

Here is one thing that I want to know more about the Old Testament.

_____

_____

_____

_____

We are blessed to be God's People!

Prayers and Practices

Glory Be to the Father

Glory be to the Father
and to the Son
and the Holy Spirit
as it was in the beginning
is, now and ever shall be
world without end. Amen.

Our Father

Our Father, who art in heaven,
hallowed be thy name;
thy kingdom come;
thy will be done on earth
    as it is in heaven.
Give us this day our daily bread;
and forgive us our trespasses
as we forgive those
    who trespass against us;
and lead us not into temptation,
but deliver us from evil. Amen.

Hail Mary

Hail Mary, full of grace,
the Lord is with you!
Blessed are you among women,
and blessed is the fruit
    of your womb, Jesus.
Holy Mary, Mother of God,
pray for us sinners,
now and at the hour of our death.
Amen.

Morning Offering

O Jesus, I offer you all my prayers, works,
and sufferings of this day for all the
intentions of your most Sacred Heart. Amen.

Memorare

Remember, most loving Virgin Mary,
never was it heard
that anyone who turned to you for help
was left unaided.

Inspired by this confidence,
though burdened by my sins,
I run to your protection
for you are my mother.
Mother of the Word of God,
do not despise my world of pleading
but be merciful and hear my prayer.
Amen.

Apostles' Creed

I believe in God, the Father almighty,
    Creator of heaven and earth,
and in Jesus Christ, his only Son, our Lord,
    who was conceived by the Holy Spirit,
    born of the Virgin Mary,
suffered under Pontius Pilate,
    was crucified, died and was buried;
he descended into hell;
on the third day he rose again from the dead;
he ascended into heaven,
    and is seated at the right hand
      of God the Father almighty;
from there he will come to judge
    the living and the dead.

I believe in the Holy Spirit,
the holy catholic Church,
the communion of saints,
the forgiveness of sins,
the resurrection of the body,
and life everlasting. Amen.

Find other versions of some of these prayers at **www.webelieveweb.com**

Nicene Creed

I believe in one God,
the Father almighty,
maker of heaven and earth,
of all things visible and invisible.

I believe in one Lord Jesus Christ,
the Only Begotten Son of God,
born of the Father before all ages.
God from God, Light from Light,
true God from true God,
begotten, not made, consubstantial
with the Father;
through him all things were made.
For us men and for our salvation
he came down from heaven,
and by the Holy Spirit was incarnate
of the Virgin Mary,
and became man.

For our sake he was crucified
under Pontius Pilate,
he suffered death and was buried,
and rose again on the third day
in accordance with the Scriptures.
He ascended into heaven
and is seated at the right hand
of the Father.
He will come again in glory to judge
the living and the dead
and his kingdom will have no end.

I believe in the Holy Spirit, the Lord,
the giver of life,
who proceeds from the Father and the Son,
who with the Father and the Son is
adored and glorified,
who has spoken through the prophets.

I believe in one, holy, catholic
and apostolic Church.
I confess one Baptism for the
forgiveness of sins
and I look forward to the resurrection of the
dead and the life of the world to come.
Amen.

Gloria

Glory to God in the highest,
and on earth peace to people of good will.

We praise you,
we bless you,
we adore you,
we glorify you,
we give you thanks for your great glory,
Lord God, heavenly King,
O God, almighty Father.

Lord Jesus Christ, Only Begotten Son,
Lord God, Lamb of God, Son of the Father,
you take away the sins of the world,
have mercy on us;
you take away the sins of the world,
receive our prayer;
you are seated at the right hand of the Father,
have mercy on us.

For you alone are the Holy One,
you alone are the Lord,
you alone are the Most High,
Jesus Christ,
with the Holy Spirit,
in the glory of God the Father.
Amen.

Evening Prayer

Dear God, before I sleep
I want to thank you for this day,
so full of your kindness and your joy.
I close my eyes to rest
safe in your loving care.

The Canticle of Mary, the Magnificat

"My soul proclaims the greatness of the Lord;
    my spirit rejoices in God my savior.
For he has looked upon his handmaid's lowliness;
    behold, from now on will all ages call me
      blessed.
The Mighty One has done great things for me,
    and holy is his name.
His mercy is from age to age
    to those who fear him.
He has shown might with his arm,
    dispersed the arrogant of mind and heart.
He has thrown down the rulers from their thrones
    but lifted up the lowly.
The hungry he has filled with good things;
    the rich he has sent away empty.
He has helped Israel his servant,
    remembering his mercy,
according to his promise to our fathers,
    to Abraham and to his descendants forever."

(Luke 1:46–55)

Stations of the Cross

1. Jesus is condemned to die.
2. Jesus takes up his cross.
3. Jesus falls the first time.
4. Jesus meets his mother.
5. Simon helps Jesus carry his cross.
6. Veronica wipes the face of Jesus.
7. Jesus falls the second time.
8. Jesus meets the women of Jerusalem.
9. Jesus falls the third time.
10. Jesus is stripped of his garments.
11. Jesus is nailed to the cross.
12. Jesus dies on the cross.
13. Jesus is taken down from the cross.
14. Jesus is laid in the tomb.

Note:

The Prayer to the Holy Spirit is found on page 107.

The Prayer for Vocation is found on page 267.

Sacramentals are found on pages 148-149.

The gifts and fruits of the Holy Spirit are found on pages 112-115.

The Angelus

The angel spoke God's message to Mary,
and she conceived of the Holy Spirit.
Hail Mary....

"I am the lowly servant of the Lord:
let it be done to me according to your word."
Hail Mary....

And the Word became flesh
and lived among us.
Hail Mary....

Pray for us, holy Mother of God,
that we may become worthy of the promises
of Christ.

Let us pray.
Lord,
fill our hearts with your grace:
once, through the message of an angel
you revealed to us the incarnation of your Son;
now, through his suffering and death
lead us to the glory of his resurrection.
We ask this through Christ our Lord.
Amen.

Hail, Holy Queen

Hail, holy Queen, mother of mercy,
hail, our life, our sweetness, and our hope.
To you we cry, the children of Eve;
to you we send up our sighs,
mourning and weeping in this land of exile.
Turn, then, most gracious advocate,
your eyes of mercy toward us;
lead us home at last
and show us the blessed fruit of your womb,
  Jesus:
O clement, O loving, O sweet Virgin Mary.

Act of Contrition

My God,
I am sorry for my sins with all my heart.
In choosing to do wrong
and failing to do good,
I have sinned against you
whom I should love above all things.
I firmly intend, with your help,
to do penance,
to sin no more,
and to avoid whatever leads me to sin.
Our Savior Jesus Christ
suffered and died for us.
In his name, my God, have mercy.

Prayer of Saint Francis

Lord, make me an instrument of your peace:
where there is hatred, let me sow love;
where there is injury, pardon;
where there is doubt, faith;
where there is despair, hope;
where there is darkness, light;
where there is sadness, joy.

O divine Master, grant that I may not so
much seek
to be consoled as to console,
to be understood as to understand,
to be loved as to love.
For it is in giving that we receive,
it is in pardoning that we are pardoned,
it is in dying that we are born to eternal life.
Amen.

Saint Francis of Assisi

Note:

Our Lady of Guadalupe is found on page 151.

The Rosary is found on pages 226-227.

The Ten Commandments

1. I am the LORD your God: you shall not have strange gods before me.
2. You shall not take the name of the LORD your God in vain.
3. Remember to keep the holy the LORD'S day.
4. Honor your father and your mother.
5. You shall not kill.
6. You shall not commit adultery.
7. You shall not steal.
8. You shall not bear false witness against your neighbor.
9. You shall not covet your neighbor's wife.
10. You shall not covet your neighbor's goods.

The Beatitudes

Blessed are the poor in spirit,
    for theirs is the kingdom of heaven.
Blessed are they who mourn,
    for they will be comforted.
Blessed are the meek,
    for they will inherit the land.
Blessed are they who hunger and
        thirst for righteousness,
    for they will be satisfied.
Blessed are the merciful,
    for they will be shown mercy.
Blessed are the clean of heart,
    for they will see God.
Blessed are the peacemakers,
    for they will be called children of God.
Blessed are they who are persecuted for
        the sake of righteousness,
    for theirs is the kingdom of heaven.
(Matthew 5:3–10)

The Precepts of the Church

The pope and bishops have established some laws to help us know and fulfill our responsibilities as members of the Church. These laws are called the precepts of the Church.

It is helpful to think of the precepts as rules or principles intended as a guide for behavior. They teach us how we should act as members of the Church. These precepts also make sure that the Church has what it needs to serve its members and to grow.

1. You shall attend Mass on Sundays and holy days of obligation and rest from servile labor.
2. You shall confess your sins at least once a year.
3. You shall receive the Sacrament of the Eucharist at least during the Easter season.
4. You shall observe the days of fasting and abstinence by the Church.
5. You shall help to provide for the needs of the Church.

Catholic Social Teaching

There are seven themes of Catholic social teaching.

Life and Dignity of the Human Person

Human life is sacred because it is a gift from God. Because we are all God's children, we all share the same human dignity. As Christians we respect all people, even those we do not know.

Call to Family, Community, and Participation

We are all social. We need to be with others to grow. The family is the basic community. In the family we grow and learn values. As Christians we are involved in our family life and community.

Rights and Responsibilities of the Human Person

Every person has a fundamental right to life. This includes the things we need to have a decent life: faith and family, work and education, health care and housing. We also have a responsibility to others and to society. We work to make sure the rights of all people are being protected.

Option for the Poor and Vulnerable

We have a special obligation to help those who are poor and in need. This includes those who cannot protect themselves because of their age or their health.

Dignity of Work and the Rights of Workers

Our work is a sign of our participation in God's work. People have the right to decent work, just wages, safe working conditions, and to participate in decisions about work.

Solidarity of the Human Family

Solidarity is a feeling of unity. It binds members of a group together. Each of us is a member of the one human family. The human family includes people of all racial and cultural backgrounds. We all suffer when one part of the human family suffers whether they live near or far away.

Care for God's Creation

God created us to be stewards, or caretakers, of his creation. We must care for and respect the environment. We have to protect it for future generations. When we care for creation, we show respect for God the Creator.

Note:

An Examination of Conscience is found on page 184.

The Corporal and Spiritual Works of Mercy are found on page 39.

The Holy Days of Obligation are found on page 147.

The Virtues are found on pages 248-253.

An Act of Faith is found on page 249.

An Act of Hope is found on page 251.

An Act of Love is found on page 253.

Glossary

Act of Contrition (p. 188)
a prayer that allows us to express our sorrow and promise to try not to sin again

Annunciation (p. 220)
the name given to the angel's visit to Mary at which the announcement was made that she would be the Mother of the Son of God

Anointing of the Sick (p. 201)
the sacrament by which God's grace and comfort are given to those who are seriously ill or suffering because of their old age

Apostles (p. 26)
men chosen by Jesus to share in his mission in a special way

Assumption (p. 223)
the belief that when Mary's work on earth was done, God brought her body and soul to live forever with the risen Christ

Baptism (p. 57)
the sacrament in which we are freed from sin, become children of God, and are welcomed into the Church

bishops (p. 288)
the successors of the Apostles who are ordained to continue the Apostles' mission of leadership and service in the Church

Blessed Trinity (p. 21)
the Three Persons in One God: God the Father, God the Son, and God the Holy Spirit

catechumenate (p. 68)
a period of formation for Christian initiation that includes prayer and liturgy, religious instruction, and service to others

Christian initiation (p. 47)
the process of becoming a member of the Church through the Sacraments of Baptism, Confirmation, and Eucharist

Church (p. 26)
all those who believe in Jesus Christ, have been baptized in him, and follow his teachings

common vocation (p. 47)
the call to holiness and evangelization that all Christians share

Concluding Rites (p. 138)
the last part of the Mass in which we are blessed and sent forth to be Christ's servants in the world and to love others as he has loved us

Confirmation (p. 100)
the sacrament in which we receive the Gift of the Holy Spirit in a special way

conscience (p. 184)
our ability to know the difference between good and evil, right and wrong

Consecration (p. 137)
the part of the Eucharistic Prayer when, by the power of the Holy Spirit and through the words and actions of the priest, the bread and wine become the Body and Blood of Christ

conversion (p. 173)
a turning to God with all one's heart

Corporal Works of Mercy (p. 39)
acts of love that help us care for the physical and material needs of others

deacons (p. 289)
baptized men who are not priests but are ordained to the work of service for the Church

ecumenism (p. 300)
the work to promote unity among all Christians

eternal life (p. 63)
living in happiness with God forever

Eucharist (p. 121)
the Sacrament of the Body and Blood of Christ, Jesus is truly present under the appearances of bread and wine

evangelization (p. 34)
proclaiming the Good News of Christ by what we say and do

faith (p. 249)
the virtue that enables us to believe in God and all that the Church teaches us; it helps us to believe all that God has told us about himself and all that he has done

fidelity (p. 277)
faithfulness to a person and to duties, obligations, and promises; in marriage, the loyalty and the willingness to be true to each other always

gifts of the Holy Spirit (p. 112)
wisdom, understanding, counsel, fortitude, knowledge, piety, and fear of the Lord

holiness (p. 47)
sharing in God's goodness and responding to his love by the way we live; our holiness comes through grace

holy day of obligation (p. 147)
a day we are obliged to participate in the Mass to celebrate a special event in the life of Jesus, Mary, or the saints

Holy Orders (p. 287)
the sacrament in which baptized men are ordained to serve the Church as deacons, priests, and bishops

hope (p. 251)
the virtue that enables us to trust in God's promise to share his life with us forever; it makes us confident in God's love and care for us

Immaculate Conception (p. 223)
the belief that Mary was free from Original Sin from the moment she was conceived

Incarnation (p. 58)
the truth that the Son of God became man

Introductory Rites (p. 132)
the part of the Mass that unites us as a community. It prepares us to hear God's Word and to celebrate the Eucharist

Jesus' mission (p. 24)
to share the life of God with all people and to save them from sin

Kingdom of God (p. 24)
the power of God's love active in our lives and in the world

Last Judgment (p. 39)
Jesus Christ coming at the end of time to judge all people

laypeople (p. 262)
all the baptized members of the Church who share in the mission to bring the Good News of Christ to the world

liturgy (p. 34)
the official public prayer of the Church

Liturgy of the Eucharist (p. 137)
the part of the Mass in which the Death and Resurrection of Christ are made present again. Our gifts of bread and wine become the Body and Blood of Christ, which we receive in Holy Communion.

Liturgy of the Hours (p. 147)
public prayer of the Church made up of psalms, readings from Scripture and Church teachings, prayers and hymns, and celebrated at various times during the day

Liturgy of the Word (p. 135)
the part of the Mass in which we listen and respond to God's Word; we profess our faith and pray for all people in need

love (p. 253)
the greatest of all virtues that enables us to love God and to love our neighbor

marks of the Church (p. 296)
the four characteristics of the Church: one, holy, catholic, and apostolic

marriage covenant (p. 275)
the life-long commitment between a man and a woman to live as faithful and loving partners

Matrimony (p. 272)
the sacrament in which a man and woman become husband and wife and promise to be faithful to each other for the rest of their lives

Paschal Mystery (p. 37)
Christ's suffering, Death, Resurrection from the dead, and Ascension into Heaven

Passover (p. 121)
the feast on which Jewish People remember the miraculous way that God saved them from death and slavery in ancient Egypt

Penance and Reconciliation (p. 177)
the sacrament by which our relationship with God and the Church is strengthened or restored and our sins are forgiven

priesthood of the faithful (p. 260)
Christ's priestly mission in which all those who are baptized share

priests (p. 289)
ordained ministers who serve the Christian faithful by leading, teaching, and most especially celebrating the Eucharist and other sacraments

prophet (p. 61)
someone who speaks on behalf of God, defends the truth, and works for justice

Real Presence (p. 125)
Jesus really and truly present in the Eucharist

religious (p. 264)
women and men who belong to communities of service to God and the Church

sacrament (p. 45)
an effective sign given to us by Jesus through which we share in God's life

sacramentals (p. 149)
blessings, actions, and objects that help us respond to God's grace received in the sacraments

Sacred Chrism (p. 74)
perfumed oil blessed by the bishop

sacrifice (p. 123)
a gift offered to God by a priest in the name of all the people

saints (p. 63)
followers of Christ who lived lives of holiness on earth and now share in eternal life with God in Heaven

salvation (p. 58)
the forgiveness of sins and the restoring of friendship with God

sanctifying grace (p. 45)
the gift of sharing in God's life that we receive in the sacraments

sin (p. 177)
a thought, word, deed or omission against God's law

Spiritual Works of Mercy (p. 39)
acts of love that help us care for the needs of people's hearts, minds, and souls

stewards of creation (p. 303)
those who take care of everything that God has given them

virtue (p. 249)
a good habit that helps us to act according to God's love for us

Index

The following is a list of topics that appear in the pupil's text.
Boldface indicates an entire chapter or section.

In this section, you will find questions and answers that review the content in your *We Believe: Catholic Identity Edition* book this year. Each question in this section covers the key Catholic teachings in your book, in chapter order. Answer each question to review what you have learned—whether you use this section at home, in school, or in the parish. The answers provided will strengthen your understanding of your Catholic faith and help to reinforce your Catholic Identity.

The *CCC* references after each answer indicate where to find further information about that answer in the *Catechism of the Catholic Church.*

Q: Who is Jesus?

A: Jesus Christ is the Second Person of the Blessed Trinity. The Blessed Trinity is the Three Persons in One God: God the Father, God the Son, and God the Holy Spirit. Jesus Christ is the Son of God who became man. CCC, 254, 422

Q: What is Jesus' mission?

A: Jesus' mission is to share the life of God with all people and to save them from sin. CCC, 714

Q: What is the Church?

A: The Church is all those who believe in Jesus Christ, have been baptized in him, and follow his teachings. CCC, 752, 759

CCC = Catechism of the Catholic Church

Q: What is the Good News?

A: The Good News is that God loves all people. He sent his only Son, Jesus Ch[rist]
to show us how to live and to save us from sin. Jesus shares the very life o[f God]
with us and gives us the hope of life forever with God. *CCC, 714, 763*

Q: What is the mission of the Church, given to her by Jesus Christ?

A: The work, or mission, of the Church is to share the Good News of Christ and to
spread the Kingdom of God. *CCC, 768*

Q: What is the Kingdom of God?

A: The Kingdom of God is the power of God's love active in our lives and in
the world. *CCC, 2046*

Q: What is the liturgy?

A: The liturgy is the official public prayer of the Church. *CCC, 1069, 1136*

Q: What is the Paschal Mystery?

A: The Paschal Mystery is Christ's suffering, Death, Resurrection from the dead,
and Ascension into Heaven. By his Paschal Mystery, Jesus saves us from sin
and gives us life. *CCC, 654, 1067, 1085*

Q: What is a sacrament?

A: A sacrament is an effective sign given to us by Jesus through which we share in
God's life. *CCC, 1131*

Q: What are the Seven Sacraments?

A: The Seven Sacraments are: Baptism, Confirmation, Eucharist, Penance and
Reconciliation, Anointing of the Sick, Holy Orders, and Matrimony. Baptism,
Confirmation, and Eucharist are the Sacraments of Christian Initiation.
Penance and Reconciliation and Anointing of the Sick are the Sacraments of
Healing. Holy Orders and Matrimony are the Sacraments at the Service of
Communion. *CCC, 1210*

Q: What is the Sacrament of Baptism?

A: Baptism is the sacrament in which we are freed from sin, become children
of God, and are welcomed into the Church. *CCC, 1212, 1213*

Q: What symbols are used in the celebration of Baptism?

A: Water, a baptismal candle, a white garment, and Sacred Chrism are used at Baptism. *CCC, 1238, 1241, 1243*

Q: What is the Church's year called?

A: The Church's year is called the liturgical year. *CCC, 1168*

Q: What does the liturgical year celebrate?

A: The liturgical year celebrates the whole life of Christ, most especially his Paschal Mystery. *CCC, 1171–1173*

Q: What is Ordinary Time?

A: Ordinary Time is a special season of the liturgical year in which we learn about the life of Christ and grow as his followers. It is celebrated twice during the liturgical year. It includes special days honoring Mary and the saints. *CCC, 1163, 1168, 1173*

Q: What is Pentecost?

A: Pentecost is the day on which the Holy Spirit came to the Apostles. It was the beginning of the Church. *CCC, 1076*

Q: What happens in the Sacrament of Confirmation?

A: In the Sacrament of Confirmation we are sealed with the Gift of the Holy Spirit. We become more like Christ and are strengthened to be his witnesses. *CCC, 1294–1296, 1303*

Q: What are the Gifts of the Holy Spirit?

A: The Gifts of the Holy Spirit are wisdom, understanding, counsel, fortitude, knowledge, piety, and fear of the Lord. *CCC, 1831*

Q: What is the Sacrament of the Eucharist?

A: The Eucharist is the Sacrament of the Body and Blood of Christ. *CCC, 1333, 1374*

Q: What are the four parts of the Mass?

A: The four parts of the Mass are the Introductory Rites, the Liturgy of the Word, the Liturgy of the Eucharist, and the Concluding Rites. *CCC, 1346, 1348*

Q: What happens at the Consecration of the Mass?

A: At the Consecration, by the power of the Holy Spirit and through the words and actions of the priest, the bread and wine become the Body and Blood of Christ. *CCC, 1333, 1353*

Q: How do we pray?

A: We pray by opening our hearts and minds to God. We can pray alone or with others, in silence or aloud. *CCC, 2559, 2698–2699*

Q: What are sacramentals?

A: Sacramentals are blessings, actions, and objects that help us respond to God's grace received in the sacraments. Examples of sacramentals include blessings of people; objects such as a crucifix or rosary; and actions such as the Sign of the Cross. *CCC, 1670*

Q: What are popular devotions?

A: Popular devotions are prayer practices that are not part of the Church's official public prayer, or liturgy, but are part of the heritage of prayer in the Church. *CCC, 1674*

Q: What is Advent?

A: Advent is a liturgical season of joyful expectation and preparation for the birth of God's Son, Jesus Christ, at Christmas. *CCC, 524*

Q: What do we celebrate during the season of Christmas?

A: During the season of Christmas, we rejoice in the Incarnation—the truth that the Son of God became man. *CCC, 1171*

Q: What is the Sacrament of Penance and Reconciliation?

A: The Sacrament of Penance and Reconciliation is the sacrament by which our relationship with God and the Church is strengthened or restored and our sins are forgiven. *CCC, 980*

Q: What is the Sacrament of the Anointing of the Sick?

A: The Sacrament of the Anointing of the Sick is the sacrament by which God's grace and comfort are given to those who are seriously ill or suffering because of their old age. *CCC, 1499, 1514*

Q: Why does the Church remember and honor Mary?

A: The Church honors Mary because she is the Mother of Jesus Christ, the only Son of God. She is Jesus' first and most faithful disciple, and the greatest of all the saints. *CCC, 971*

Q: What is Lent?

A: Lent is a season of the liturgical year in which we prepare for the great celebration of Easter through prayer, penance, and good works. *CCC, 1438*

Q: What is the Easter Triduum?

A: The Easter Triduum, a time during the liturgical year, is our greatest celebration of the Paschal Mystery. It is the three days from Holy Thursday evening to Easter Sunday evening. *CCC, 1168*

Q: What are the theological virtues?

A: The theological virtues are faith, hope, and love. They are called theological because *theo* means "God," and these virtues are gifts from God. *CCC, 1813*

Q: What is the priesthood of the faithful?

A: The priesthood of the faithful is the sharing in Christ's priestly mission by all those who are baptized. We live our priesthood when we pray daily, participate in the liturgy, and offer our lives to God. *CCC, 1591*

Q: What is the mission of the laity?

A: The mission of the laity is to bring the Good News of Christ to the world. *CCC, 898–900*

Q: How do women and men live out their vocation of religious life?

A: Women and men in religious life belong to communities of service to God and the Church. They make vows, or promises, of poverty, chastity, and obedience to God. *CCC, 925–927*

Q: What are ways we can listen to God's call to our vocation?

A: We can listen to God's call through prayer, advice from good people, and the recognition of our God-given abilities and talents. *CCC, 2826*

Q: What is the Sacrament of Matrimony?

A: The Sacrament of Matrimony is the sacrament in which a man and a woman promise to always love and be faithful to each other. They make a life-long commitment to live as loving partners and promise to lovingly accept children as a gift from God. *CCC, 1601*

Q: What is the Sacrament of Holy Orders?

A: Holy Orders is the sacrament in which baptized men are ordained to serve the Church as bishops, priests, or deacons. *CCC, 1538*

Q: What are the marks of the Church?

A: There are four marks, or characteristics, of the Church. The Church is one, holy, catholic, and apostolic. *CCC, 811*

Q: What do we celebrate at Easter?

A: Easter is the liturgical season during which we celebrate the Resurrection of Jesus Christ. It is a special time to rejoice over the new life we have in Christ. *CCC, 1169*

Resources
for the Family

I n this section, you will find a treasury of
resources to help build up your Catholic
Identity at home, in your parish, and in
the community. Learn more about key Catholic
teachings from the themes of your child's
Celebrating Catholic Identity retreats: **CREED**,
LITURGY & SACRAMENTS, **MORALITY**, and
PRAYER. For each theme, you will find
Catholic prayers, practices, and devotions to
share with those you love—and make a part of
your daily lives as a Catholic family!

Family: "the place where parents pass
on the faith to their children."
—Pope Francis
Apostolic Exhortation *Evangelii Gaudium*, 66

343

Spirituality and Your Fifth-Grade Child

Fifth graders have an increased capacity for reflecting on their spiritual lives. They can see how their explanations for who God is and how God works in the world are sometimes affirmed by their friends and sometimes challenged by them. Support your child in living out his or her faith at home and among his or her peers. If possible, find times to pray and reflect together, perhaps at mealtime or before bedtime.

Your fifth grader is beginning to think abstractly. Concepts such as love, peace, and justice are becoming more defined. Fifth graders also have a keen sense of what is fair and what is not. Seize opportunities to encourage justice in family situations to help your child to see that treating others justly leads to peace.

Fifth graders are also greatly influenced by the values of their peer group. Be alert to behavior that might reflect peer pressure. Affirm behavior and attitudes that demonstrate respect and kindness.

Fifth graders are ready to assume certain responsibilities for their lives and their faith. They are also able to make stronger connections between their decisions and the living of the Ten Commandments and the Beatitudes. Teach personal responsibility by allowing them freedom to make personal choices. Provide guidance in their efforts at decision-making.*

*See *Catechetical Formation in Chaste Living,* United States Conference of Catholic Bishops, #19

One God, Three Persons

If your family were asked, "What is the central mystery of our faith?" how would you respond? The central belief of our faith, and our life of faith, is the Blessed Trinity. We believe in Three Persons in One God: God the Father; God the Son, who is Jesus Christ; and God the Holy Spirit. Whenever we make the Sign of the Cross, we express this belief. Whenever we pray and celebrate the liturgy, we pray and celebrate in the name of the Blessed Trinity. The Blessed Trinity is a mystery of faith. It is a belief that we will not fully understand until we share life forever with God in Heaven.

As a family pray this prayer of praise to God. Note which words praise God as Father, Son, and Holy Spirit.

The Divine Praises

Blessed be God.
Blessed be his holy name.
Blessed be Jesus Christ, true God and true man.
Blessed be the name of Jesus.
Blessed be his most Sacred Heart.
Blessed be his most precious Blood.
Blessed be Jesus in the most holy sacrament of the altar.
Blessed be the Holy Spirit, the Paraclete.
Blessed be the great mother of God, Mary most holy.
Blessed be her most holy and Immaculate Conception.
Blessed be her glorious Assumption.
Blessed be the name of Mary, Virgin and Mother.
Blessed be St. Joseph, her most chaste spouse.
Blessed be God in his angels and in his saints.

Angels Among Us

Angels are creatures created by God as pure spirits. They do not have physical bodies. Angels serve God as his messengers. They serve God in his saving plan for us and constantly give him praise. Everyone has a guardian angel. Encourage your child to pray to his or her guardian angel.

Prayer to My Guardian Angel

Angel of God,
my guardian dear,
to whom God's love
commits me here,
ever this day be at my side,
to light and guard,
to rule and guide.

Amen.

119   Luke, |10| ⟶ **Book**
⟶ **Chapter**

⟶ **Verse**

Praise of the Father ⟨21⟩ *t u**At that very moment he rejoiced [in] the holy Spirit and said, "I give you praise, Father, Lord of heaven and earth, for although you have hidden these things from the wise and the learned you have revealed them to the childlike. Yes, Father, such has been your gracious will. 22 *v*All things have been handed over to me by my Father. No one knows who the Son is except the Father, and who the Father is except the Son and anyone to whom the Son wishes to reveal him."

⟶ **Passage**

Passage Title —

Titles are sometimes added to show themes of the chapters, but these titles are not part of the actual words of the Bible.

A passage is a section of a chapter made up of a number of verses.

This passage shows Luke 10:21–22, which means: the Gospel of Luke, chapter ten, verses twenty-one to twenty-two.

Reading the Bible ... in Five Easy Steps

The Bible is a collection of seventy-three books written under the inspiration of the Holy Spirit. The Bible is divided into two parts: the Old Testament and the New Testament. In the forty-six books of the Old Testament, we learn about the story of God's relationship with the people of Israel. In the twenty-seven books of the New Testament, we learn about the story of Jesus Christ, the Son of God, and of his followers. The Bible is divided into books, which are divided into chapters, which are divided into verses. When you are given a Scripture passage to read, here are five easy steps that will help you to find it! With your child, follow these steps to look up **Lk 10:21–22.**

1. **Find the book.** When the name of the book is abbreviated, locate the meaning of the abbreviation on the contents pages found at the beginning of your Bible. *Lk* stands for Luke, one of the four Gospels.

2. **Find the page.** Your Bible's contents pages will also show the page on which the book begins. Turn to that page within your Bible.

3. **Find the chapter.** Once you arrive at the page where the book begins, keep turning the pages forward until you find the right chapter. The image above shows you how

a chapter number is usually displayed on a typical Bible page. You are looking for chapter **10** in Luke.

4. **Find the verses.** Once you find the right chapter, locate the verse or verses you need within the chapter. The image above also shows you how verse numbers will look on a typical Bible page. You are looking for verses **21** and **22**.

5. **Start reading!**

A Church in the Home

Talk with your child about what he or she knows about the Sacraments at the Service of Communion. Share that the Sacrament of Matrimony provides a man and a woman with the opportunity to share God's love. They express that love in faithfulness to each other and in openness to having children and bringing them up in a loving family.

Each family is called to be a domestic Church, or a "Church in the home." It is in the family that we learn to pray and worship God together, to forgive and be forgiven, and to be disciples of Jesus. Think of this as a call to live like the Holy Family: Jesus, Mary, and Joseph. Jesus grew up in a loving, faith-filled home. Jesus was obedient to his parents. Mary, Joseph, and Jesus' family followed Jewish traditions, prayed, and celebrated the religious feasts of their time. Like the Holy Family, our families should love and respect one another. Pray together the following prayers.

Prayer to the Holy Family

Jesus, Mary and Joseph, in you we
    contemplate
the splendor of true love, to you we
    turn with trust.
Holy Family of Nazareth, grant that
    our families too
may be places of communion and
    prayer, authentic schools of the Gospel
        and small domestic Churches.

(From Pope Francis's *Prayer to the Holy Family*, December 29, 2013)

Prayer to Saint Joseph

Grant, we pray, almighty God,
that by Saint Joseph's intercession your
Church may constantly watch over
the unfolding of the mysteries of
human salvation,
whose beginnings you entrusted
to his faithful care.
Through our Lord Jesus Christ,
your Son,
who lives and reigns with you
in the unity of the Holy Spirit,
one God, for ever and ever.

Amen.

The Communion of Saints

One of the most comforting Catholic beliefs is our belief in the Communion of Saints. The Communion of Saints is the union of all the baptized members of the Church on earth, in Heaven, and in Purgatory. This belief is comforting because we remain united with our loved ones who have died, and are all united with the saints in Heaven, who intercede for us.

This unity is most clearly expressed in the Mass when the priest prays the Eucharistic Prayer. We also express this unity with the Communion of Saints when we pray the Litany of the Saints. This litany is prayed at the Sacrament of Baptism, as well as the Easter Vigil, the Mass celebrated the night before Easter Sunday. Learn and share the prayer with your family today.

A Celebration of Saints, by Brother Mickey O'Neill McGrath

Litany of the Saints

Lord, have mercy.	Lord, have mercy.
Christ, have mercy.	Christ, have mercy.
Lord, have mercy.	Lord, have mercy.
Holy Mary, Mother of God,	pray for us.
Saint Michael,	pray for us.
Holy angels of God,	pray for us.
Saint Peter and Saint Paul,	pray for us.
Saint John,	pray for us.
Saint Stephen,	pray for us.
Saint Perpetua and Saint Felicity,	pray for us.
Saint Prisca,	pray for us.
Saint Gregory,	pray for us.
Saint Augustine,	pray for us.
Saint Basil,	pray for us.
Saint Benedict,	pray for us.
Saint Francis and Saint Dominic,	pray for us.
Saint Catherine,	pray for us.
Saint Teresa,	pray for us.
All holy men and women,	pray for us.

(Adapted from the *Litany of the Saints*)

Living with Dignity

Review with your child what he or she has learned about human dignity:

- that we are made in the image of God.

- that God calls us to recognize one another's dignity.

- that we can work toward human dignity by promoting justice and respect.

- that we can be instruments of God's peace.

Remind your child that Jesus treated all people equally and respected the dignity of every person.

Jesus gave us commandments that help us to follow the way he lived, respecting the dignity of all people. Read and remember these commandments as a family. Let them guide all your relationships—at home, at school, in the parish, and in the community.

Great Commandment

"You shall love the Lord, your God, with all your heart, with all your soul, and with all your mind. This is the greatest and the first commandment. The second is like it: You shall love your neighbor as yourself."

(Matthew 22:37–39)

New Commandment

"I give you a new commandment: love one another. As I have loved you, so you also should love one another. This is how all will know that you are my disciples, if you have love for one another."

(John 13:34–35)

How to Become a Saint

Yes, it is true, everyone in your family can become a saint! Having been made holy by your Baptism and united to Christ, you are actually called to be a saint. Saints were ordinary human beings, just like you, who were faithful disciples of Jesus. They are followers of Christ who lived lives of holiness on earth and now share in eternal life with God in Heaven. From the example of the saints' lives, we can learn ways to love God, ourselves, and others. We can learn how to be disciples of Jesus, as the saints were.

Have you or your child ever wondered how the Church decides who is named a saint? Here is a brief summary of this process.

Nuns displaying portraits of Saints John Paul II and John XXIII at the canonization ceremony for these popes

The Canonization Process

If someone who has died was known for living an especially holy life, or was martyred for his or her Catholic faith, the bishop of this person's diocese may begin the process to consider the person for sainthood.

- The first step is an investigation into the person's life. People who knew him or her will be interviewed. The bishop will collect information on things the person said, wrote, and did. The information will be sent to the Vatican. When a person becomes a candidate for sainthood, he or she is known as "Servant of God."

- A group of cardinals at the Vatican, the Congregation for the Causes of Saints, will study the information about the candidate's life. They will consider whether the person is a role model for living Catholic virtues. If so, the person will be declared "Venerable."

- The next step is declaring the candidate "Blessed." This is called *beatification*. Beatification occurs if it can be shown that a miracle occurred in connection with the candidate or if the person died a martyr for the faith. An example of a miracle might be a sudden cure or healing, with no reasonable medical explanation, when someone prayed for the candidate's help. The Vatican carefully reviews the evidence on any miracles.

- If a second miracle can be credited to the candidate, he or she can be named a saint, or canonized.

Practicing Devotions

Does anyone in your family practice devotions such as praying the Rosary? Devotions are a type of prayer that are not part of the liturgy of the Church but are rich and diverse expressions of faith that have been handed down to us through the centuries. Examples of devotions include novenas and the Stations of the Cross. Catholics of many different cultures and traditions practice devotions. Devotions can draw us into the mystery of Christ among us.

A novena is a devotion of praying for nine consecutive days. The word *novena* comes from a Latin word meaning "nine." Novenas have been prayed since the earliest days of the Church. In fact, Mary and the Apostles prayed together for a period of nine days between Jesus' Ascension and his sending of the Holy Spirit on Pentecost (see Acts of the Apostles, Chapter 1). Often people pray a novena for a special need or intention. Here is one prayer you might pray with your family as a novena.

Prayer to the Sacred Heart of Jesus

O most Sacred Heart of Jesus, fountain of every blessing, I adore You, I love You and with a true sorrow for my sins, I offer You this poor heart of mine. Make me humble, patient, pure and wholly obedient to Your will. Grant, good Jesus that I may live in You and for You.

Protect me in the midst of danger, comfort me in my afflictions, give me health of body, assistance in my temporal needs, Your blessing on all that I do, and the grace of a holy death. Amen.

The Chaplet of the Divine Mercy

The Chaplet of the Divine Mercy is a devotion that is prayed using rosary beads. Saint Faustina Kowalska, who lived from 1905 to 1938 in Poland, gave this practice of praying for the mercy of Jesus Christ to the Church. The Church celebrates Divine Mercy Sunday on the Second Sunday of Easter.

End

4 After five decades, pray three times:

Holy God, Holy Mighty One, Holy Immortal One, have mercy on us and on the whole world.

3 On the ten small beads of each decade, pray:

For the sake of His sorrowful Passion, have mercy on us and on the whole world.

2 Then, on the large bead before each decade, pray:

Eternal Father, I offer You the Body and Blood, Soul and Divinity of Your dearly beloved Son, Our Lord Jesus Christ, in atonement for our sins and those of the whole world.

1 To pray the chaplet, begin with the Sign of the Cross, an Our Father, three Hail Marys, and the Apostles' Creed, just as you would when beginning the Rosary.

Start